THE DEAD CENTER

THE DEAD CENTER

*Reflections on Liberalism and Democracy
After the End of History*

Luke Savage

OR Books
New York · London

© 2022 Luke Savage

Published by OR Books, New York and London

Visit our website at www.orbooks.com

All rights information: rights@orbooks.com

First printing 2022

Cataloging-in-Publication data is available from the Library of Congress.
A catalog record for this book is available from the British Library.

Typeset by Lapiz Digital Services. Printed by BookMobile, USA, and CPI, UK.

paperback ISBN 978-1-68219-333-4 • ebook ISBN 978-1-68219-334-1

In loving memory of Michael Brooks

Contents

Introduction

The Dead Center

I had the slight misfortune of being born just as the future was being canceled. Though technically a child of the 1980s, my first real memories are from the last decade of the 20th century—the strange and formative period which both inaugurated our current political order and infused it with a world-historic sense of self-confidence. On the face of it, this meant coming of age amid a wave of new enthusiasm for liberal institutions and liberal politics, as a new generation of politicians like Bill Clinton and Tony Blair heralded the final triumph of markets and proclaimed the obsolescence of the activist state. What it meant in practice, however, turned out to be much more intangible and altogether more far-reaching. Just as Francis Fukuyama's now infamous turn of phrase "the end of history" implied, the new consensus would also aggressively contort the horizons of our political imaginary around itself: anointing liberal capitalism as the superlative global orthodoxy while declaring even the most modest social democratic alternatives obsolete.

In a very real way, this revolution succeeded. When I first entered the political left as a teenager, I often found it to be a subdued and dispiriting place—its outlook tempered by decades of retrenchment and suffused with a version of the same political fatalism that had infected liberals. There was, or so it then seemed, no future that could be conceived of beyond a continuous and inescapable present. The only question was whether this elicited a feeling of wide-eyed excitement or one of resigned despair.

Today, for leftists and liberals alike, that sense of finality has given way to something altogether more uncertain and ambiguous. At the level of culture and ideology, the inheritance of the 1990s continues to shackle our institutions and our politics, but the epochal zeal and hubris that first greeted its arrival has long since fizzled away. Having so brazenly announced the end of history itself, the liberal order has suffered an almost-continuous stream of crises and existential traumas since the financial crash of 2008, the past six years alone inflicting the body blows of Britain's Brexit vote, the election of Donald Trump, and a series of surprisingly strong challenges from the left.

The result, as I variously argue throughout this book, is a political project that remains entrenched but has completely lost its bearings and finds itself congenitally unable to articulate anything resembling a substantive or coherent vision—even as its rudderless tribunes adopt the rhetoric of urgency and crisis.

****

My own backstory isn't especially novel, but its component parts have played an undeniable role in shaping and informing my political outlook today. I studied politics academically while, like many students, getting involved in them personally. Both during and after university, I volunteered on several campaigns for Canada's social democratic New Democratic Party (NDP) and worked in various capacities as a party staffer. (I also stood as a sacrificial lamb candidate for its Ontario wing for a few weeks in 2014, my only direct foray into politics to date.)

Some way along, I stumbled into a career as a writer. I say "stumbled" only because the course was never really planned. Though I had spent a year editing the University of Toronto's venerable student newspaper *The Varsity*, I never really imagined myself working "in the media." In one way or another, that's more or less what I've now been doing for the past six or seven years: a uniquely turbulent period in global politics and one that's also seen the birth of the first popular, intellectually mature, and polit-ically ambitious left-wing current of my lifetime. Absent this somewhat unexpected development, many of the essays that make up this book—the majority of which were originally published in *Jacobin*—would probably never have been written.

When I first came to know it, the left was more of a desiccated rem-nant than a living, breathing political identity accessible to the average person. With some notable exceptions, even many self-styled radicals were just dissident liberals by any other name. To be a socialist was to belong to an eccentric and marginal tendency, and political radical-ism (such as it existed) was an often-confused mix of neo-anarchism, post-ideological posturing, and free-floating anti-establishment senti-ment. Insofar as the left had a purpose, it amounted either to defending past gains or registering dissent within an order whose basic premises and institutions were considered unassailable.

Without exaggerating the success or reach of a politics that are still very much in the minority, things feel very different today. The neolib-eral settlement, and its quasi-theological claim to represent the best of all possible worlds, is no longer axiomatic as it once was: a development made all-too evident by the remarkable interest in democratic socialist politics now prevalent among many under forty.

Though it would be reductive to isolate a single moment or point of rupture, the financial meltdown of 2008 and its aftermath is certainly a worthy enough place to begin the story of liberalism's loss of confidence. Appropriately enough, 2008 also saw the ascendancy of Barack Obama: a figure who for many (including my nineteen-year-old self) represented the best hope for a different kind of world after the crisis—a crisis that plenty outside of elite circles, whether versed in the inscrutable workings of high finance or not, understood to be the product of deep structural flaws in the architecture of the world economy.

The administration's willful decision to forgo any serious reorder-
ing of the political settlement and the subsequent global march into austerity caused untold human suffering and emboldened the most sinister
currents on the political right. But it also helped instill in a generation
of downwardly mobile young people a hardened skepticism of centrist
platitudes, political saviorism, and liberal doublespeak. As you'll see from
many of the essays in this collection, the inveterate conservatism of so
many would-be progressive figures has played a major and undeniable
role in the development of my own politics. Though I certainly cannot
claim to speak for others, I suspect this trajectory is one that many millennial readers in particular will identify with.

Life on the left, of course, is ultimately about much more than finding
fault with centrist triangulation or rolling one's eyes in the direction of
individual liberal politicians. Unless grounded in materialist analysis and
undergirded by firm egalitarian commitments, anti-liberal critiques can
all-too easily slide into shallow contrarianism or various genres of ersatz
iconoclasm that are really just conservatism by another name. Events of
the past decade, however, have been remarkably clarifying for those of
us who once believed that the leaders of a conventional institution like
the Democratic Party could, or even wanted, to deliver progress in any
meaningful sense of the word.

Among other things, the breathtaking liberal hostility to both of
Bernie Sanders's presidential campaigns was emblematic of an orientation whose guiding ethos remains hierarchical and corporatist, whatever
its official branding may suggest to the contrary. The same applies in my
native Canada, where Trudeaumania 2.0 has proven to be every bit as
hollow, politically staid, and change-averse a phenomenon as early critics like myself argued it would be. In Britain, the other Anglo-American
democracy to make an appearance in this book, the stunning and
unlikely success of Jeremy Corbyn in the Labour Party's 2015 leadership

election was met with a reaction from establishment pundits and media oligopolies so hysterical that it made the attacks on Sanders look tame by comparison.

Such hostility has been every bit as instructive as the corresponding lack of vision offered by liberals themselves. In the 1990s, figures like Blair and Clinton took up the task of dismantling the old order with gusto and conviction. Theirs was a self-consciously ideological effort animated by a genuine zeal for the so-called Third Way and a real, if misplaced, enthusiasm for an unbroken future of rule by the dictates of exchange value.

Even in victory, the bewildered progeny of Clinton and Blair possess none of this spirit—their energies occupied instead with symbolic gestures, triangulating sound bites, and cynical attempts to garnish what is by now a thoroughly technocratic project with a patina of popular allure. Beyond soaring platitudes and vague appeals to fairness; beyond empty bromides about transcending partisanship and finding a mythical common ground; beyond an ethereal language of inclusion, and the hazy promise of some newly shared prosperity which supposedly awaits us all just over the next electoral horizon, it has become difficult to say what, if anything, the contemporary liberal project is actually *about*. As a political practice today, what is generally called liberalism is functionally small-c conservative. In rhetoric, gesture, and affect, the liturgies of change and progress remain, but any sincere belief in them has melted into air.

Since 2008, liberal elites have floundered in a series of vain efforts to recover their lost élan and, more urgently, devise new ways of getting ordinary people excited about the focus-tested pablum churned out by their increasingly remote and hyper-professionalized political machines. To this end, the only strategy that has found any success—amid a less than negligible record of failure—has involved the creation and marketing of carefully airbrushed personalities who, in turn, audition to play protagonists in the gaudy and hypermediated spectacle which today passes for democratic politics.

With very few exceptions, these cipher politicians are actors in the plainest and most literal sense: the almost incidental byproducts of a vast and lumbering cultural machinery that has vetted them and provided most of the script in advance. As sentient human brands, their job is primarily to sell that script to electorates—who are, in turn, now conceived more like aggregations of consumers sortable into market niches than citizens of a democratic polity with clashing values and interests.

These themes strongly inform the lengthiest section of this book, which features essays on a number of individual politicians (many of which were written during the 2019-20 Democratic primary race). But you'll also find them running throughout the portions devoted to neoliberalism and the media, both of which are component parts of the same story. If politics has increasingly been reduced to the level of spectacle and many of its participants to the status of performers-qua-commodities, elite pundits—ever the stubborn guardians of trite orthodoxy and received wisdom—deserve a very real share of the blame.

As I do my best to argue, this has at least as much to do with the modern media's overall construction as it does with the individual pundits or talking heads involved. The press, much like the political class whose activities it is charged with overseeing, is subject to a host of market pressures and incentives that strongly encourage both the embrace of spectacle and the enforcement of particular ideological boundaries.

This is where neoliberalism—our narcotic inheritance from the age of Reagan, Thatcher, Clinton, and Blair—comes in. Freed from the various limits and counterweights it faced in the decades after the Second World War, the twenty-first century has seen us enter a world in which profit-driven corporate enterprise is really and truly allowed to consume anything and everything in its path. The upshot, or at least one of them, is that market economies have increasingly become market *societies*, the space within them not subject to the tidal forces of commodification and profit-seeking growing ever smaller by the day.

Notwithstanding the various terms associated with diffidence or passivity I often use in relation to many of this book's subjects (surrender, retreat, etc.), it is worth stating outright that this was always more or less the point. Neoliberalism is first and foremost a political project, and its greatest champions genuinely do accept, and even celebrate, the constraints on democracy it imposes, the hierarchies that it creates, and the overbearing influence that markets now exert over daily life.

Accepting these things as natural and inevitable necessarily limits the scope and substance of politics as well. When the realm of what can be debated or contested has been so radically narrowed, all that's left is to tinker with minor reforms and try to weave them into a broad cultural narrative, most typically by drawing on the signifiers and attributes attached to a single personality at its center. It's little wonder, really, that so many liberal politicians today come across as smarmy and inauthentic. The project they've signed up for effectively precludes anything else.

****

The essays in this book are generally about specific events and specific people. Given the period in which many were written, much of *The Dead Center* will read as a quasi-campaign diary set against the backdrop of the Trump era, the 2020 Democratic primaries, the ensuing presidential election, and its immediate aftermath. As will periodically be apparent, a good number were written during a period in which I sincerely believed liberal democratic capitalism was about to undergo, at minimum, a kind of social democratic quarter-revolution on the heels of left electoral victories in Great Britain and the United States. While this obviously did not happen, I remain quite doggedly hopeful about the political possibilities that the past six years have opened up—and the future prospects of the populist social democracy that so nearly brought the left to power in two of the world's wealthiest and most influential English-speaking countries.

As for our present, it can only be called a strange interregnum. Largely thanks to Donald Trump and his disastrous handling of the pandemic, centrist Democrats in the United States have secured for themselves another mandate. As I write these words, the cul-de-sac of the American legislative process ironically continues to exhibit all the dysfunction of the Brezhnev-era USSR—the impossibly wealthy ideologues who populate its cloistered and putrescent upper ranks stubbornly determined to prove, above all else, that their decaying system still works. Despite the various media prognostications of a bold new era in the making, the Biden presidency's early maneuvers strongly suggest it intends to follow the blandly managerial template set out by its predecessor in 2008—a path almost certain to yield similar results. Even on a straightforward issue like voting rights, liberal leaders have proven unable to legislate basic reforms or wield their (probably fleeting) congressional majority to protect the franchise from right-wing onslaught. The Biden presidency—for all the buzz it elicited in the administration's early months by hinting at big spending and new social programs—has always been more about restoring the comparatively placid cultural consensus of the pre-2016 era than ushering in a twenty-first-century version of the New Deal. If Trump's improbable victory fostered (or rather hardened) many dangerous and self-defeating impulses among mainstream liberals—a renewed obsession with bipartisanship; a dopey willingness to embrace Trump's conservative critics, whatever their actual beliefs, into the liberal fold; a neurotic instinct to treat left and right populism as politically and morally equivalent; a credulous deference to the wisdom of credentialed experts and traditional elites; a preference for cosmetic social harmony over genuine equality—the ascendance of Bidenism ultimately represents their crystallization. As has been the case again and again throughout my adult life, a moment of soporific cultural regress has arrived with all the pageantry of a swinging new era.

The difference is that now it seems possible to conceive of an alternative. For all the withering cynicism I appear to exhibit in this book, most of its essays were written in a spirit of optimism—not so much about the inevitability of an urgently needed political transformation but rather the real and tangible possibility of one. In some ways, *The Dead Center* might seem like an odd title to give a collection published following, among other things, the defeat of the Sanders movement and the ascendancy of Joe Biden. For what it's worth, I offer it less as a description of immediate prospects than as an urgent claim about the future.

The liberal narrative of politics persists in large part because the story it tells is a seductive and comforting one. In an age of surging inequality, far-right reaction, and impending climate apocalypse, liberalism offers an elegant and appealing psychological compromise: a frictionless vision of social, racial, and economic justice achieved through conventional institutions without the redistribution of wealth and power, the disruption of actual change, or the bother of mass popular democracy. Whatever the self-styled realists who make up its leaders and intellectuals might insist to the contrary, this is a cynical and bleak outlook masquerading as a cheery and optimistic one.

Twenty-first-century liberal capitalism rests on the contradictory premise that it will soon be possible to cure cancer and colonize Mars, but that even the most modest social democratic reforms are a naive and quixotic fantasy. If we are serious about winning a more just, equal, and peaceful world, we must reject the fatalism which insists that real progress isn't possible, and that no future exists beyond the lean horizons of our present. If we are serious about winning a more just, equal, and

peaceful world, we must reject the fatalism which insists that real progress isn't possible, and that no future exists outside the lean horizons of
our present.

Beyond the failures, contradictions, and injustices of our frail political order, I believe that it does.

A Note to the Reader

The essays in this book are accompanied with their original times and places of publication. Those unmarked with the latter are being published for the first time. Like most writers, I am rarely fully satisfied with my own prose upon revisiting them and, as such, have made minor edits to many previously published pieces. All essays were written solely by me, with the exception of "The Fraudulent Universalism of Barack Obama."

PART I

Salvos

[The] prevalence of liberalism yields, to be sure, some obvious and sub-stantial benefits. It makes us properly skeptical of the excessive claims and fanaticisms that accompany ideologies . . . And it allows for the hope that any revival of American radicalism will acknowledge not only its break from, but also its roots in, the liberal tradition. At the same time, however, the dominance of liberalism contributes heavily to our intellectual conform-ity. Liberalism dominates, but without confidence or security; it knows that its victories at home are tied to disasters abroad; and for the élan it cannot summon, it substitutes a blend of complacence and anxiety. It makes for an atmosphere of blur in the realm of ideas, since it has a stake in seeing momentary concurrences as deep harmonies. In an age that suffers from incredible catastrophes it scoffs at theories of social apocalypse—as if any more evidence were needed; in an era convulsed by war, revolution and counterrevolution it discovers the virtues of "moderation." . . . Liberalism as an ideology, as "the haunted air," has never been stronger in this country; but can as much be said of the appetite for freedom?[1]

    —Irving Howe

A socialist is just someone who is unable to get over his or her astonishment that most people who have lived and died have spent lives of wretched, fruit-less, unremitting toil. [2]

    —Terry Eagleton

Liberalism in Theory and Practice

In political activity . . . men sail a boundless and bottomless sea; there is neither harbour for shelter nor floor for anchorage, neither starting-place nor appointed destination. The enterprise is to keep afloat on an even keel.

—Michael Oakeshott[3]

No one of my generation and background will forget where they were on the evening of November 4, 2008. Outside my then-residence at the University of Toronto, people streamed into the quad with tears running down their faces. It was a moment like no other I have experienced. The seemingly impossible had happened: Barack Obama had been elected president of the United States. Within minutes of CNN projecting the result, a collective feeling that was equal parts euphoria and disbelief seemed to burst forth all over. It took weeks, maybe even months, to dissipate.

The election of Barack Obama certainly isn't my first political memory, but it may well have been my first really formative one. As embarrassing as it is to write more than a decade later, I'll readily admit to having been swallowed up in the excitement and emotionally sold on the romantic promise of "Change We Can Believe In." It offered a compelling narrative incorporating everything my political imagination craved at the time: an image of progress as I then understood it; a charismatic leader to take us out of the darkness and into the promised land; the negation of the hated Bush presidency and all it stood for, from the reign of the Christian Right and its dimwitted rubes to the evils of Fallujah and

Abu Ghraib. I wasn't even American, but Obama's victory still felt like a moment of grand, even historic, affirmation.

I bring this up not because I have since become a left-wing writer and seek penance, or want to issue some kind of embarrassed mea culpa (we were all nineteen once), nor as part of some reductive effort to trace the roots of my own politicization back to a single event or moment. I came to my politics the way most people do: by way of a confused and often contradictory jumble of ideas and idioms gradually clarified through learning and experience.

On a basic level, I am a socialist because I simply cannot fathom reconciling myself to a society where so many needlessly suffer because of circumstances beyond their control; where human dignity is distributed on the basis of luck and a social caste system is allowed to permeate every aspect of daily life; and where all of this is considered perfectly normal and acceptable in a civilization that has split the atom and sent people to the Moon.

But while it would be nice to attribute everything about my politics to pure moral sentiment, it would be a lie. Because the less noble truth, if I'm honest with myself and the reader, is that something else has played a formative role in animating my politics and anchoring me on the left: namely, a searing dislike for liberalism as the hegemonic outlook in our culture and a deep, abiding disdain toward the political class that so self-righteously upholds it.

Maybe I was predisposed to democratic socialism; I always considered myself to be "on the left," even as a teenager. In any case, it's become clear in retrospect that watching the liberal class respond to events over the past decade has been a powerful stimulus in my politicization.

Which is to say, I didn't acquire radical politics simply through reading Marx in college (though it certainly aided the process). Nor did I become irredeemably frustrated with liberalism merely by absorbing some abstract argument about its flaws. I didn't have a Road to Damascus revelation while thumbing through some volume by Chomsky or David Harvey. And while I would certainly count them as formative to my political evolution, it wasn't the likes of Ralph Miliband and Tony Benn—let alone Bernie Sanders or Jeremy Corbyn—who ultimately imbued me with a burning hatred for anything and everything that calls itself "moderate" or "centrist."

No, that instinct owes much more to watching Barack Obama summon forth a tidal wave of popular goodwill, then proceed to invite the same old cadre of apparatchiks and financiers back into the White House to carry on business as usual despite the most punishing economic crisis since the Great Depression; to seeing the "War on Terror" become a permanent fixture of the global landscape long after its original architects had been booted from the halls of power, courtesy of supposedly enlightened humanitarians; to witnessing a potentially monumental hunger for change be sacrificed on the altar of managerialism and technocratic respectability. It comes from watching a smiling Nick Clegg stand next to David Cameron in the Rose Garden at Number 10 Downing Street before rubber-stamping a series of lacerating cuts to Britain's welfare state and betraying a generation of students in the process; to seeing the dexterity by which Canada's liberals gesture to the left then govern from the right; and from seeing the radical demands of global anti-austerity movements endlessly whittled down and regurgitated as neoliberal slam poetry to be recited at Davos by the airbrushed centrist innovators du jour.

These triangulations, and many others like them, helped me realize that the malaise was the product of a congenital trait rather than a temporary blip. The problem, in other words, wasn't that contemporary liberalism was failing to live up to its ideals, but that it was living up to them all too well.

From an early age I had been trained by mainstream political culture to think of liberalism as an orientation synonymous with change, progress, even dissent. This, in theory at least, remains its official branding in our moment of looming climate catastrophe and ascendant right-wing nationalism. Yet throughout the particularly dark decade spanning 2008–2018, liberals have positioned themselves as the persistent agents of caution, hesitation, and reassurance, often directing greater hostility toward constituencies on the left than those on the right to which they are ostensibly opposed. Faced with the choice between a radical, populist figure and an orthodox machine politician in 2016, the executive officers at Liberalism Inc. made this antipathy all too clear—and we are now living the disastrous consequences.

In an era where a deranged former reality star can possess nuclear launch codes, many liberal elites still adamantly insist that *things have actually never been better* and that, beneath the chaos of our tumultuous present, the species is doggedly marching in a straight line toward Something Very Exciting Indeed. (This is why the beaming Steven Pinker, not the dour Jordan Peterson, is arguably the figure who best reflects our liberal order in crisis—watching the world burn around him and proclaiming like some postmodern Professor Pangloss as the flames lick his feet that, actually, *this is fine.*)

Modern liberalism, of course, has in its past a rich and diverse philosophical tradition from which socialists and conservatives alike have occasionally been able to draw resources and inspiration. But perhaps because it's been a victim of its own success or because it has failed to meaningfully adapt since its most recent high watermark in the 1990s, today's liberal mainstream seems less concerned with ideas than with temperament and more driven by mood than mind.

This may be the reason liberal thought endlessly obsesses over the language used in political debate and often seems to place a higher value on its tone and quality than on its content or outcome. It is also why, I suspect, today's grinning Trudeaus and Obamas seem so much more preoccupied with how things are perceived to be going than with how they actually are, and value the sanctity of procedures over the implications they may ultimately have for ordinary people's lives.

The animating mission here is less to combat injustice than to efficiently manage discontent: to take the temperature of the popular mood, strain it of radical aspiration, then serve it back wrapped in the most aesthetically pleasing package liberalism's practitioners can assemble, and pray like hell nobody notices when the gold paint loses its luster at the first sign of a market hiccup, budget deficit, foreign intervention, or real challenge from the left.

Over time, the act wears thin and the package must be redesigned according to the evolving tastes of prospective consumers in the voting electorate. Borrowing from the world of marketing, liberal politics have thus become an endless and growingly absurd quest to ever so slightly reconfigure rhetoric and blandly repackage the same old policies and ideas as exciting new chapters in our twenty-first-century story.

Thus, teflon politicians like Massachusetts representative Joe Kennedy III have trained themselves to confidently issue bold pronouncements that amount to little more than glorified rebranding efforts—the latest being a radically new system of thought the congressman calls "moral capitalism."[4] (In its own way, this is an even better metaphor for liberalism in crisis than Pinker's quixotic Enlightenment: the third-generation scion of an aristocratic dynasty trying to seize the mantle of novelty with a slogan you might see used to advertise a seminar near the airport that turns out to be a pyramid scheme.) It's an impulse identical to the one that drives Hollywood mega studios to reboot the same franchises over and over again, and it's also what enables some liberals to believe they will discover the negation of the Trump era in Oprah, Michael Bloomberg, or Beto O'Rourke.

In theory, modern liberalism is a set of ideas about human freedom, markets, and representative government. In practice, or so it now seems to me, it has largely become a political affect, and a quintessentially conservative one at that: a set of reflexes common to those with a Panglossian faith in capitalist markets and the institutions which attempt to sustain them amid our flailing global order. In theory, it is an ideology of progress. In practice, it has become the secular theology of the status quo; the mechanism through which the gilded buccaneers of Silicon Valley, Wall Street, and multinational capital rationalize hierarchy and exploitation while fostering resignation and polite deference among those they seek to rule.

Etiquette before equality, manners before morals, procedure ahead of program, conciliation over conflict, private vice over public good, the modern liberal increasingly does politics as the Tory philosopher Michael Oakeshott once recommended: keeping things on an even keel and refusing to set a definitive course. The problem is that, while its sun-kissed officers so cheerfully steady things from above deck, the ship is sinking and many of the passengers below have already drowned.

—*A version of this essay first appeared in* Jacobin, *December 2018.*

Why Liberals Pretend They Have No Power

At a press conference in September, House Speaker Nancy Pelosi fielded questions about the increasingly perilous state of affairs which now forms the backdrop to November's election. Denouncing Donald Trump's refusal to commit to a peaceful transfer of power should he be defeated, Pelosi was unequivocal: "You are not in North Korea; you are not in Turkey . . . You are in the United States of America. It is a democracy, so why don't you just try for a moment to honor your oath of office to the Constitution of the United States?"[5] Only moments later, Pelosi dismissed calls that she leverage her role as speaker to shut down the US government in an effort to block Trump's incoming nominee for the Supreme Court—offering up, by way of explanation, the transparently cop-out defense that the country's public employees need their paychecks too much for the regular operation of Congress to be disrupted.[6]

The contrast between the two comments was stark. The first, after all, elicited a sense of moral and political urgency, gravely implying (not without cause) that the very foundations of America's democratic and constitutional order are in danger. The second, particularly if we accept that premise, amounted to nothing less than an abdication of responsibility from one of the country's most powerful figures during a moment of national crisis. A sitting president openly flouting the rules of democracy represents a serious enough threat on its own; if the prospect of a Supreme Court appointment weeks before an election whose outcome could well be decided by that very body is not an appropriate moment for vigorous opposition, then what is?

This tension underscores a deeper paradox of liberalism that has arguably reached its apex in the Trump era. Since the president's election four years ago, the political and intellectual leaders of America's supposedly reform-minded opposition have issued repeated warnings about the existential threat that Trump poses to democracy. Amid it all, senior Democrats have mostly maintained both the regular operation of government and a standard of congressional etiquette that suggests normalcy more than it does any state of exception: applauding the president's speeches, approving his military budgets,[7] awarding him new domestic spying powers,[8] and even fast-tracking his judicial nominees.[9] A line from one 2019 CNBC report[10] detailing the overwhelming House approval of Trump's marquee NAFTA renegotiation sums up the absurdity of this posture: "Democrats also wanted to show they can work with Trump only a day after they voted to make him the third president impeached in American history." Determined opposition to Trump has sometimes been so nonexistent that Democratic partisans have had to invent it, as when an image of Pelosi during the 2019 State of the Union address went viral on the entirely spurious grounds that the speaker had intended for her clapping to look sarcastic.[11]

Liberalism in the Trump era has thus become a kind of strange pantomime act in which elite politicians deploy the rhetoric of imminent threats and national emergency only to behave like hapless passengers trapped aboard a sinking ship. Although it has certainly found its most potent expression in Washington since 2016, this posture of feigned powerlessness has gradually come to infect the broader culture and ideology of American liberalism as a whole.

Even in solidly blue states where Democrats face none of the institutional impediments that confront them in Washington, DC, robust progressive legislative agendas are rare.[12] Powerful figures such as New York Governor Andrew Cuomo[13] and California Governor Gavin Newsom[14] issue bulletins about climate change that read more like desperate pleas from activists than statements by sitting governors with the power to make and alter laws. (In response to the recent wildfires raging across the West Coast, Newsom announced that he has "no time for climate-change deniers," despite having approved some forty-eight new fracking permits since April.[15] Cuomo tweeted, "This is what climate change looks like. The proof is right in front of us. This is a national emergency—it's now or never.") The Democratic Party's 2020 nominee for president, meanwhile, is a former vice president who pledges to reform corporate America through "non-legislative" means[16] and proudly champions the idea that "nothing fundamental" needs to change.[17] On issues as varied as the environment, racial oppression, and immigrant rights, the culture of liberalism has rarely been so suffused with a language of moral urgency and social justice; as an institutional and ideological presence in American life, its politics have rarely been so unambitious or shy of confrontation.

The contradictory posturing of today's most powerful liberals is not fully attributable to the shock and disorientation brought about by the 2016 election; its roots go back to the Clinton era at least—the period (not incidentally) when Democratic leaders formally abandoned their commitment to the New Deal and absorbed key parts of a Republican agenda.

American liberalism has always had a technocratic streak, but the disappointments experienced by liberals since the end of the 1960s enabled a new generation of more conservative Democrats to restructure the liberal coalition[18] and redefine both its style and its political priorities. In the past few decades, the party has largely avoided embracing a clearly defined progressive program or engaging in the politics of confrontation. Whereas the consensus once put in place by Franklin D. Roosevelt was secured through open conflict[19] with powerful forces in American society, the lodestars of the new liberalism became compromise and conciliation with the right. While FDR forged a lasting political settlement around welfarism and an activist state against the wishes of much of America's corporate establishment, the Clinton administration would famously denounce the scourge of "Big Government"[20] and declare "the end of welfare as we know it."[21] The Bill Clinton adviser Dick Morris summed up the administration's strategy in a memo as follows: "Fast-forward the Gingrich agenda."[22]

Accordingly, key parts of the conservative agenda were absorbed into American liberalism, which would now make a virtue out of both bipartisan compromise and ideological triangulation. This style found its ultimate expression in Barack Obama, who masterfully paired a sonorous rhetoric of optimism with, to paraphrase the political scientist Corey Robin, a "moral minimalism" that rendered Democrats not so much unprepared for a fight with their Republican foes as indisposed to the very idea of one.[23] Beginning with the hopeful cadence of "Yes we can!" and ending, after a slew of congressional defeats, with the election of Donald Trump, the Obama era has served to convince many liberals of the need to compromise even further—anything remotely ambitious being doomed to fail on the altars of conservative partisanship and Republican obstruction. (Rampant opposition to Medicare for All from centrist Democrats, despite its considerable popularity, has been justified on these grounds for years.)

Partly in response to the limitations of Obama-era liberalism, the left (notably, though not exclusively, in Bernie Sanders's two presidential campaigns) has embraced something like an inverse strategy: mobilizing around ambitious, popular policies and openly naming the forces and interests that stand in their way.

The standard rejoinder is that the American left is detached from the political realities of a system that makes changing anything exceptionally difficult. On short-term pragmatic grounds, this argument obviously has a certain force: Pelosi can't single-handedly stop the president from behaving dangerously in advance of November's election any more than Newsom or Cuomo can arrest the progress of climate change. Democrats might grind the federal government to a halt to prevent Amy Coney Barrett's nomination to the Supreme Court, only to find themselves out-flanked by Trump and Senate Majority Leader Mitch McConnell. But until such an effort is mounted, we will never know what it might achieve. The same logic applies in the longer term to popular policies such as Medicare for All and the Green New Deal.

It's all well and good to recognize the structural constraints imposed by America's political system, and the difficulty of passing major reforms in the face of organized opposition. But for too many of America's leading liberal politicians, "realism" has become an identity unto itself, unmoored from any programmatic orientation toward the future or sustained effort to bring about significant change.

Transformation on the scale necessary to undo the ravages of the Trump presidency will certainly be difficult to achieve, the fight for larger objectives such as health-care reform and a green industrial revolution harder still. But, given what the leaders of twenty-first-century liberal-ism themselves tell us about the state of things, what is the alternative? There's no reason to surrender when you can fight.

—*A version of this essay first appeared in* The Atlantic, *October 2020.*

David Brooks's Capitalist Fatalism

In a recent op-ed for the *New York Times*, David Brooks offers a characteristic dismissal of socialist politics entitled "I Was Once a Socialist. Then I Saw How It Worked."[24] As its title suggests, the piece (an adapted version of remarks Brooks gave at the Munk Debates in Toronto last week) is framed as a story of grown-up hardheadedness prevailing over the naive idealism of youth. Channeling the famous and unbearably smug quote (erroneously) attributed to Winston Churchill,[25] Brooks presents his own political evolution as the triumph of head over heart; a slow coming to terms with the world as it really is rather than how we think it ought to be.

This biographical garnish matters mostly because the assumed binary between socialist naivete and capitalist realism heavily informs the more substantial parts of Brooks's argument (more on those in a moment). But it is also relevant because the definition of socialism Brooks gives himself as an intellectual sparring partner is so unforgivably thin: "The best version of socialism," he writes, "is defined by Michael Walzer's phrase 'what touches all should be decided by all.'"

As a basic ethical principle this isn't bad, except it turns out that what Brooks means in practice is an incredibly straw-manned version of mid-century statism characterized by centralized economic planning. In the opening stanzas, he tells us he was a socialist in college who once read *The Nation* and old issues of the *New Masses* (a publication associated with the Communist Party USA that stopped circulating some thirteen years before he was born). Aside from this rather anecdotal claim, it's unclear in what sense Brooks was ever seriously engaged with socialist thought, let alone activism. He tells us that a youthful, socialist version of himself once debated Milton Friedman, though the bespectacled twenty-two-year-old who appears in the clip[26] was already employed at the *Wall Street Journal* (by twenty-four, he'd moved to the *National Review*) and can be heard making arguments against excessive state regulation and complaining about the FDA.

It's hardly the stuff of Phil Ochs songs, which perhaps explains why Brooks's understanding of socialism seems so narrow: if you've never really held or practiced a political ideology, you're liable to give it less of a fair hearing than someone who has, even if they've eventually abandoned it. In any case, whether we take Brooks at his word or not, his espoused biography turns out to be a brittle skeleton for the arguments that follow—which have less to do with an intellectual critique of socialism as such than a quasi-spiritual faith in the superiority of capitalism.

For our purposes, it is worth isolating the separate, though interwoven, dimensions of Brooks's piece: the first, a series of fairly basic historical and theoretical claims; the second, a set of deep structural assumptions about politics and what might crudely be called human nature. Whatever one thinks of Brooks as a thinker or stylist, he does have a knack for making conservatism legible and intuitively appealing to his (now mostly liberal) audience. In this respect, the piece is a useful illustration, both of how one of America's most influential public intellectuals thinks about politics, and the flawed worldview it ultimately represents.

Brooks's most tangible point (in many ways the fulcrum of his entire argument) is stated plainly enough: socialism, whatever its laudable humanitarian commitments might be in the abstract, simply doesn't work for technical reasons:

> My socialist sympathies didn't survive long once I became a journalist. I quickly noticed that the government officials I was covering were not capable of planning the society they hoped to create. It wasn't because they were bad or stupid. The world is

just too complicated. I came to realize that capitalism is really good at doing the one thing socialism is really bad at: creating a learning process to help people figure stuff out … It has a competitive profit-driven process to motivate you to learn and innovate, every single day. [27]

This assessment makes a certain degree of sense if we limit our definition of socialism to "state bureaucrats doing things" and, even then, the argument has some obvious problems. The state-managed utilities created in many countries after the Second World War had an observably better track record than the market versions which have since emerged following the privatization mania of the 1980s and '90s. Some elements of a modern industrial society are natural monopolies in the sense that they serve their original purpose better when owned and managed by a single actor and tasked to operate in the public good. (If you want to see how badly the introduction of so-called market dynamism into former public utilities has really gone, look no further than Britain's rail system[28] or transit in Auckland.[29])

Which brings us to a second issue with Brooks's argument from efficiency, namely that capitalism tends toward private monopoly in a way that renders claims about learning or risk deeply troubled at best. "Competition" is a ludicrous concept when applied to corporate giants like Amazon or Google, which are themselves involved in large-scale economic planning of their own. A modern capitalist economy is one structured around highly concentrated ownership far more than dynamic competition, of socialized risk and mostly privatized gain. It's also a wretched notion to apply to basic human needs like health care: sick people don't need a system that gives investors the biggest return on the lowest investment, they need a doctor. Furthermore, the absurdity of venture capital schemes like WeWork and Theranos should have everyone asking serious questions about how efficiently modern capitalism allocates resources (criticize the limitations of Soviet planning all you want, but don't call the economic model that gave us the Fyre Festival and financial derivatives "efficient").

Much as the rest of the piece descends from this basic premise, Brooks's real argument has more to do with a kind of capitalist fatalism than any serious critique of the socialist project or engagement with the highly varied institutional configurations socialists have advocated or defended as necessary extensions of its core egalitarian concerns (configurations that simply aren't reducible to "state bureaucrats running the whole economy"). The piece's subheading reads, "Two cheers for capitalism, now and forever," which is a much clearer distillation of its actual thesis than anything the author has to say about government inefficiency or market incentives. In heart and mind, Brooks believes that inequality is an indelible fact of life that cannot be undone by human agency. He tells us as much when he asks the following rhetorical questions:

> Why do we have to live with such poverty and inequality? Why can't we put people over profits? What is the best life in the most just society? Socialism is the most compelling secular religion of all time. It gives you an egalitarian ideal to sacrifice and live for. [30]

Faced with all the obvious flaws and injustices of capitalist societies, Brooks opts to casually acknowledge them while insisting they mean that the glass is half full rather than half empty. The implicit assumption that human nature is so immutably flawed that the best we can hope for is the least bad of universally imperfect alternatives is an animating feature of modern conservatism (and one expressed to Brooks by none other than Milton Friedman during their debate in the 1980s), as is the related idea that all attempts to meaningfully transform human societies represent a naive utopianism doomed to fail. In the case of Brooks's op-ed, perhaps unsurprisingly, we find this fatalism masquerading as hardheaded intellectual maturity, and we needn't embrace an overly sentimental view or reductive conception of "human nature" to reject it.

Far from being a dogmatic commitment to a particular set of institutional arrangements or an irrational faith in the sorcery of bureaucrats, the socialist analysis simply holds that inequality is neither a natural nor an inevitable feature of life but rather the product of identifiable contradictions in the structures of our economy and society. Even in the richest nations today, millions are denied the opportunity to realize their full potential as human beings: not because they're intrinsically weaker, less intelligent, or less hardworking than others, but because capital forces them to be its unwilling instruments. Denying power and agency to the many while granting them in abundance to a wealthy few, it ravenously commodifies everything it can about our daily lives—from our time and energy to our opportunities to be educated and even to reproduce—while enriching a gilded minority whose singular imperative is to enrich itself further.

Believing there's an alternative isn't fanciful, and it certainly isn't utopian as Brooks would have us believe. The seeds of this revelation, in fact, are contained within his very own argument courtesy of a rhetorical sleight of hand that finds him praising Scandinavia (whose model, he reminds us, ultimately still involves markets). Though Brooks tries to cover for himself with the parochial claim that Scandinavian-style social democracy would never work in America for cultural reasons, he nevertheless gives us a clear example (among many others throughout the world) of injustice undone by human agency.

Take even a cursory look at the social outcomes of countries like Finland or Denmark compared to those of the United States and you'll find they're a direct product of decidedly non-market institutions. Generations of Swedish trade unionists didn't fight for the collective ownership of wealth, a more robust welfare state, or the right to be represented at work to make themselves "better capitalists" (as Brooks so absurdly puts it), but because they knew the poverty and immiseration that once dominated their societies was no more natural than feudalism—and could similarly be undone.

This, more than anything else, is what being a socialist is fundamentally about: embracing and recognizing the injustices owed to hierarchy and exploitation, rejecting the fatalism of those who insist they are inevitable, and uniting in solidarity with your fellow human beings until they're finally undone for good.

—*A version of this essay first appeared in* Jacobin, *December 2019.*

What Canada Can Teach Us About Liberals Everywhere

For as long as I can remember, the same refrain has greeted any criticism of liberal timidity made from the left. Though it comes in many shades and variations, the basic contours are always identical. To put it as plainly as possible: Those of us on the left are instructed, again and again, that liberals—whatever their failures or shortcomings might seem to be—are always behaving as progressively as the world will allow. Out of power, this means that liberal politicians must always triangulate or moderate their message to win back ground from the right. In power, as it inevitably turns out, they must do exactly the same to retain it. But fear not, partisans of this narrative will always declare: The liberal path is merely a longer and, ultimately, more effective route to the same destination—born of a canny strategic calculus that takes into account the frustrating realities of social change and the many obstacles, institutional and political, facing anyone who seeks to make the world a better place.

To be a liberal, then, is to master the art of explaining why, regrettable as it may be, things either cannot change or cannot change at the speed demanded by those of us on the left. This argument comes in many forms, but invariably employs the same basic formula: namely, an expressed affinity for a progressive cause or concern tempered by a series of stated obstacles that make realizing it difficult, impossible, or unrealistic—even (or perhaps, especially) when a liberal administration is in power.

Midway through his excellent 2016 book *Listen, Liberal*, Thomas Frank puts these arguments to the test in a memorable chapter examining blue states, i.e., those where Democratic hegemony is unchallenged and liberal politicians are presumably free to put the progressive values they quietly hold elsewhere into action without fear of institutional resistance or Republican obstruction. The chapter's opening passage succinctly lays out one of liberal partisans' most common and exhausting defenses:

> When you press Democrats on their uninspiring deeds—their lousy free trade deals, for example, or their incomprehensible Wall Street reform legislation—when you press them on any of these things, they reply automatically that this is the best anyone could have done. After all, they had to deal with those awful Republicans, and those awful Republicans wouldn't let the really good stuff through. They filibustered in the Senate. They gerrymandered in the congressional districts. And, besides, it's hard to turn an ocean liner. Surely you don't think the tepid-to-lukewarm things Clinton and Obama have done in Washington really represent the fiery Democratic soul. [31]

If we accept these claims, Frank points out, it follows that blue states like Rhode Island and Massachusetts should be flourishing, progressive utopias—Democrats in those states, after all, aren't forced to defer to corporate interests, gut social programs, or worship at the altar of high finance (as they so regrettably must do everywhere else).

But, as it turns out, the typical blue state is no progressive utopia after all. New York, in many ways the centrifuge of the Democratic machine, suffers from soaring levels of poverty and inequality, not to mention rampant corruption. Despite providing safe seats for Democratic politicians at every level of government, party apparatchiks and donor networks actively work to shut down and defeat progressive and left challengers—the better to ensure that the halls of power are staffed with a never-ending cavalcade of Joe Crowley and Andrew Cuomo clones in perpetuity.

I know all too well how Mr. Frank and others on the American left feel looking at this dismal state of affairs and hearing the same bad arguments mobilized to maintain it again and again. That's because Canadian federal politics are effectively the blue state thesis put to the test on an even grander scale—with even more depressing results.

In the American context, the obstacles to progress are generally said to be institutional roadblocks like gerrymandering, voter suppression, Republican obstruction, and the incremental realities imposed by America's conservatively inclined system of government (two directly elected houses, counter-majoritarian checks and balances, term limits). Given the power afforded to large corporations and other moneyed interests to grease the wheels of campaigns and ballot initiatives with endless donations, the inevitability of organized private resistance to progressive politics is also regularly cited as an intractable impediment for liberals. There's also popular opinion, which tends to be portrayed (often in a very misleading fashion) as inherently conservative or, at any rate, as too conservative to permit much beyond the most tepid centrism.

Wrong as these arguments are, they do at least have the virtue of being rooted in reality. America's political institutions are deeply obstructionist and Republicans, outside of solid blue states, manifestly do rig the system at every opportunity—suppressing the votes of poor and racialized people, gerrymandering districts, and blocking legislation they dislike whenever possible. The power of corporations is undeniably vast and plays an active role in tilting the political process thanks to America's comically awful campaign finance system. And, while popular opinion is certainly nowhere near as conservative as it is often made out to be, there's little doubt that millions of Americans harbor reactionary views on both social and economic issues and could be mobilized to resist a reform-minded Democratic president or Congress with minimal effort from the demagogues at Fox News.

PART I

In Canada, the picture looks quite a bit different.

Unlike the United States, Canada is a constitutional monarchy with a parliamentary system of government modeled on the UK's. Majority governments where a single party controls the House of Commons are far more common than minority ones and, as a matter of course, party discipline tends to be incredibly strict. (Canada also has an unelected Upper House though, since sitting governments are free to appoint whomever they please to any vacancies, this is rarely a serious obstacle.)

Thanks to Canada's first-past-the-post electoral system, governments don't even need to win 50 percent of the popular vote to wield what is effectively unrestricted legislative power—the sitting Liberal government, led by Justin Trudeau, received less than 40 percent in the federal election that brought it to power four years ago, and it still secured 184 out of 338 seats.

Since 2003, the country's campaign finance system has also been incredibly restrictive. PACs and Super PACs are not a part of the political landscape, spending limits are rigorously enforced, donations and advertising from unions and corporations are banned outright, and the maximum individual contribution to a political party is capped at less than $2,000. District boundaries are drawn by an independent elections commission and the ability of corporations or other interest groups to flood the airwaves with advertising is restricted during campaigns.

What all this means is that Canadian federal governments have comparatively few obstacles to passing transformative legislation, if indeed it's their intention. Except in extreme cases, a prime minister with a majority in the House probably won't face a backbench rebellion and isn't going to run afoul of big donor money in the event they push legislation that private interests dislike. Public opinion, of course, might be an obstacle. Governments aren't generally prone to pursuing policies that are wildly unpopular. But majority public opinion in Canada appears

37

predisposed to supporting big new social programs and higher taxes on the rich. (Recent polling, for example, has found that more than two-thirds of Canadians support a wealth tax[32] and a big majority support the creation of a national universal prescription drug program.[33])

For even more evidence of this, we need to look no further than Justin Trudeau's own campaign messaging in 2015—which gestured, rhetorically at least, toward an activist and progressively minded platform. In office, however, Trudeau has largely governed from the neoliberal center: paying lip service to the problems and injustices facing Canadian society while doing little if anything to meaningfully alleviate them and, in some cases, actively moving things in the opposite direction. Unlike its predecessor, his administration has been willing to acknowledge the threat of climate change, but nonetheless remains fiercely committed to the construction of new oil pipelines. It has tabled a poverty reduction strategy—touted as the first in Canadian history—which in practice amounts to nothing more than a series of new metrics for measuring poverty and includes no resources for actually reducing it.[34] In a cynical sleight of hand, its signature tax hike on the rich was neatly paired with a tax cut for the slightly less rich, the upshot being that those in the top 10 percent of incomes saw the greatest benefit.[35] Having promised to reform Canada's archaic electoral system, it reversed course midstream and denounced the very efforts it had sworn to take up as risky and dangerous.[36]

Despite four years of a Liberal government in office preaching the rhetoric of progressive reform, little about Canadian society has fundamentally changed and there's every reason to believe things will stay that way if the government is re-elected with another majority. And yet, members of the Canadian left can probably expect all the familiar sermons to be repeated when they inevitably protest. Despite the relative lack of obstacles they face compared to America's Democrats, Canada's Liberals have long offered the same sermons to progressively minded voters about the need for "pragmatism" and the necessity of never breaking too much with the status quo, even as they rhetorically acknowledge its injustices.

This cycle is bound to continue until a critical mass finally understands the grim reality that liberalism has far more to do with arresting and stifling social change than it does with pursuing or promoting it. Which is to say: Even when you remove all the obstacles and constraints; even given a carte blanche to reform without impediment; even when doing the right thing would be greeted with resounding popular support; there is simply no fiery spirit hiding behind the familiar liberal timidity.

Even calling it timidity, in fact, is too generous. A timid person, after all, neglects to pursue a desired goal out of fear. The liberal refusal to actualize progressive goals, on the other hand, is quite plainly a conscious choice. Canada is all the evidence we need.

—A version of this essay first appeared in Current Affairs, *October 2019.*

PART II

Bipartisan Bromides

The unreal, artificial character of our politics reflects their insulation from the common life, together with a secret conviction that the real problems are insoluble.[37]

　　—Christopher Lasch

Bipartisan usually means that a larger-than-usual deception is being carried out.

　　—George Carlin

The Curse of Bipartisanship

Let us try a thought experiment. Let's suppose that on a day in the near future all of America's political elites spontaneously agree to be cordial in public, with the media's biggest talking heads quickly following suit. Let's imagine they also sign a document agreeing to finally put their differences aside and work together in the common interests of the American people. Let's suppose (bear with me) that the document officially commits them to put evidence, common sense, and moderation ahead of petty squabbles and country ahead of party. To immortalize this historic treaty, they establish a new statutory holiday called Unity Day—a kind of centrist Bastille Day—commemorating the end of political contention and marking the eternal reign of Reason. At the event's inauguration, statues are unveiled in honor of the philosophes of the pundit gallery whose collective wisdom finally toppled partisanship's ancient régime. In an image that will surely echo throughout the ages, a bespectacled David Brooks stands atop the National Mall to unveil a towering monument to moderation. Henceforth, the word "partisan" will be Washington's most vicious slur and all but a few eccentrics will conduct themselves in a manner that ensures they are never tarred by it.

Having imagined all of this, it's worth asking how much life for the average person would meaningfully change if this little farce were to become reality.

If a single cliché unites all of establishment political discourse in America, it might be the idea that the greatest obstacle to progress is Partisanship in Washington, i.e., powerful people's inability to get along. Variations of this hallowed fable, and the whole extended family that makes up the Too-Much-Partisanship Industrial Complex, are found all over Capitol Hill, cable news, and throughout all of the nation's papers of record. It's the rationale behind countless astroturfed initiatives under-taken by political operatives upon their retirement. It's the subtext of every breathlessly written cover story proclaiming a dangerous new era of polarization and warning us about the threat posed by populist dema-gogues. It's the epistemology genetically programmed into the most cre-tinous breed of op-ed writer when they emerge, fully formed and lanyard clad, from the primordial pundit ooze.

For their part, politicians themselves, supposedly the greatest cul-prits in fostering a hyper-partisan environment, frankly can't seem to stop decrying it while declaring their intention to put differences aside in the name of some idealized common good that always seems just out of reach. Democratic Senator Amy Klobuchar wants to "bring back bipartisan talks" on health care.[38] So does Republican Senator Lamar Alexander.[39] So does Donald Trump![40] Paul Ryan and Nancy Pelosi, in a joint interview, proudly informed the public that "most of what we actu-ally pass is bipartisan," with Pelosi lamenting that "what's newsworthy is what is controversial."[41] Calls for bipartisanship are the white noise of institutional American politics, perpetually emanating from the Beltway in a dull and ceaseless drone.

The basic story goes something like this: ordinary Americans are fed up with the petty squabbling that dominates DC. Reckless partisan-ship prevents compromise on the issues that matter and most voters, who are manifestly non-ideological (whatever this entails), simply want to see their out-of-touch political representatives work across the aisle for a change. Brinkmanship prevails and nothing, or so the expression goes, "gets done."

This trope, at once tired and ubiquitous, hinges on the idea that most people share a common set of desires and values and could agree on things if only the gosh darn politicians and talking heads would stop stoking division. There are no unbridgeable divides, only needlessly inflamed rhetoric. Politics is not a contest of right and left, rich and poor, insiders and outsiders, exploiters and exploited, just a meritocracy of discourse and ideas. This was the message that first landed Barack Obama in the national spotlight, with his 2004 "Red America, Blue America" speech. It was Jon Stewart's core message during 2010's Rally to Restore Sanity, which he framed as being about "tone, not content."[42] It inspired the almost satirical "No Labels" initiative undertaken by former Bush and Clinton advisors David Frum and William Galston, whose great emancipatory battle cry to the restless masses was "a grassroots answer to gridlock."[43] More recently, it provided the backdrop for center-left think tank Third Way's bizarre safari into Trump country—a multi-city "listening tour"[44] that will probably be cited by subsequent generations of sociologists as a case study in confirmation bias (its chief finding, of course, being that ordinary Americans want Washington to Put Aside Differences And Get Things Done.)

The bipartisanship fable is one with real, if superficial, appeal. For one thing, a part of its critique is undeniably true: the talking heads on cable news manifestly *do* spend much of their time stoking division for its own sake and tying themselves into knots to defend their chosen side in America's never-ending culture war. For that reason, the story offers temptingly simple solutions to what ails American politics. If powerful people's lack of collegiality and compromise is the problem, after all, the fixes are obvious. Washington's grownups need merely to pull up their sleeves and use their indoor voices; cable news pundits need only become a bit less shrill; campaign cycles less reliant on attack ads. These things being the case then somewhere, just out of sight, there lies our hypothesized bipartisan promised land—a place where most agree on all the big questions and every national debate is as high-minded as a friendly joust at the Oxford Union. All the while, absolutely nothing about the fundamental structures underpinning America's politics or economy need actually change.

The most glaringly obvious hole in the bipartisanship story is that those at the top of American politics and culture already do, often visibly, get along pretty well. They exchange banter at the same awards dinners, appear on the same late night talk shows, occupy the same area codes, and tend to pay the same, criminally low, rates of income tax.

Despite the supposedly unbridgeable chasm of the partisan divide, examples of elite chumminess abound. Only four short years ago, Ivanka Trump was fundraising for Cory Booker.[45] Samantha Power, who once harshly criticized Henry Kissinger's human rights record, joined him at a 2014 Yankees game and accepted an award in his name.[46] Just days after they had exchanged fire over the value of black lives on national TV, the *Daily Show*'s Trevor Noah was sending Tomi Lahren (who compared Black Lives Matter to the KKK) a conciliatory batch of cupcakes.[47] The legendary "Notorious RBG" was close friends with Antonin Scalia, whose recent posthumous book contains a gushing foreword from Ginsburg on how "some very good people have ideas with which we disagree."[48] Van Jones, who was supposedly too much of a radical leftist to serve in the Obama administration, has just penned a book on how to "come together," a philosophy he has practiced by taking gleeful selfies with Eric Trump.[49]

The 2016 presidential election, which supposedly brought to the surface a uniquely divided America, is perhaps the perfect case in point. Prior to their formal political rivalry, the Clinton and Trump families enjoyed a friendly relationship for over a decade, the former infamously attending the latter's wedding in 2005. Even the election and its aftermath have failed to fully corrode these bonds. Mere hours before her shock defeat, Clinton made it known that she hoped to patch things up with Trump—a man who had threatened to "lock her up" and who she and her supporters had routinely characterized as an existential threat to the republic itself.

(Their daughters, incidentally, also vowed to continue as "good friends" and last August, Bill, Hillary, and Tiffany Trump were all cordially invited to the wedding of Sophie Lasry, the daughter of hedge fund billionaire Marc Lasry.)[50]

It should come as no surprise that people closest to the center of power are often the ones most fond of extolling the virtues of bipartisanship and consensus. This is, after all, more or less the reality many of them already inhabit, and the one they more or less need to inhabit if they want to be upwardly mobile—genuinely controversial ideas are unlikely to get you a promotion. The Beltway may not be a place of total agreement, but it's certainly one where internal conflict rarely has serious consequences for those directly involved. Debates with outcomes that potentially affect millions of lives can provide raw material for jocular cocktail chatter at the nearest capitol bar or even become an occasion for the affable exchange of baked goods. Friendships may be strained, prestige may be lost, and members of the two competing political and cultural tribes may have to trade offices every few years, but the price of failure for those at the top still tends to be a teaching gig in the ivory tower, a lucrative job in lobbying or finance or, in the worst case scenario, a multimillion dollar book deal from Simon & Schuster.[51] Even the most loathed former presidents are generally afforded the equivalent of secular sainthood, especially—as in the case of George W. Bush—if their successors prove to be even worse. Given these rather lowly stakes, it's easy to understand why so many elites find bipartisanship appealing.

In the wake of Trump, high profile Democrats have taken to evangelizing bipartisanship in an increasingly absurdist fashion. After the Republican Senate passed its robber baron tax package last December, a lachrymose Chuck Schumer took to Twitter to lament "what could have been" describing tax reform as "an issue that is ripe for bipartisan compromise"[52] (Schumer has long favored massive corporate tax cuts), while the Democratic Party's official Senate account praised Ronald Reagan's approach to tax policy.[53] Despite a sweeping victory over Republicans in Virginia, newly elected Democratic Governor Ralph Northam is now preaching bipartisanship ("Virginians deserve civility . . . they're looking for a moral compass right now")[54] and exploring ways he can work with those across the aisle to reduce spending on Medicaid. In a recent intervention, Bill Clinton even issued the groundbreaking suggestion that Americans work to "expand the definition of 'us' and shrink the definition of 'them.'"[55]

Bipartisan posturing of this kind would be absurd in a healthy democracy even at the best of times—after all, one of the reasons we elect people is so that they can debate and disagree and, if you're not fighting with anyone, you're not fighting for anything. But, given the stated agenda of the current administration, not to mention countless other Republican-led administrations across the country, bipartisanship is perilous and counterproductive almost by definition.

Despite some obvious areas of discord, it's not as if American elites have spent the past several decades disagreeing, cordially or otherwise, on a particularly large scale. Both parties have largely promoted a corporatist agenda and their respective leaderships have been united in their mutual support for policies of unending war, mass incarceration, means-testing, and privately administered for-profit health care. The same plutocrats bankroll everyone's reelections: even the Koch brothers have given hundreds of thousands of dollars to Democrats.[56] Hedge fund managers vastly preferred Clinton over Trump, and Wall Street can go back and forth depending on who seems marginally more favorable to their interests. (They adored Obama in 2008, but switched to ex-private equity executive Mitt Romney in 2012.)[57]

The operating premise of those who promote bipartisanship, in other words, is flawed. The problem isn't that elites are so acrimonious they can't agree or forge a consensus, but rather that they continue to be harmonious enough to do both, often with devastating consequences.

Bipartisan consensus is the reason tens of millions of Americans still can't afford health care and why so many elections are ultimately bought and sold rather than won or lost. It's how Washington elites from the center-left to the center-right can look upon a country where thousands die every year because they can't afford to go to the doctor and quite earnestly conclude that the remedy is another wretched compromise between the federal government and a junta of bloodsucking private insurance firms. It's the reason Americans have found themselves engaged in a state of destructive, open-ended war, and it is why debates about military intervention invariably revolve around how to prosecute it most competently rather than whether to prosecute it at all. It's why the country's public schools and infrastructure are allowed to crumble while trillions in subsidies go to genocidal gizmos that would give Dr. Strangelove pause. It's why wealth inequality is soaring while wages continue to stagnate and why prisons are overflowing with the poor, racialized, and mentally ill while rapacious bankers who commit fraud and collapse the economy are deemed too big to jail.

And it's how, amid all this, it remains possible and indeed downright respectable to believe that the greatest obstacle to a decent society is bad manners.

—*A version of this essay first appeared in* Current Affairs, *January 2018.*

Liberalism's Veil of Ignorance

Review of A Citizen's Guide to Beating Donald Trump *by David Plouffe (Penguin Random House, (2020)*

As a matter of professional necessity, I am regularly obliged to watch clips from cable news. To say I don't particularly enjoy the experience would be something of an understatement. In fact, on the rare occasions it becomes necessary to watch an entire program, I am aghast that so many people opt to do so voluntarily, idly wondering if I've committed an unpardonable sin and slipped into some lesser circle of Hell, a place where the damned must pay eternal penance by listening to talking heads deliver insights about politics so trite they might as well be sports commentary. ("The economy's going to be a big factor in 2020, no doubt about it," "When it comes to candidates, the most important thing is always character," "In campaigns, messaging matters but on election day it's all about the ground game . . .", etc., etc., ad infinitum as the flames lick my ankles.)

On an aesthetic level, David Plouffe's *A Citizen's Guide to Beating Donald Trump* reads like several hours of punditry in precisely this vein, transcribed for those who prefer to consume the august medium of cable news in literary form. Tedious even by the cavernously low standards of the many Why Trump Is Bad cash-grab books that have popped up since 2016, the author delivers more or less what a skeptical left-wing observer might assume from its title: a mass market political treatise containing instructions for what the average person can do to ensure Donald Trump's defeat in November.

Many of these turn out to be prosaic beyond belief—so much so that even the most hardened Obama partisans are liable to be disappointed.

Despite Plouffe's ostensible bona fides as a political master strategist (he did, after all, manage Barack Obama's stupendously successful presidential campaign in 2008) the book is more Idiot's Guide than Art of War, brimming with banal observations like "the [Democratic] nominee must win the economic argument against Donald Trump among those voters who will decide the election," all written in the same drably declarative prose. Elsewhere, for example, in a chapter evocatively entitled "Create," the author observes "It is absolutely mandatory that we weaponize our own social media and email lists," waiting until midway through the book to deliver one of its most memorable aphorisms: "Registering won't get you to victory if our people don't then vote." Machiavelli or Sun Tzu could hardly have put it better.

Nearly the whole of *A Citizen's Guide to Beating Donald Trump* reads this way, the mundane instructions that make up most of the text punctuated with occasional war stories from the Obama campaign and the odd personal anecdote. The word Russia, perhaps unsurprisingly, makes plenty of appearances. (I counted nine, more if you include the various allusions to Putin, Moscow, and, for some reason, Belarus.) It's mercifully not until page 98 that the phrase "Orange Menace" rears its head and somewhere near the book's halfway point before we are finally subjected to the inevitable *West Wing* reference.[58]

At least some of the mundanity is owed to the book having been written in the summer of 2019, long before the heat of the primary season and well before important details of the general election matchup were known. This, says Plouffe, is intentional:

> I have no idea . . . who the nominee will be. I don't know how various issues, including the economy, the tariff wars, the border wall, North Korea, Iran, and impeachment will play out over the next year . . . My timing is intentional because knowing the candidate does not matter in terms of getting ready for the main

event, the general election . . . Please, please, do not waste vital
energy and time worrying about events we do not control. . .[59]

This veil-of-ignorance approach is meant to be the book's strength: the
very thing that makes it a practically minded handbook which the average
person can use to become an effective militant in the anti-Trump struggle of 2020. But with the details of policy and ideology—not to mention
more basic facts like who the Democratic candidate is and what they're
running on—entirely absent, *A Citizen's Guide to Beating Donald Trump* is
reduced to making a series of prescriptions so obvious and pedestrian it's
by no means clear that they justify its existence.

Be an enthusiastic Democrat. Make phone calls. Register to vote and
tell your friends to do the same. Contribute money. Host debate-watch
parties. Email your friends and post pro-Democratic messages on social
media, preferably putting the campaign's message-box in your own voice
so it sounds more "authentic." Interact with voters and use the exchanges
to create lists. If you canvass your neighborhood, post a photo of the canvass on Instagram, etc. A few paragraphs are even dedicated to explaining basic concepts like how data collection works, what a battleground
state is, and the difference between the popular vote and the electoral
college.

Like many elite liberals, Plouffe is evidently under the impression
that people who fail to vote Democrat primarily do so out of ignorance or
because they've internalized misinformation. To this end, a key section is
devoted to tutoring readers on the finer points of how to argue with fellow
citizens online:

> You see something in your Facebook feed from one of your
> old college friends about a "study" demonstrating that if the
> Democrat is victorious, crime will rise 50 percent and rapes
> and murders from undocumented immigrants will triple. Take

a minute to shake your head in frustration, sigh in sadness, but then respond calmly and by sharing content that shows the Democrat's commitment to increasing funds for local enforcement; stats showing that immigrants commit fewer crimes than those native born; our candidate's commitment to solving at long last the immigration challenge with comprehensive reform, including smart, humane, technology-based border security. [60]

(Plouffe, of course, simply assumes the Democratic nominee will have exactly these commitments come election time—a fact which tells us something about his own political preferences, and what he believes is possible.)

In an accidentally funny passage that comes shortly after, Plouffe imagines how a savvy Democratic partisan might respond to a caricatured red-state relative posting conspiracy theories about liberal politicians and infanticide. Should this happen, he advises, "the wisest course" is to "inwardly vent your frustration and sadness, then get down to business," explaining things to the hypothetical Crazy Uncle John as follows:

Uncle John, I respect that you support Trump. As you know, I do not support Trump. While I don't support everything about the Democratic nominee, I think on balance our country would be better off with that nominee in the White House than four more years of Trump. But let's make it an honest debate. You have plenty of arguments to make on Trump's behalf that are true and maybe persuasive to some. The article/video/infographic you just shared to suggest the Democratic nominee supports infanticide is a lie. No credible person in our country, much less a presidential candidate, supports infanticide. My candidate is pro-choice, yes. Donald Trump used to be pro-choice; now he says he's pro-life. So there's that difference. My candidate wants abortion to be safe, legal, and rare. Trump would like to see it outlawed—for every woman. Check out this article below from *The Wall Street Journal*, hardly a liberal source, that captures the candidate positions on abortion and makes clear the infanticide charge is a hideous lie. [61]

Even Plouffe is obliged to concede that this approach may not actually change any minds: ("Maybe it will have an impact on someone in the chain. Maybe not."). Nonetheless, it's amusing to think that a veteran of so many election campaigns believes the best antidote to misinformation is calm recitation of facts and logic. (Still more amusing is to imagine Plouffe's strategy taken to its logical conclusion: "Listen @DeusVult_1776, I respect that you believe Trump is on a divinely ordained mission to prevent the Satanic Islamicist Soros cult from carrying out Agenda 21. While I don't support everything about our Democratic nominee . . . ")

This brings us to a bigger problem with Plouffe's veil of ignorance approach: namely, that it leaves nothing for the average person to do besides mindlessly campaign for whoever the Democratic Party nominates. Once again, the author tells us, this is intentional—the book's foundational premise being that there is simply nothing more important than getting Donald Trump out of the White House. "There is only one fact," Plouffe writes, "that you need to focus on now: our candidate will be infinitely preferable to the incumbent."[62]

Though Plouffe doesn't know it, this sentiment is what makes his book an accidentally lucid treatise on the hollowness of elite liberal politics in 2020. That's because, despite it being partially true (Democratic presidents do tend to be preferable to Republican ones, though "infinitely" is really pushing it) it's also a credo maintained by Democratic partisans regardless of circumstance. Try to recall a time when the likes of David Plouffe deemed it acceptable to mount serious criticisms of the Democratic Party and its leaders, and you will inevitably struggle. The Republican bogeyman invariably justifies whatever the latest triangulation happens to be, and renders anything but the most obsequious deference to the party and its apparatchiks akin to collaboration with the enemy.

Lesser-evilism has been an animating principle among American liberals for as long as I can remember, and it rather conveniently fails to disappear even after election seasons have concluded. Which is to say: Plouffe's veil-of-ignorance approach may justify itself by invoking the exceptional danger of the Trump presidency, but the same exceptional danger was also said to be with us in 2000, 2004, 2008, 2012, and 2016. Democrats being preferable to Republicans, or so it follows, there's little reason for the socially concerned person to ever do more than try and elect the former, and dull any moral reservations about the kinds of things they regularly do when in office. Once this line of reasoning has been fully internalized, the whole enterprise of political and social activism as we know it becomes indistinguishable from unthinking partisanship for the Democratic Party and its leaders, the rank-and-file liberal reduced to little more than a campaign drone who blindly follows directives handed down from above. (Though there are many reasons centrist liberals have exhibited such a burning hatred for Bernie Sanders, his movement's steadfast refusal to assume this hierarchical and deferential posture is undoubtedly among the most significant.)

This is the actual purpose of liberalism's veil of ignorance: to subordinate policy, ideology, and even basic morality to the wider goal of electing Generic Democrat and keeping any Republican out of office. Tellingly, Plouffe's supposed manual for a citizen's crusade rarely even mentions actual issues and, when it does, it's invariably in the service of helping elect said Democrat regardless of their commitments or platform—which we do not know. And in any case, it is suggested this doesn't matter (though the author somehow did know the Democratic nominee's border and immigration policies in summer 2019).

For something supposedly motivated by disgust at the state of things in Trump's America, Plouffe's book is notably short on genuine moral outrage or substantive political concern outside the electoral event scheduled for November 2020. Vital issues like the influence of organized money in politics, climate change, mass incarceration, and health care are scarcely even mentioned, if indeed they're mentioned at all.

A handbook for fighting conservative reaction that doesn't discuss ideology, program, or social vision beyond the nearest electoral horizon? You'd be hard-pressed to find a better précis of America's gilded, ideologically exhausted, and over-professionalized liberal project than that.

—A version of this essay first appeared in Current Affairs, *July 2020.*

How Liberals Fell in Love with
The West Wing

In the history of prestige TV, few dramas have had quite the cultural stay-ing power of Aaron Sorkin's *The West Wing*. Set during the two terms of fictional Democratic president and Nobel Laureate in Economics Josiah "Jed" Bartlet (Martin Sheen), the show depicts the inner workings of a sympathetic liberal administration grappling with the daily exigencies of governing. Every procedure and protocol, every piece of political bro-kerage—from State of the Union addresses to legislative tugs of war to Supreme Court appointments—is recreated with an aesthetic authentic-ity enabled by ample production values (a single episode reportedly cost almost $3 million to produce) and rendered with a dramatic flair that stylizes all the bureaucratic banality of modern governance.

The same, of course, might be said of other glossy political dramas such as Netflix's *House of Cards* or *Scandal*. But *The West Wing* aspires to more than simply visual verisimilitude. Breaking with the cynicism or amoralism characteristic of many dramas about politics, it offers a vision of political institutions that is ultimately affirmative and approv-ing. What we see throughout its seven seasons are Democrats govern-ing as Democrats imagine they govern, with the Bartlet administration standing in for liberalism as liberalism understands itself.

More than just a fictional account of an idealized Democratic pres-idency, *The West Wing* is a revealing projection of the shibboleths that animate Beltway liberalism and the political milieu that produced them.

****

During its run from 1999 to 2006, *The West Wing* garnered immense popularity and attention, capturing three Golden Globe Awards and twenty-six Emmys and building a devout fan base among Democratic partisans, Beltway acolytes, and people of the liberal-ish persuasion the world over. Since its finale more than a decade ago, it has become an essential part of the liberal cultural ecosystem, its importance arguably on par with *The Daily Show*, *SNL*, and the rap musical about the founding fathers with which it shares many fans.

If anything, its influence has only continued to grow with age. In the summer of 2016, a weekly podcast hosted by seasons 4–7 star Joshua Malina launched with the ultimate goal of running through all 154 episodes (at a rate of one per week), and almost immediately garnered millions of downloads; an elaborate fan wiki with almost two thousand distinct entries is maintained and regularly updated, magisterially documenting every mundane detail of the *West Wing* cosmos save the characters' bowel movements; and, in definitive proof of the silence of God, superfan Lin-Manuel Miranda has recently recorded a rap named for one of the show's most popular catchphrases ("What's next?").

While certainly appealing to a general audience thanks to its expensive sheen and distinctive writing, *The West Wing*'s greatest zealots have proven to be those who professionally inhabit the very milieu it depicts: Washington political staffers, media types, centrist cognoscenti, and various others drawn from the ranks of those who tweet "Big, if true" in earnest and think a lanyard is a talisman that grants wishes and wards off evil.

The West Wing "took something that was for the most part considered dry and nerdy—especially to people in high school and college—and sexed it up," former David Axelrod advisor Eric Lesser told *Vanity Fair* in a longform 2012 feature about the "Sorkinization of politics" (Axelrod himself having at one point advised *West Wing* writer Eli Attie). It "very much served as inspiration," said Micah Lasher, a staffer who then worked for Michael Bloomberg.[63]

Thanks to its endless depiction of procedure and policy, the show naturally gibed with the wonkish libidos of future *Voxsplainers* Matt Yglesias and Ezra Klein. "There's a cultural meme or cultural suggestion that Washington is boring, that policy is boring, but it's important stuff," said Klein, adding that the show dramatized "the immediacy and urgency and concern that people in this town feel about the issues they're working on." "I was interested in politics before the show started," added Yglesias. "But a friend of mine from college moved to DC at the same time as me, after graduation, and we definitely plotted our proposed domination of the capital in explicitly *West Wing* terms: Who was more like Toby? Who was more like Josh?"[64]

Far from the Kafkaesque banality which so often characterizes the real-life equivalent, the mundane business of technocratic governance is made to look exciting, intellectually stimulating, and, above all, honorable. The bureaucratic drudgery of both White House management and governance, from speechwriting, to press conference logistics, to policy creation, are front and center across all seven seasons. A typical episode script is chock full of dweebish phraseology—"farm subsidies," "recess appointments," "census bureau," "congressional consultation"—usually uttered by swift-tongued, Ivy League-educated staffers darting purposefully through labyrinthine corridors during the infamous "walk-and-talk" sequences. By recreating the look and feel of political processes to the tee and garnishing them with a romantic veneer, the show gifts the Beltway's most spiritually committed adherents with a vision of how many would probably like to see themselves.

In serving up this optimistic simulacrum of modern US politics, Sorkin's universe has repeatedly intersected with real-life US politics. Following the first season, and in the midst of the 2000 presidential election contest, *Salon*'s Joyce Millman wrote: "Al Gore could clinch the election right now by staging as many photo-ops with the cast of *The West Wing* as possible."[65] A poll published during the same election found that most voters preferred Martin Sheen's President Bartlet to Bush or Gore.[66] A 2008 *New York Times* article predicted an Obama victory on the basis of the show's seasons 6–7 plot arc. The same election year, the paper published a fictionalized exchange between Bartlet and Barack Obama penned by Sorkin himself.[67] 2016 proved no exception, with the *New Statesman*'s Helen Lewis reacting to Donald Trump's victory by saying: "I'm going to hug my *West Wing* boxset a little closer tonight, that's for sure."

Appropriately, many of the show's cast members, leveraging their on-screen personas, have participated or intervened in real Democratic Party politics. During the 2016 campaign, star Bradley Whitford—who portrays frenetically wily strategist Josh Lyman—was invited to "reveal" who his [fictional] boss would endorse: "There's no doubt in my mind that Hillary would be President Bartlet's choice. She's—nobody is more prepared to take that position on day one. I know this may be controversial. But yes, on behalf of Jed Bartlet, I want to endorse Hillary Clinton."[68] Six leading members of the cast, including Whitford, were even dispatched to Ohio to stump for Clinton (inexplicably failing to swing the crucial state in her favor).

During the Democratic primary season Rob Lowe (who appeared from 1999–2003 before leaving in protest at the ostensible stinginess of his $75,000-per-episode salary) even deployed a clip from the show and paraphrased his own character's lines during an attack on Bernie Sanders's tax plan: "Watching Bernie Sanders. He's hectoring and yelling at me WHILE he's saying he's going to raise our taxes. Interesting way to communicate."[69] In season 2 episode "The Fall's Gonna Kill You," Lowe's character Sam Seaborn angrily lectures a team of speechwriters: "Every time your boss got on the stump and said, 'It's time for the rich to pay their fair share,' I hid under a couch and changed my name . . . The top 1 percent of wage earners in this country pay for 22 percent of this country. Let's not call them names while they're doing it, is all I'm saying."

What, then, is the actual ideology of *The West Wing*? Just like the real American liberalism it represents, the show proved to be something of a weathervane throughout its seven seasons on the air. Debuting during the twilight of the Clinton presidency and spanning much of Bush II's, its politics predictably vacillated in response to events while remaining grounded in a general liberal ethos. Having writing credits for all but one episode in *The West Wing*'s first four seasons, Sorkin left in 2003, with executive producer John Wells characterizing the subsequent direction as more balanced and bipartisan. The Bartlet administration's actual politics—just like those of the real Democratic Party—therefore run the gamut from the stuff of Elizabeth Warren-esque wonkery to the straightforward neoliberal bilge of a Beltway think tank financing its reports with assistance from UnitedHealth or Goldman Sachs.

But promoting or endorsing any specific policy orientation is not the show's true raison d'être. At the conclusion of its seven seasons, it remains unclear if the Bartlet administration has succeeded at all in fundamentally altering the contours of American life. In fact, after two terms in the White House, Bartlet's gang of hyper-educated, hyper-competent politicos do not seem to have any transformational policy achievements whatsoever. Even in their most unconstrained and idealized political fantasies, liberals manage to accomplish nothing.

Insofar as there is an identifiable ideology, it isn't one definitively wedded to a particular program of reform, but instead to a particular aesthetic of political institutions. The business of leveraging democracy for any specific purpose comes second to how its institutional liturgy and processes look and, more importantly, how they make us feel—virtue being attached more to posture and affect than to any particular goal. Echoing Sorkin's 1995 film *The American President* (in many ways the progenitor of *The West Wing*), it delights in invoking "seriousness" and the supposedly hard-headed pragmatism of grownups.

Consider a scene from season 2's "The War at Home," in which Toby Ziegler (Richard Schiff) confronts a rogue Democratic senator over his objections to Social Security cuts prospectively to be made in collaboration with a Republican Congress. The episode's protagonist certainly isn't the latter, who tries to draw a line in the sand over the "compromising of basic Democratic values" and threatens to run a third-party presidential campaign, only to be admonished acerbically by Ziegler: "If you think demonizing people who are trying to govern responsibly is the way to protect our liberal base, then speaking as a liberal . . . go to bed, would you please? . . . Come at us from the left, and I'm gonna own your ass."

The administration and its staff are invariably depicted as tribunes of the serious and the mature, their ideological malleability taken to signify their virtue more than any fealty to specific liberal principles. Even when the show ventures to criticize the institutions of American democracy, it never retreats from a foundational reverence for their supposed enlightenment and the essential nobility of most of the people who administer them. As such, the presidency's basic function is to appear presidential and, more than anything, Jed Bartlet's patrician aura and respectable disposition make him the perfect avatar for the *West Wing* universe's often maudlin deference to the liturgy of "the office." "Seriousness," then—the superlative quality in the Sorkin taxonomy of virtues—implies presiding over the political consensus, tinkering here and there, and looking stylish in the process by way of soaring oratory and White-collar chic.

****

Its relatively thin ideological commitments notwithstanding, there is a general tenor to the *West Wing* universe that cannot be called anything other than smug. It is a smugness born of the view that politics is less a terrain of clashing values and interests than a perpetual pitting of the clever against the ignorant and obtuse. The clever wield facts and reason, while the foolish cling to effortlessly exposed fictions and the braying prejudices of provincial rubes. In emphasizing intelligence over ideology, what follows is a fetishization of "elevated discourse" regardless of its actual content or conclusions. The greatest political victories involve semantically dismantling an opponent's argument or exposing its hypocrisy, usually by way of some grand rhetorical gesture. Categories like left and right become less significant, provided that the competing interlocutors are deemed respectable and practice the designated etiquette. The Discourse becomes a category of its own, to be protected and nourished by Serious People conversing respectfully while shutting down the stupid with heavy-handed moral sanctimony.

In Toby Ziegler's "smart and not," "qualified and not" formulation,[70] we can see a preview of the (disastrous) rhetorical strategy that Hillary Clinton would ultimately adopt against Donald Trump. Don't make it about vision, make it about qualification. Don't make it about your plans for how to make people's lives better, make it about your superior moral character. Fundamentally, make it about how smart and good and serious you are, and how bad and dumb and unserious they are.

In this respect, *The West Wing*'s foundational serious/unserious binary falls squarely within the tradition that has since evolved into the "epic own/evisceration" genre characteristic of social media and late-night TV, in which the aim is to ruthlessly use one's intellect to expose the idiocy and hypocrisy of the other side. In a famous scene from season 4's "Game On," Bartlet debates his Republican rival, Governor Robert Ritchie (James Brolin). Their exchange, prompted by a question about the role of the federal government, is the stuff of a Keith Olbermann wet dream:

Ritchie: My view of this is simple. We don't need a federal Department of Education telling us our children have to learn Esperanto, they have to learn Eskimo poetry. Let the states decide, let the communities decide on health care and education, on lower taxes, not higher taxes. Now he's going to throw a big word at you—"unfunded mandate," he's going to say if Washington lets the states do it, it's an unfunded mandate. But what he doesn't like is the federal government losing power. I call it the ingenuity of the American people.

Bartlet: Well first of all let's clear up a couple of things: unfunded mandate is two words, not one big word. There are times when we are 50 states and there are times when we're one country and have national needs. And the way I know this is that Florida didn't fight Germany in World War Two or establish civil rights. You think states should do the governing wall-to-wall, now that's a perfectly valid opinion. But your state of Florida got 12.6 billion dollars in federal money last year from Nebraskans and Virginians and New Yorkers and Alaskans, with their Eskimo poetry—12.6 out of the state budget of 50 billion. I'm supposed to be using this time for a question so here it is: Can we have it back please?

In another famous scene from the season 2 episode "The Midterms," Bartlet humiliates homophobic talk radio host Jenna Jacobs by quoting scripture from memory, destroying her by her very own logic.

If Richie and Jacobs are the obtuse yokels to be epically taken down with facts and reason, the show also elevates several conservative characters to reinforce its post-partisan celebration of The Discourse. Republicans come in two types: slack-jawed caricatures, and people whose high-mindedness and mutual enthusiasm for Putting Differences

Aside make them the Bartlet administration's natural allies or friends regardless of whatever conflicts of values they may ostensibly have. Foremost among the latter is Arnold Vinick (Alan Alda), a moderate, pro-choice Republican who resembles John McCain (at least the imaginary "maverick" John McCain that liberals continue to pretend exists) and is appointed by Bartlet's Democratic successor Matthew Santos (Jimmy Smits) to be secretary of state. (In reality, there is no such thing as a "moderate" Republican, only a polite one. The upright and genial Paul Ryan, whom President Bartlet would have loved, is on a lifelong quest to dismantle every part of America's feeble social safety net.)

Thus, Bartlet Democrats do not see Republicans as the "enemy," except to the extent that they are rude or insufficiently respectful of the rules of political decorum. In one season 5 plot, the administration opts to install a Ruth Bader Ginsburg clone (Glenn Close) as chief justice of the Supreme Court. The price it pays—willingly, as it turns out—is giving the other vacancy to an ultra-conservative justice, for the sole reason that Bartlet's staff find their amiable squabbling stimulating. (Ziegler: "I hate him, but he's brilliant. And the two of them together are fighting like cats and dogs . . . but it works.")

Through its idealized rendering of American politics and its institutions, *The West Wing* offers a comforting avenue of escape from the grim and often dystopian reality of the present. If the show, despite its age, has continued to find favor and relevance among liberals, Democrats, and assorted Beltway acolytes alike, it's because it reflects and affirms their worldview with far greater fidelity and catharsis than any of its contemporaries.

But if anything gives that worldview pause, it should be the events of the past eight years. Liberals got a real-life Josiah Bartlet in the figure of Barack Obama, a charismatic and stylish politician elected on a wave of popular enthusiasm. But Obama's soaring speeches, quintessentially presidential affect, and deference to procedure did little to fundamentally change the country or prevent his Republican rivals from storming the congressional barricades at their first opportunity. Confronted in 2016 by a mercurial TV personality bent on transgressing every norm and truism of Beltway thinking, Democrats responded by exhaustively informing voters of his indecency and hypocrisy, attempting to destroy him countless times with *his own logic* but ultimately leaving him completely intact. They smugly taxonomized as "smart" and "dumb" the very electorate they needed to win over, and retreated into an insular fantasy in which political success comes from having the most detailed policy statements and the most polished arguments rather than organizing or building power. If you can simply just crush Trump in debates, as Bartlet does to Ritchie, then you've won.

Now, facing defeat and political crisis, the guiding liberal instinct has not been self-reflection but a further retreat into Ivy League dogmas and orthodoxies. Like fans at the climax of *The West Wing's* original run, they sit waiting for the decisive gestures and gratifying crescendos of a series finale, only to find their favorite plotlines and characters meandering without resolution. Shockingly, life is not a television program, and Aaron Sorkin doesn't get to write the ending.

The West Wing is many things: a uniquely popular and lavish effort in prestige TV; an often crisply written drama; a fictionalized paean to Beltway liberalism's foundational precepts; a wonkish celebration of institutions and processes; an exquisitely tailored exercise in political fanfiction. But, in 2017, it is foremost a series of glittering illusions to be abandoned.

—*A version of this essay first appeared in* Current Affairs, *June 2017.*

2004 Redux

Review of Irresistible, *directed by Jon Stewart (Focus Features, 2020)*

One of the defining moments of Jon Stewart's career remains his famous 2004 appearance on CNN's *Crossfire*. Like many of my fellow millennials, I watched the clip dozens of times, and parts of it would linger in my memory for years—it having a far greater resonance than any of the televised debates from that year's election season, all of which I forgot about in a matter of days.

Revisit the footage in 2020, and it's still easy to see why it had such an impact. Skewering hosts Tucker Carlson and Paul Begala as a pair of "hacks," Stewart eviscerated the noxious partisan theater that passes for debate on cable TV—correctly bemoaning a media culture that prizes empty adversarialism and histrionics over the genuine exchange of ideas. Pointed and funny, it was an example of what Stewart did best during his many years as host of *The Daily Show*: expose the political and media class with a hatred that often seemed genuinely pure.

Though I didn't clue in at the time, the famous *Crossfire* episode was emblematic of another, somewhat less laudable streak running throughout Stewart's career: one altogether closer to the why-can't-we-all-just-get-alongism favored by the same Beltway talking heads he has so long disdained. "Why do we have to fight?" pleaded Stewart in his opening salvo against Carlson and Begala—a sentiment he would channel some six years later at the Rally to Restore Sanity, an event convened to denounce a rancor its hosts more or less contended was being imposed from above. As Robin Marie Averbeck would later put it in a 2014 essay for *Jacobin*:

The festival reached its height as the spectators were treated to a video montage of fire-breathing pundits from all the major news networks denouncing their political opponents. The message was clear: Those who tell you there are fundamental differences between Americans that are worth getting emphatically angry about are lying to you. This divided America—an America that contains people with radically different values and radically different ideas of what a just, moral society looks like—does not exist. If it seems otherwise, it is simply because, as one sign at the rally put it, we fail to use our "inside voices."

Though his dislike for America's political and media class has invariably seemed genuine, there has always been a parallel streak in Stewart that earnestly views political differences as artificial—partisan conflict being something inflicted on ordinary Americans by a ratings-obsessed media in partnership with a political class that stokes culture war for its own sake.

He isn't wrong, of course, to contend that both institutions are hopelessly out of touch. Nor was he wrong to argue in 2004 that shows in the mold of *Crossfire* or *Hardball* do absolutely nothing to inform or foster meaningful debate. The problem is that even if you could somehow strip away the partisan White noise of cable news and the theatrical bickering that makes up most of America's political debate, you would still find a deeply unequal society riddled with division and conflict. As Averbeck put it succinctly in 2014: "For all their shameless spectacle-making, the talking heads of the national news media do get one thing right: There are substantial, and fundamental, oppositions between Americans."

****

Just like his appearance on *Crossfire*, the comedian's new film *Irresistible* casts a jaundiced eye toward the culture of the Beltway. Following

70

high-rolling Democratic political consultant Gary Zimmer (played competently by Steve Carell) in the aftermath of the 2016 presidential election, its intended targets will be instantly familiar to anyone who has followed Stewart's career: partisan hacks, cable news, and, perhaps most significantly, the influence of big money in politics.

As Zimmer, who we learn has served in the upper ranks of the Hillary Clinton campaign, convalesces following the Democratic Party's defeat, he sees a YouTube video showing a retired marine colonel eloquently defending the rights of undocumented people at a city council meeting in the small town of Deerlaken, Wisconsin (which has hemorrhaged citizens since the closure of a local military base). Hack and opportunist that he is, Zimmer's political instincts are instantly tickled, and he soon convinces a nameless committee of DNC flunkies to dispatch him to flyover country and recruit the viral Colonel Jack Hastings (Chris Cooper) to run in Deerlaken's mayoral election. Zimmer's aims are entirely cynical, his desire to help the Democrats reconnect with the heartland being entirely concerned with optics and branding, and rural Wisconsin being little more than a laboratory for the DNC's consultant class to test-drive its messaging. Referring to Hastings, he gushes, "He looks like a conservative, he talks like a progressive!"

Much of the film's humor is drawn from the latte-sipping Zimmer's confusion in the face of rustic heartland authenticity. In Washington, he's a high-flying consultant; in Deerlaken, a fish out of water befuddled by Midwestern mores. His awkward attempts to interact with the locals only serve to showcase how little he understands about small-town America.

This conceit, well intentioned though it is, feels exhausted after the first fifteen minutes. As a result, precious few of the gags pack the intended satirical punch. In one scene, Zimmer is shocked to discover that his hotel lacks Wi-Fi; in another, he is thrown off when a local tells him to "have a good one"; in another, he awkwardly tries to blend in by ordering a hamburger and a Budweiser, then can't seem to master twisting off the cap. The film seems so determined not to condescend to its salt-of-the-earth characters that it feels the need to bludgeon us with the same caricature of Beltway elitism over and over again—variously making sure to let us know that Zimmer enjoys caprese salads, listens to NPR, and rides around on a private jet. All well-meaning enough, sure. But about as subtle as an *SNL* sketch riffing on the phrase "Cheeto in Chief" (and mostly just as unfunny).

The same can be said for many of the film's gags about big money and the media, though, for what it's worth, a few of these do manage to land. In one cutaway, a single CNN panel hosts what looks like a dozen guests who are all talking at once; in another, an anchor can be heard saying "Coming up, we'll be looking at this year's hot races and how those will affect races four years from now." The only major appearance of Stewart's old nemesis, Fox News, on the other hand, feels like a dead joke from 2004 that's been kept alive in cryostasis—an angry host declaring of Colonel Hastings throwing in his lot with the Democrats: "I know if I had served, I wouldn't like it." (There are many issues with military jingoism on the right, but too few jar-headed right-wingers having served in uniform to make said jingoism legitimate is about as peak Kerry-era liberalism as you can get, and it already sucked in 2004.)

Zimmer's mission is complicated by the sudden presence of an old rival and romantic interest (Faith Brewster, played by Rose Byrne) in Deerlaken at the head of a massive and well-funded RNC campaign to boost the incumbent Republican mayor. As the campaign comes down to the wire, he informs Hastings and his daughter Diana (Mackenzie Davis) that despite the DNC's money and resources—Zimmer takes Hastings to a big-money fundraiser in New York and secures him several super PACs— his candidacy must go negative in the final days if it intends to cross the finish line.

Here, the film finally appears to be settling on its, albeit decidedly unsubtle, thesis: that a corrupt, bipartisan political establishment treats small-town America as a sideshow while its storefronts shutter and its jobs are exported abroad (though why Stewart chose the closure of Deerlaken's army base to illustrate the Rust Belt experience is unclear, given that the military tends to be the only institution in American life that never experiences austerity). On election day, we see the likes of antifa, Black Lives Matter, the coal and gun lobbies, and MAGA-heads gather outside the local polling stations, but Zimmer is confused when none of the town's five thousand inhabitants seem to be voting. At day's end, the race is tied at one vote apiece.

Then comes a bizarre twist: the whole election has been a sham, seemingly instigated by every citizen of Deerlaken. Zimmer's entire mission, in fact, has been planned by Diana Hastings from day one to bring money into the local economy and pull one over on the clowns in DC. This has the rather strange implication that Colonel Hastings's speech had been every bit as fake as the election, a piece of scripted content denouncing a chauvinist bylaw that never existed. In a confusing series of epilogues dated six months later, it appears that Zimmer has returned to Washington and begun a relationship with his love interest and rival in the RNC, while Diana has been elected mayor of Deerlaken. Just before the credits roll, the film's apparent final message is summed up in the words "Money lived happily ever after, reveling in its outsized influence over American politics."

If much of *Irresistible*'s satire is unsubtle, this tremendously convoluted ending only serves to undermine its intended message, leaving the confused viewer asking questions about exactly what it is that they've just seen. The would-be rubes have won, or so it would seem, but only insofar as they've successfully gamed the campaign finance industrial complex to the town's advantage. More confusingly, Deerlaken's political divides turn out to be entirely fake, superimposed by a political and media class too riven with partisanship and drunk from the poisoned chalice of the almighty dollar to care about average folk. There's no local red/blue divide, no right-wing backlash against the undocumented, no cultural schism over access to abortion (we briefly see one portrayed, but the twist implies this is also fake).

This raises the further question of what exactly we're supposed to make of the lobbyists, BLM activists, and others who show up for Deerlaken's fake mayoral election. Are they local citizens in costume? A part of the national political cavalcade that has descended upon the town? The film's last act is so tangled that there's probably no straightforward answer. Either way, we are left with the impression of a community so civically and culturally homogenous that it has no need for politics (all five thousand citizens, including the incumbent mayor, having been in on the ruse). In a film pitting rubes against elites and trying its darndest to side with the former, it's a startlingly reductive portrait of small-town America—and an example of exactly the kind of patronizing coastal stereotype Stewart's film seems determined to militate against.

As he always has, Jon Stewart still displays good intentions and exhibits a laudable disdain of media bullshit, corruption, and the hollow spectacle of a bipartisan establishment that revels in both. But if *Irresistible* is any indication, his vision has yet to extend itself beyond the chimera of post-partisanship that has always rested so uncomfortably alongside his well-founded scorn for the political and media elite.

—A version of this essay first appeared in Jacobin, *July 2020.*

The Never Trump Delusion

On February 15, 2016, the longtime house journal of American conservatism published nearly two dozen essays with the express purpose
of repudiating the then-ascendant Republican presidential candidate
Donald Trump. Featuring contributions from such prominent voices in
the conservative movement as Bill Kristol and Glenn Beck, the *National
Review*'s now infamous "Against Trump" issue denounced the soon-to-be
president as no less than a "philosophically unmoored political opportunist"—a dangerous demagogue antithetical to everything conservatism
stood for whose quest for the GOP nomination had to be thwarted at any
cost.

Trump, it hardly needs saying, hastily conquered both the American
conservative movement and its principal political arm, the Republican
Party. And, in a development which should have surprised no one, at least
half of those who had contributed to February 2016's official censure not
only fell in line but soon became some of Trumpism's most zealous and
committed partisans.[71]

This includes Eric Erickson, the conservative talk-radio host who
once condemned Trump as "a racist" and "a fascist," adding that it was
no surprise "so many people with swastikas in their Twitter profile pics"
support him. "I will not vote for Donald Trump. Ever." wrote Erickson—
who recently published a piece entitled "I Support the President."[72]

It includes William F. Buckley's nephew L. Brent Bozell III, who in his
National Review essay argued, "Trump might be the greatest charlatan
of them all"[73] and now aides in his efforts to delegitimize critical press.
It includes Glenn Beck, who once called the president "an immoral man

who is absent decency or dignity"[74] and now views him as the ultimate Daddy figure.[75]

With so many erstwhile critics now firmly onside, an approval rating among self-identified Republicans that would make any ribboned despot blush, and a phalanx of sycophants and palace courtiers hanging on his every word, it can safely be said that Donald Trump has enshrined his ideology and personal style as the lingua franca of American conservatism.

Yet turn on cable news or open any of the country's leading newspapers, and there's a good chance you'll be served with a radically different narrative about the orientation of prominent conservative figures toward the current Republican president. I'm speaking, of course, about the so-called Never Trump Conservative: a phenomenon at once so ubiquitous and so illusory it will one day feature in media studies courses as a teachable moment about the dangers of believing everything you see on TV.

Since 2016, figures like David Frum, Bill Kristol, and former McCain apparatchik Steve Schmidt have made themselves the toast of cable networks and publishing houses—despite hailing from a constituency so lilliputian in number that a candidate waving its banner would struggle to win an election in a single one of America's more than three hundred area codes. Start a tendency called Originalists for Anarchy or Paleocons for Full Communism, and you could probably garner a roughly equal number of real-world converts with the same money and institutional support behind you.

There is indeed, of course, a group of self-identified conservatives who publicly declare their opposition to Donald Trump. Earlier this week, several of them (including Schmidt) even published an op-ed in the *New York Times* announcing something they call *The Lincoln Project*.[76] the latest product relaunch to hit the market courtesy of the perpetually inflated NeverTrump brand.

While Schmidt and co. do at least find time to condemn their fellow Republicans, congressional and otherwise, for backing the atrocious Trump, the authors also take care to make sure that their critique of the president never quite rises to the level of political substance. Read the whole thing yourself and you'll find little more than a mound of meaningless fluff adorned with hollow appeals to patriotism and wounded national pride; a giant Have You No Decency, Sir-esque screed masquerading as the Gettysburg Address.

Not once do the piece's authors see fit to mention the president's racism. Not a single word is allocated to brutalized refugees in detention camps or his appointment of a man credibly accused of sexual assault to the Supreme Court. Despite interminable pablum about the greatness of American democracy there is nothing whatsoever about gerrymandering, voter suppression, or the various wider efforts at disenfranchisement. Go to the group's website and you'll find little more than a few images of Honest Abe, a box in which to enter your name and email address, a statement which says, "The Lincoln Project is holding accountable those who would violate their oaths to the Constitution and would put others before Americans," and a link back to the *New York Times* op-ed you just finished reading. There is no substantive critique of Trump, no proffered manifesto or program to counter his politics, and certainly no condemnation that rises above the extremely generalized idea of opposing the president, even if it means holding your nose and voting for the odd Democrat.

"This effort," the authors announce,

> . . . asks all Americans of all places, creeds and ways of life to join in the seminal task of our generation: restoring to this nation leadership and governance that respects the rule of law, recognizes the dignity of all people and defends the Constitution and American values at home and abroad . . . The American presidency transcends the individuals who occupy the Oval Office.

Their personality becomes part of our national character. Their actions become our actions, for which we all share responsibility. Their willingness to act in accordance with the law and our tradition dictate how current and future leaders will act. Their commitment to order, civility and decency are reflected in American society.

A dewy-eyed Aaron Sorkin pulling a cognac-fueled all-nighter ahead of *The Newsroom*'s pilot episode could hardly have put it better.

So, to return to our original point, while there is indeed a group of people who might reasonably be called Never Trump Conservatives, their omnipresence on our TV and computer screens obscures the extent to which they represent a media phenomenon rather than a real political constituency. There is simply no popular base for Never Trump conservatism within the Republican Party or the wider conservative movement, and the quixotic gaggle of former neocons, Bush administration alumni, and right-wing intelligentsia that forms the skeleton of this would-be resistance front has about as much flesh on the bone as a desiccated corpse in the Gobi Desert.

As a political strategy designed to defeat Trump, it has little to commend it—among other reasons, because it was already tried in 2016 and failed so spectacularly. The media's effusive elevation of the Never Trumpist sect also obscures the extent to which its critique is, and has always been, laughably hollow. Revisit the *National Review* editorial board's supposedly principled censure of Trump and you'll discover it was largely an attack from the right motivated by angst that he would be a poor salesman for conservatism who lacked sufficient commitment to the reactionary cause.[77] Which is to say: if the conservatives who still denounce Trump seem to offer little in the way of a countervailing agenda, it's because they don't actually have one. David Frum's bestselling polemic against the president also attacks him from the right[78] and Jonah

Goldberg's book similarly struggles to find much of substance to disagree with him about.[79] (One only need glance at the history of American conservatism to understand why there's so little daylight between its so-called "mainstream" and the ever-more feral incarnations it seems to birth with each successive decade.)

Above all else, the tedious ubiquity of the Never Trump Conservative is an indictment of those who moderate the organs of liberal tastemaking and opinion-forming. In what might have been a moment of critical introspection, America's liberals made a conscious choice to reaffirm rather than interrogate their core assumptions and beliefs about the country and its institutions: preferring instead to take superficial comfort in the same fairy tales of bipartisanship and American exceptionalism that accompanied Donald Trump's initial rise and the Democratic establishment's ultimately futile effort to beat him. To this end, millions have been served the seductive and highly marketable fiction of a righteous conservative movement in exile, eager to partner in a patriotic coalition with liberals to restore America's lost national honor.

It is a dangerous myth to be sure. But, faced with an increasingly vocal and progressive current demanding more from the country's anti-Republican opposition than the empty bromides it has long deployed in lieu of a policy agenda, it's also an awfully convenient one.

—*A version of this essay first appeared in* Jacobin, *December 2019.*

PART III

Dramatis Personae

The NYL—the New Young Leader . . . is said to have the courage to dispense with the double-talk and circumlocution of the Old Guard . . . Those who promote the NYL make up the highly successful new elite . . . Lawyers, professors, businessmen are not at all at odds with the structure of our society. What they look for in the NYL is the crystallization and expression of a consensus. This is why his goals must remain without real content . . . He must embody the end of ideology. At the same time, if the NYL is courageous in eschewing the language of equivocation, he speaks out not to break the consensus but to present more effectively the goals that are hidden in the gobbledygook of the traditional politician or bureaucrat . . . In the saga of the new leader, the battle is exclusively between the young and "with it" and the old with their outworn ideas and sensibilities. But this in no way involves a critique of the structures of our society or an attack on the privileges they entrench. Instead, the attack is launched in the name of these structures or on behalf of their ideal image of themselves as the breeding ground of enlightened, technocratic innovators . . . This wraith-like change embodied by the NYL is a matter of style, feeling, ideas; it glides through any structure of society without any resistance. The dramatic struggle between the old and new is thus largely theatrical.

—Charles Taylor

As neoliberalism wages war on public goods and the very idea of a public, including citizenship beyond membership, it dramatically thins public life without killing politics. Struggles remain over power, hegemonic values, resources, and future trajectories. This persistence of politics amid the destruction of public life and especially educated public life, combined with the marketization of the political sphere, is part of what makes contemporary politics peculiarly unappealing and toxic—full of ranting and posturing, emptied of intellectual seriousness, pandering to an uneducated and manipulable electorate and a celebrity-and-scandal-hungry corporate media.

—Wendy Brown

The Fraudulent Universalism of Barack Obama

Review of A Promised Land *by Barack Obama (Crown, 2020)*
Co-authored with Nathan J. Robinson

In anticipation of the release of Volume I of his presidential memoirs, Barack Obama published a playlist featuring some "memorable songs from my administration."[80] The selections seemed calculated to offend nobody. There was something for all tastes: Frank Sinatra, Bob Dylan, Beyoncé, U2, Gloria Estefan, The Beatles, Miles Davis, Brooks & Dunn, Fleetwood Mac, Stevie Wonder, Jay-Z, B.B. King, and even Eminem all had their place. Rock, country, Latin pop, R&B, hip hop, blues, jazz. At once popular, middlebrow, and ever-so-slightly refined. Nobody needed to feel neglected, everyone was included. The divides between Country America and Hip Hop America were bridged. Who could possibly criticize the playlist? It was utterly unobjectionable. Perfect. A collage of American heartland sounds. Aretha Franklin covering The Band's "The Weight," with Duane Allman on guitar—Southern rock meets Detroit gospel! What better proof that our divides are illusory, that red-blue and Black-White are artificial categories, that we are better off when we borrow from all traditions and recognize each other's humanity? One cannot help but recall Matt Taibbi's scorching 2007 description of Obama as "an ingeniously crafted human cipher" whose "'man for all seasons' act is so perfect in its particulars that just about *anyone* can find a bit of himself somewhere in the candidate's background."[81]

The playlist is therefore a fitting accompaniment to the book, *A Promised Land*, which covers the period from Obama's early life up until the end of his first term. *A Promised Land* is not just a recounting of events, but a lengthy argument for the author's political vision and an attempt to explain why he made the choices that he did. Notwithstanding its (mostly unconvincing) effort to appear self-critical and introspective, the book is as much a response to critics as a straightforward chronicle; a defense of a legacy, a record, and a political outlook whose detractors, on both left and right, have only grown more vociferous with the passage of time. Part memoir and part apologia, *A Promised Land* thus offers tremendous insight into how the most gifted and popular liberal politician in living memory sees the world—and the considerable limitations of his vision. From beginning to end, it proves an epic demonstration of Obama's skills as a political storyteller, his remarkable knack for making the status quo appear novel and the calculated seem earnest. Above all else, it show-cases his masterful ability to speak the language of conservatism in the register of idealism and progress.

The Man from Everywhere and Nowhere

Any fair critic of the author needs to acknowledge that he is an immensely talented writer. Just as he once dazzled crowds with flourishes of sono-rous rhetoric, Obama here offers readers a style of prose completely atypical of the average political memoir. As legions of ghostwriters can attest, most politicians and public figures are ill-equipped to produce a single readable paragraph without conscripting a phalanx of uncred-ited wordsmiths in the effort. Even the more gifted and independently minded among them would struggle to bring such literary flair to the often-mundane business of governance, campaigning, and retail politics. In Obama's hands, however, all three are seamlessly woven into a sweep-ing narrative tapestry in which very little seems labored or out of place.

PART III

While they certainly include plenty of extraneous description—
recounting, in forensic detail, the exact appearance of meeting tables at
international summits (adorned with "a national flag, a microphone with
operating instructions; a commemorative writing pad and pen of varying quality") or lengthy taxonomies of various physical objects found in
the Oval Office ("the busts of long-dead leaders and Remington's famous
bronze cowboy; the antique grandfather clock . . . the thick oval carpet
with stern eagle stitched in its center, and the Resolute desk, a gift from
Queen Victoria in 1880 ornately carved from the hull of a British ship that
a US whaling crew helped salvage after a catastrophe . . .")[82]—the seven
hundred pages that make up *A Promised Land* are brimming with lyrical
passages like the following description of the White House Rose Garden
from the book's opening chapter:

> Oh, how good that garden looked! The shady magnolias ris-
> ing high at each corner; the hedges, thick and rich green; the
> crab apple trees pruned just so. And the flowers, cultivated in
> greenhouses a few miles away, providing a constant explosion
> of color—reds and yellows and pinks and purples; in spring, the
> tulips massed in bunches, their heads tilted towards the sun; in
> summer, lavender heliotrope and geraniums and lilies; in fall,
> chrysanthemums and daisies and wildflowers. And always a
> few roses, red mostly but sometimes yellow or white, each one
> flush in its bloom. [83]

Delivered from the fingertips of a Hillary Clinton or a John Kerry, the
preceding description would probably hit with the cacophonous thud of
an elbow smashing the keys on a grand piano; its imagery stale, its delivery mannered, and its rhythm a jarring staccato. Wielded by Obama, however, even a description of the White House Rose Garden quickly turns
into an epochal meditation on fatherhood, duty, longing, the passage of

time, and the wondrousness of America—the author somehow evoking George Washington, Martin Luther King Jr., and Norman Rockwell's 1946 oil painting *Working on the Statue of Liberty* in a single paragraph that follows ("The men in the painting, the groundskeepers in the garden—they were the guardians, I thought, the quiet priests of a good and solemn order").[84]

There are numerous sections in this vein, the book leaping with ease across vast expanses of space, time, history, geography, ideology, and culture—from the battlefields of Gettysburg and Appomattox to the palace intrigues of ancient Egypt; from the jazzy rhythms of Manhattan's Village Vanguard to the writings of Langston Hughes and Fyodor Dostoyevsky; from the cloistered world of White House cabinet deliberations to the open-air retail politics of the Iowa caucuses. As elegant as his paean to the Rose Garden, Obama's more literary passages ultimately achieve something else: the fusion of his thoughts and biography with anything and everything he finds around him. On a rhetorical level, the effect is incredibly potent, giving the impression of a thoughtful leader perpetually grappling with the infinite complexities and nuances of a world rendered in glorious technicolor. Aesthetically pleasing though it may be, this mode of storytelling does more to obscure than illuminate the author's actual beliefs, its imagery and style being so polychromatic that *anyone* can, indeed, find their own preferences or tastes represented somewhere between the lines.

Obama's choose-your-own-adventure schtick undeniably explains much about his popularity and appeal, a reality to which he himself seems exquisitely attuned. "I was new and unexpected," the author writes of his rapid ascent from senator to president, "a blank canvas onto which supporters across the ideological spectrum could project their own visions of change."[85] Removed from their immediate context, in fact, parts of *A Promised Land* could almost be read as self-aware metacommentary on the nature of political cipherhood. Take the following passage, which comes early in the book amid a section about his early life reflections on hierarchies of race and class:

> All of this pulled me in different directions. It was as if, because of the very strangeness of my heritage and the worlds I straddled, I was from everywhere and nowhere at once, a combination of ill-fitting parts, like a platypus or some imaginary beast, confined to a fragile habitat, unsure of where I belonged. [86]

Or this one, which follows a passage about campaigning in Chicago neighborhoods endlessly varied in their class and ethnic makeup:

> My stump speech became less a series of positions and more a chronicle of these disparate voices, a chorus of Americans from every corner of the state . . . I'd drive on to the next town, knowing that the story I was telling was true; convinced that this campaign was no longer about me and that I had become a mere conduit through which people might recognize the value of their own stories, their own worth, and share them with one another. [87]

This, he said, "worried me" because "the continuing elevation of me as a symbol ran contrary to my organizer's instincts."[88] But he acknowledges that it was an "image that my campaign and I had helped to construct," having deliberately encouraged people to make his candidacy "a vessel for a million different dreams"[89] and himself an epoch-defining symbol of all hope and all change.

Again and again, Obama describes important events and incidents in the same fashion, each one a pluralist cornucopia bursting with people from every conceivable background, orientation, and walk of life (with even the zany cosplayers of the world somehow managing to earn their due). Just ahead of 2008's crucial Iowa caucuses, he recalls: "People streamed into the main building from every direction, a noisy festival of humanity. No age, race, class, or body type appeared unrepresented. There was even one ancient-looking character dressed as Gandalf from *The Lord of the Rings*, complete with a long white cloak, a pluming white beard, and a sturdy wooden staff . . ."[90]

A regular variation involves the author offering up what seem to be opposing ideas or concepts only to flatten out their differences to the point that they might as well not exist. His foreign policy team, for example, is initially described as a contrasting blend of those who favored hard power and "more liberal members" inclined toward soft power and multilateralism. This relatively straightforward dichotomy, however, is qualified by the caveat that all members "considered themselves internationalists to one degree or another," who "believed that American leadership [is] necessary to keep the world moving in a better direction" and that American influence comes "in many forms." The difference between these apparently juxtaposed geopolitical outlooks is then ironed out still further as Obama informs us that:

> Even the more liberal members of my team . . . had no qualms about the use of 'hard power' to go after terrorists and were scornful of leftist critics who made a living blaming the United States for every problem around the globe. Meanwhile, the most hawkish members of my team understood the importance of public diplomacy and considered the exercise of so-called soft power, like foreign aid and student exchange programs, to be essential ingredients in an effective US foreign policy.

When it came to making foreign policy decisions, Obama says, "the question" simply had to do with "emphasis" and the divide, insofar as one existed, was partly generational—older members of the team favoring more conventional foreign policy thinking and younger members, "seared by both the horrors of 9/11 and the images of Iraqi prisoners abused by US military personnel at Abu Ghraib," being less inclined toward "the Washington playbook." Any remaining conceptual friction is then smoothed out even more by the author's assurance that "none of the younger staffers" ("no less patriotic than their bosses") "were firebrands," and that they "respected the institutional knowledge of those with deep foreign policy experience."[91]

All told, the passage is emblematic of Obama's remarkable capacity to evoke tremendous nuance and complexity while saying very little, any apparent difference or conflict between the ideas he is discussing smoothed over by way of elegant rhetorical synthesis. (Thus in this case, for those following along, we ultimately get a foreign policy team whose members are sorted into binarily opposing camps—young/old, hard/soft, unilateral/multilateral—with these distinctions being collapsed under the vague umbrella of "internationalism," then modified by the caveat that proponents of soft power also believed in hard power and vice versa. This formulation is then *further* qualified by the proviso that younger members who wanted to break from the staid orthodoxies of the Washington playbook nonetheless held the foreign policy establishment they ostensibly disliked in high esteem.)

Predictably enough, the author's own political identity is rendered in much the same way: as a finely balanced synthesis of contrasting traditions, beliefs, temperaments, and impulses—at once progressive and pragmatic, idealist and realist, grand in vision but keenly aware of norms and political constraints, attuned to injustice but moderate in word and deed; a harmonious union of various constituent identities and ideological hues as infinitely varied as the wards that make up Chicago's 13th State Senate district or the flowers in the White House Rose Garden; as infinitely varied as America itself. Reflecting on his first hundred days in office, for example, Obama calls himself "a reformer, conservative in temperament if not in vision."[92] Reformism and conservatism may appear to be opposites, but no matter—in Obama they are unified and the contradiction is dissolved. Study enough of Obama's words and speeches, in fact, and they all begin to read as transliterations of his most memorable flourish, "hard and soft power" in Chapter 13 of *A Promised Land* serving a roughly equivalent function to "red states and blue states" in 2004's DNC keynote address:

> *E pluribus unum.* Out of many, one . . . there is not a liberal America and a conservative America—there is the United States of America. There is not a Black America and a White America and Latino America and Asian America—there's the United States of America. The pundits, the pundits like to slice-and-dice our country into Red States and Blue States; Red States for Republicans, Blue States for Democrats. But I've got news for them, too. We worship an awesome God in the Blue States, and we don't like federal agents poking around in our libraries in the Red States. We coach Little League in the Blue States and yes, we've got some gay friends in the Red States. There are patriots who opposed the war in Iraq and there are patriots who supported the war in Iraq . . .[93]

From his debut book *Dreams from My Father* to the present day, Obama's tendency to invoke grand, dialectical oppositions then resolve them with abstract appeals to unity or similitude has been a hallmark of his style. Combined with his flair for lofty, even mythical imagery and ability to fuse his thoughts and biography with everything around him, the upshot is a rendering of events in which every strand of history, culture, and ideology appears to realize itself in Barack Obama: a man whose life and presidency represent the synthesis of every strain of American life hitherto in tension. The same basic pattern recurs again and again throughout Obama's prose and speeches in great Enigma Variations of rhetorical triangulation—as everything from his music preferences to his foreign policy team find the old dichotomies dismantled and an underlying harmony revealed. At times this rhetoric has even sounded like Biblical prophecy, as when Obama expressed his confidence that future generations would "look back and tell our children that . . . this was the moment when the rise of the oceans began to slow and our planet began to heal"[94] (upon being elected, Obama immediately appointed BP's climate change–denying chief scientist to his Department of Energy).[95,96] If that sounds like hyperbole, consider how some of Obama's smartest and most enthusiastic supporters responded to his words. A twenty-four-year-old Ezra Klein wrote in January of 2008 that:

> Obama's finest speeches do not excite. They do not inform. They don't even really inspire. They **elevate**. They enmesh you in a grander moment, as if history has stopped flowing passively by, and, just for an instant, contracted around you, made you aware of its presence, and your role in it. He is not the Word made flesh, but the triumph of word over flesh, over color, over despair. The other great leaders I've heard guide us towards a better politics, but Obama is, at his best, able to call us back to our highest selves, to the place where America exists as a glittering ideal, and where we, its honored inhabitants, seem capable of achieving it, and thus of sharing in its meaning and transcendence. [emphasis Klein's][97]

Obama emphatically insists he was uncomfortable with those who expressed outsized hopes in him and discussed him in messianic terms, but admits that his campaign deliberately "helped to construct"[98] this association in the public's mind between *the election of Barack Obama to the presidency* and *the fulfillment of America's promise and the end to people's troubles.* The route to the "promised land" was through his presidency. It was hope itself, change itself. Elect me, he said, and we will end our divisions, part the seas, and move to a new stage of history. Say what you will, but this is a powerful piece of personal branding. Not for nothing did *Advertising Age* give Obama its 2008 Marketer of the Year award, the forty-fourth president winning out over Apple and Zappos.[99]

Yes We Can . . . What?

Try as he might, Obama's elegant obfuscations and literary digressions can only take him so far. *A Promised Land* is, after all, a response to critics and a memoir concerned with recounting the specifics of political decisions from the point of view of the man at their center—an effort which inevitably necessitates the occasional clearly stated opinion. Even here, however, the author frequently proves difficult to pin down—his narration often ventriloquizing the perspectives of others and invariably placing him somewhere, dispassionately, in between. One again recalls Taibbi in 2007 describing Obama's capacity to exude a "seemingly impenetrable air of Harvard-crafted moral neutrality" while expending tremendous rhetorical energy "showing that he recognizes the validity of all points of view [and emphasizing] that when he does take hard positions on issues, he often does so reluctantly."[100]

For all his talk of grand aspirations and hopes, then, Obama does not come across as someone with a very strong or clearly defined set of political goals. It is striking, in fact, given the book's subject matter and length, how little he says about *why* he wanted to hold elected office in the first place, with what he does offer in this regard mostly taking the form of empty platitudes. He suggests, for example, that he could "excite voters in ways" that other candidates couldn't, that he could use "a different language" than they did, that he could "shake up Washington," and "give hope to those in need."[101] As he considers running for president, Michelle asks why he feels that he of all people should hold high office. Obama hesitates, and slips into a reverie about marriage. Snapping back to reality, he then tosses out a few more possible explanations, most of them trite to the point of meaninglessness: he could "spark a new kind of politics," "get a new generation to participate," and "bridge the divisions in the country." As a final answer, he settles on the fact that young Black children would be deeply inspired by his presence in the White House.[102] This is tangible, true, and shouldn't be trivialized. But it's also not a legislative agenda.

Again and again, Obama appears reluctant to define himself by any particular political ideology. The author says he wanted to "avoid doctrinaire thinking," instead "plac[ing] a premium on what worked" and "listen[ing] respectfully to what the other side had to say."[103] As examples of his willingness to buck the conventional Washington wisdom, he cites his decision to chastise teachers' unions over their lack of "accountability" and his willingness to advocate violating Pakistani sovereignty in the pursuit of Osama bin Laden, which even Republicans were unwilling to publicly endorse. Examples of bipartisan cooperation actually yielding anything valuable meanwhile prove notably sparse, with Obama citing a collaboration in the Illinois Senate with arch-conservative Tom Coburn "on measures to increase transparency and reduce waste in government contracting."[104]

Though he often presents self-effacingly as someone who is overly "professorial" and excessively detail-oriented in matters of policy, this portrayal is the opposite of the truth. Throughout his political career (as in *A Promised Land*) Obama tended to deal in uplifting abstractions rather than concrete promises or objectives, even of the wonky kind. He relates, for example, an incident from 2007 at a Service Employees International Union (SEIU) forum on health care, where Hillary Clinton and John Edwards presented their plans for health care reform. When

Obama's turn came, he appeared empty-handed, with no actual vision for how health care should work. The then-candidate was roundly criticized, with NBC asking "is Obama all style and little substance?" and noting that he had "provided few details about how he would lead the country."[105] Ezra Klein remarked at the time that while coverage of Obama had focused on "the Illinois senator's explosive charisma, preternatural ease on the stump, and inspirational back story," at the forum he had appeared "unprepared and overwhelmed" when asked by a twenty-three-year-old questioner the very simple question of what he actually intended to do to fix health care.[106] In the end, Obama spent much of the 2008 primary arguing *against* the "individual mandate" that would later become a core part of the Affordable Care Act.[107]

One cannot help but feel Taibbi had it right when he noted in '08 that "you can't run against [Obama] on the issues because you can't even find him on the ideological spectrum."[108] Every time Obama appears as if he is about to take a stand, he qualifies it. This is even true of his 2002 speech against the invasion of Iraq, which the author quotes from in *A Promised Land*. The speech is largely remembered as an act of some political courage, given how many Democrats ultimately backed the war. In fact, even that speech began with the words: "Although this has been billed as an anti-war rally, I stand before you as someone who is not opposed to war in all circumstances," and reiterated his support for "this administration's pledge to hunt down and root out those who would slaughter innocents in the name of intolerance."[109] Similarly, Obama's 2009 Nobel Peace Prize address[110] is ostensibly a meditation on deep moral questions about peace and violence, but triangulates in similar fashion—its thesis essentially being that while peace is good, sometimes violence is necessary in order to maintain peace. When one revisits Obama's words and speeches today, it is striking just how unmemorable and lacking in content they really were, beyond vague platitudes so inoffensive it was impossible to disagree with them.[111]

Taibbi, watching Obama's rallies during his first campaign for president, observed that his "presentation is deliberately vague on most counts," his appeal being "a mood thing, not an issue thing" which ultimately stemmed from his personal qualities: "his expansive eloquence, his remarkable biography, his commanding physical presence." Taibbi grudgingly found himself rather enchanted by Obama, whose audiences "really seem to believe that his election will fundamentally change the way they feel about their country," with the candidate himself "a dynamic, handsome, virile presence, a stark contrast to the bloated hairy shitbags we usually elect to positions of power in this country."[112] Political scientist Adolph Reed, Jr. was less enthused, calling Obama a "vacuous opportunist, a good performer with an ear for how to make white liberals like him," and warning that "Obama's empty claims to being a candidate of progressive change and to embodying a 'movement' that exists only as a brand will dissolve into disillusionment."[113]

(The historical record shows that Reed was right. Upon his election, Obama sent his organizers home;[114] the movement dissolved, and many young people who had voted for Obama were soon joining Occupy Wall Street.) Tellingly, Obama often talks about what winning the presidency would *mean* rather than what it would *do*:

If we won, it would mean . . . that the America I believed in was possible, that the democracy I believed in was within reach. If we won, it would mean that I wasn't alone in believing that the world didn't have to be a cold, unforgiving place, where the strong preyed on the weak and we inevitably fell back into clans and tribes, lashing out against the unknown and huddling against the darkness.[115]

He elsewhere adds that he wanted to "deliver the goods" and show "that we could transcend the old logic, that we could rally a working majority around a progressive agenda" and address "issues like inequality or lack of educational opportunity."[116] The *enthusiastic aspiration toward nothing in particular* could be seen in his campaign slogan, "Yes We Can," a resonant affirmation of democratic possibility and collective purpose, which nonetheless begged a very obvious follow-up: Yes We Can *what*?

One passage in the book's opening chapter dramatically underscores the extent to which Obama's notion of idealism is much more an affection rooted in abstract political storytelling than an orientation toward any particular goal. Recalling the idealistic temperament of his youth, the author tells us he nonetheless clung to the idea of American exceptionalism, getting into protracted arguments "with friends who insisted the American hegemon was the root of oppression worldwide." To his credit, Obama acknowledges plenty wrong with the American experiment in practice: "The version of American history taught in schools, with slavery glossed over and the slaughter of Native Americans all but omitted . . . the blundering exercise of military power, the rapaciousness of multinationals," though he ultimately cannot resist ending the paragraph on a note of derision (". . . yeah, yeah, I got all that"). "But the *idea* of America," Obama continues, "the *promise* of America: this I clung to with a stubbornness that surprised even me. 'We hold these truths to be self-evident, that all men are created equal'—*that* was my America."[117] Extremely redolent of this passage is another which appears more than two hundred pages later when, reflecting on how the euphoric public mood that surrounded his inauguration quickly darkened amid the ravages of the financial crisis, Obama wonders, "Maybe what was needed was a burst of energy, no matter how fleeting—a happy-seeming story about who we were as Americans and who we might be, the kind of high that could provide just enough momentum to get us through the most treacherous part of the journey."[118]

The Rhetoric and the Record

Obama is fastidious in making *A Promised Land* seem like an uncommonly honest and forthright text. All the details he offers about what it feels like to be president, what the items on his desk looked like and how the White House kitchen operates, are part of an attempt to make the reader see him as *concealing nothing*. If he just offers a clear enough window into his own subjective thinking and experiences, the author hopes, we will see that he was, if flawed, at least *reasonable*, and come to share his conviction that even if he wasn't a *perfect* president, he did about the best job one could hope for given the political context in which he landed.

To this end, sections are periodically devoted to asking (what at least seem to be) probing questions about the merits of particular policies and political decisions, the very first of which appears near the book's outset:

> I confess that there have been times during the course of writing this book, as I've reflected on my presidency and all that's happened since, when I've had to ask myself whether I was too tempered in speaking the truth as I saw it, too cautious in either word or deed, convinced as I was that by appealing to what Lincoln called the better angels of our nature I stood a greater chance of leading us in the direction of the America we've been promised. [119]

There are many more paragraphs of this kind strewn throughout the book, Obama employing an approach to his own life and career every bit as ambidextrous as his attitude toward the economy or health care policy. "Why would I put her through this? Was it just vanity?" he asks himself while recalling his wife's initial opposition to his presidential ambitions, before continuing:

> ... Or perhaps something darker—a raw hunger, a blind ambition wrapped in the gauzy language of service? Or was I still trying to prove myself worthy to a father who had abandoned me, live up to my mother's starry-eyed expectations of her only son . . .[120]

On at least one occasion, Obama's tone of inquisitiveness even finds him appearing to question the essence of his own appeal and worldview:

> How useful is it to describe the world as it should be when efforts to achieve that world are bound to fall short? Was Václav Havel correct in suggesting that by raising expectations, I was doomed to disappoint them? Was it possible that abstract principles and high-minded ideals were and always would be nothing more than a pretense, a palliative, a way to beat back despair, but no match for the more primal urges that really moved us, so that no matter what we said or did, history was sure to run along its predetermined course, an endless cycle of fear, hunger and conflict, dominance and weakness?[121]

Again and again these questions pile up, their tone always pensive, probing, and self-critical. *A Promised Land* is effective in large part because it *feels* authentic and true, as if Obama is offering a thoughtful examination of his motives, successes, and failures. The capacity to engage in self-criticism, even of the harshest kind, makes it seem like he is being straight with us and offering up an objective reading of events. Thus when Obama fails to convincingly answer his own questions or begins to distort the truth in ways that seem deliberate, it begins to seem that his authenticity may be a *performance*, a calculated act rather than genuine soul-bearing.

Suspicion inevitably ensues when apparently brooding inquiries go unanswered or questions about major decisions come with passive rejoinders like "Whether I was demonstrating wisdom or weakness would be for others to judge."[122] Eventually we find ourselves starting to wonder whether Obama is just a politician trying to get us to like him, and what initially seemed honest begins to feel manipulative. For instance, Obama says that while he was *reluctant* to run for president, conversations with Ted Kennedy and Harry Reid (relayed in the form of suspiciously well-remembered monologues) helped convince him to do it. Obama wonders aloud whether he is in politics for the wrong reasons, but his story is told in such a way as to make us convinced he must have been in it for the right reasons. The textual evidence shows that he was a *reluctant* office-seeker, not a careerist, which is persuasive—until we remember that the textual evidence all comes from Obama himself.

This becomes even more obvious when we analyze the facts of Obama's presidency and compare the reality of what happened to the story Obama tells about it. It is important to examine the facts carefully against the story, because Obama spends much of his time defending himself against critics, and those defenses can be convincing when particular facts are left out. After all, Obama strongly intones that he did as well as one could reasonably expect given that he (1) is a mortal, fallible human being rather than a messiah and (2) had to operate within the constraints of a highly dysfunctional political system, opposed by a psychopathic and racist Republican party, undermined by a media with little interest in substance, and having to juggle many competing interests. He is right that those constraints exist. The Senate *is* real, the political right *is* racist and obstructionist, and the media *does* tend to focus on trivialities. It is also impossible to run a counterfactual to see what the world would have looked like if Obama had made different choices. Given how sympathetic and effective the author's self-presentation is, readers who only look at the evidence found in *A Promised Land* may well feel that criticism of him is downright unreasonable. Portraying himself as both a normal person with human failings and a progressively minded idealist, the reader is left to ask: *What different choices could he have made? One can criticize Obama, sure, but what exactly did you want?*

There are, however, many instances in which Obama made clear choices, and it can be demonstrated that those choices were wrong and that the way he presents them is dishonest. Take health care, for instance. Obama says that the Affordable Care Act was constructed the way it was because he needed to appease conservative senators. But he *also* says that he deliberately crafted his health care reform in a way that would appeal to Republicans, because he hoped that by securing bipartisan support he might make the bill seem less partisan in a way that would protect it from future attack. This is an admission that concessions were made that probably did not strictly *need* to be made to ensure the bill's passage in a Democratic Congress. Instead, they were made on a *theory* of political pragmatism, the theory that bipartisan cooperation on health care reform is possible.

This theory turned out to be flat wrong. The ACA's deliberately conservative design did not keep conservatives from viciously attacking it. Obama intentionally modeled his reform on "Romneycare" and previous plans from the right-wing Heritage Foundation.[123] In fact, it was meant to be a bill that the private insurance industry could love, because it would require every American to purchase their product and would provide generous government subsidies that would go into the companies' pockets. Obama thought that it was so *reasonable*, so little a threat to Republican ideology and interests, that they couldn't possibly be strongly opposed to it. It followed market principles! It propped up corporations! It did not socialize either insurance or care! But Republicans despised the ACA and tried to convince Americans that Obama was going to have government "death panels" deciding to pull the plug on their grannies. Not a single Republican ended up voting for the final version of the ACA in either the House or the Senate. Republicans, far from accepting Obama's olive branch, snapped it in half and set it alight. They not only resisted nearly any initiative he proposed, they portrayed a compulsively compromising centrist as a radical bent on destroying the American way of life.

Obama also downplays the fact that some of the "constraints" he was under were self-imposed, in that they came from his own unwillingness to push the envelope and be bold. He discusses, for instance, the anger of LGBTQ activists over his administration's refusal to simply unilaterally order an end to Don't Ask Don't Tell, but says that he wanted to get the military brass on board, and was worried his Republican defense secretary would resign if pushed too hard on the issue. (God forbid he lose *that guy*.) Some issues, such as his pro-privatization education "reforms,"[124] or the drone strikes on civilian populations criticized by Human Rights Watch and the ACLU, or mass deportation, are barely touched on in the book, perhaps because they were clear matters of policy choice and thus fit awkwardly with its wider effort to portray Obama as someone whose disappointing compromises were imposed upon him by circumstance.

On targeted killing, Obama does not address the human rights reports but hopes it is enough not to have taken pleasure from his actions and to have condemned his predecessor: "I took no joy in any of this . . . But the work was necessary, and it was my responsibility to make sure our operations were as effective as possible. Moreover, unlike some on the left, I'd never engaged in wholesale condemnation of the Bush administration's approach to counterterrorism."[125]

Take, as another example, the way Obama repeatedly cites the existence of the Senate filibuster as a reason why conservative Democrats needed to be appeased on health care. The case sounds ironclad, until you consider that a simple majority of senators (which the Democrats had) could have eliminated the filibuster at multiple points.[126] Obama rather amazingly admits this, but says that in 2009 nobody was contemplating changing the process. This is not the case—a 2009 *Politico* article, for example, argued that "while Democrats rail against the GOP's use of the filibuster, they seem wary of doing anything about it."[127] It was not, in fact, *impossible* to overcome Joe Lieberman's hostility to a public option: it was simply that the actions this would have required looked *radical* and violated the sacred norms of institutional Washington. The preservation of these norms is considered by some politicians to be far more important than whatever ultimate ends politics is actually directed toward. (Obama, for example, complains in the book about protesters who called George W. Bush a war criminal on Bush's last day in office. To Obama, this is simply rude, and rudeness is a vice so unconscionable that it must be avoided at all costs, even the cost of letting a war criminal get away with his war crimes without being yelled at.)

In fact, Obama made it clear that he had never been a progressive the moment he selected his staff. He had always said that he believed in *bipartisanship*, and he meant it. In his address at the Democratic National Convention in 2004, which had made his national reputation, Obama had rejected the idea that the United States needed to be "divided," suggesting that "Red America" and "Blue America" needed to sit down in a room together and understand each other. To that end, when he became president, Obama gave Republicans concessions that nobody on his side was actually asking him to give. In *A Promised Land*, he says that to show he was serious about believing that Republicans deserved to govern, he asked George W. Bush's defense secretary, Robert Gates, to stay on, even though Gates "was a Republican, a Cold War hawk, a card-carrying member of the national security establishment, a prior champion of foreign interventions I had likely protested while in college, and now defense secretary to a president whose war policies I abhorred" and "had helped oversee the arming of the Afghan mujahideen."[128] Another way of putting that is that Gates had a demonstrated record of incompetence and poor judgment, but Obama felt that keeping a discredited, right-wing figure from the administration whose record he had ostensibly run against in a powerful position would show him to be "serious" and "nonpartisan."

This was not the only such effort Obama made. He tried to appoint Bush's lead Troubled Asset Relief Program (TARP) negotiator, Judd Gregg, as his commerce secretary (Gregg declined). He admits he gave legislative concessions to Republican House whip (and later Majority Leader) Eric Cantor not because he received anything in return, but as a gesture of good faith. Obama launched a bipartisan commission on deficit reduction (deficits being a particular hobbyhorse of his)[129] that, predictably, proposed[130] cutting Social Security and raising the retirement age to sixty-nine (less than ten years before the average person is expected to croak).

Not only did Obama reach out to Republicans like Gates and Gregg, but he begged Rahm Emanuel to be his chief of staff. Emanuel was reluctant, but the president-elect insisted that he wanted no one else. Obama acknowledges that some people might find his choice insane: "Didn't he represent the same old triangulating, Davos-attending, Wall Street-coddling, Washington-focused, obsessively centrist version of the Democratic Party we had been running against? How can you trust him?" Though Obama asks the right questions, he very tellingly does not actually answer them, saying instead that "these were all variations on a question that would recur in the coming months. What kind of president did I intend to be?"[131] (Rahm Emanuel would go on to cover up the murder of a young Black man at the hands of police.)[132]

Obama similarly pleaded with Hillary Clinton to accept the position of secretary of state, despite her well-known hawkishness and vote for the Iraq War, just as he had chosen Joe Biden (one of the Bush administration's most zealous advocates in the Senate during the run-up to the invasion and its early months) as his running mate. Though Obama cites his desire to "unify a still-divided Democratic Party," concerns that Clinton might "second-guess" him "from her seat in the Senate," and a desire to "self-consciously mimi[c] Lincoln by placing a former political opponent in my cabinet," his ultimate reason for picking Clinton is pitched in the bland language of H.R.: "I thought Hillary was the best person for the job," he writes, citing her "intelligence, preparation, and work ethic."[133]

This is also more or less the justification he gives for bringing Larry Summers and Tim Geithner into his administration, despite the pair's well-known chumminess with Wall Street. Obama admits that the two men were tied to the Clintonian neoliberalism that characterized Washington "politics as usual," but says he had no choice but to pick seasoned Beltway veterans to mop up the mess of the financial crisis. This decision turned out to have serious consequences: Geithner notoriously defied[134] Obama's order to draw up a plan for bank nationalization, and both Geithner and Summers objected to conditioning aid to banks on restricting the amount that could be paid in executive bonuses, saying this would constitute an unacceptable interference with the freedom of contract and cause "irreparable damage to our market-based system."

The parts of A Promised Land about the response to the financial crisis are where the book begins to seem not just like a rationalization for mushy centrism, but a deeply dishonest rewriting of history. Ryan Cooper, in his review for the Week, notes that Obama simply leaves out inconvenient information. For instance, there were plenty of ideas floating around for how Obama could create a stimulus that would be large enough to fill the hole in the economy, but "Obama's team dismissed all of these ideas out of hand," proposing a stimulus they knew from the outset would be insufficient and not even trying to get something adequate. Cooper quotes Obama economic adviser Austan Goolsbee, who admitted that the administration could have forced banks to give homeowners more mortgage relief, or gotten restrictions on executive compensation, but had no interest in fighting for these kinds of concessions.[135]

Obama must know that, if he tells the truth about what happened, he will not come across very well, because he spins stories so that readers will not grasp the critics' arguments. Here, for instance, is how Obama explains his administration's failure to provide more relief to homeowners who were facing foreclosure:

> Affordable-housing advocates and some progressives in Congress were pushing a large-scale government program to not only reduce monthly mortgage payments for people at risk of losing their homes but actually forgive a portion of their outstanding balance. At first glance the idea had obvious appeal: a "bailout for Main Street, not Wall Street," as proponents suggested. But the sheer scale of lost home equity across the country made such a principal-reduction program cost-prohibitive. Our team calculated that even something the size of a second TARP—a political impossibility—would have a limited effect when spread across the $20 trillion US real estate market.[136]

This is nonsense, though it might easily read like cool-headed practical thinking. Why would the government need to spend money in order to make banks reduce the principal on people's mortgages? The government could just *require* banks to reduce principal. Obama is suggesting that there was no choice but to have the government *compensate* the banks for principal reductions, and that such compensation would be cost prohibitive. But there's no reason the government needed to compensate the banks; they should have taken the loss, because it was their recklessness that caused the crisis. What Obama deems impractical was only impractical under *self-imposed* constraints.

Likewise, Obama repeatedly says that the American public was crying out for what he calls "Old Testament justice" against Wall Street, because of their "understandable desire to see those who'd done wrong punished and shamed," demanding that the bankers responsible for the economic collapse face criminal prosecution. Obama explains away his administration's decision not to prosecute by saying that the law simply didn't permit it, and that he didn't wish to "stretch the definition of criminal statutes."[137] As Jesse Eisinger documents extensively in *The Chickenshit Club: Why the Justice Department Fails to Prosecute Executives,* [138] prosecutors could well have gone after bank executives but were simply too, well, chickenshit. Jed Rakoff, one of the more sensible members of the federal judiciary, discusses the failure in *Why the Innocent Plead Guilty and the Guilty Go Free.*[139] Rakoff writes that there was ample evidence of mass fraud—the "sow's ear" of dodgy mortgages could not have been turned into the "silk purse" of AAA-rated bonds unless *someone* was declining to tell the truth. It was not the law that was the problem; a better understanding of the reasoning comes from Obama's telling admission that it would have "required a violence to the social order, a wrenching of political and economic norms"[140] to put bankers in jail—after all, it simply *isn't done* in Washington, and Obama may have ended up having to put some of his own donors[141] behind bars. Furthermore, his own Attorney General Eric Holder explicitly admitted—though you won't find it in the book—that prosecutions sometimes weren't brought because of the economic effect that such prosecutions would have: "I am concerned that the size of some of these institutions becomes so large that it does become difficult for us to prosecute them when we are hit with indications that if you do prosecute, if you do bring a criminal charge, it will have a negative impact on the national economy, perhaps even the world economy."[142]

The administration declined to charge HSBC with money-laundering, for instance, because it feared that there would be negative economic consequences.[143] What was lacking was not evidence of criminality but the willingness to do something perceived as "radical," i.e., to enforce the law consistently against both rich and poor. Obama laments at one point that the "laws as written deemed epic recklessness and dishonesty in the boardroom or on the trading floor less blameworthy than the actions of a teenage shoplifter." But that's a lie. The laws as *written* criminalize fraud equally no matter who you are. The laws as *applied* by Obama's prosecutors treat the two cases differently because, as Holder indicates, prosecuting teens doesn't hurt the economy. What this amounts to is making some banks "too big to jail," meaning that they can commit crimes with impunity because prosecuting them is considered bad for the economy. This makes a mockery of "the rule of law," of course, because it means that the richer you are the more crimes you are allowed to commit, because of your role in the economy.

The misrepresentations pile up throughout *A Promised Land*. Obama leaves out a number of facts that might prove embarrassing or be difficult to explain away as well-meaning failures. For instance, Bernie Sanders goes unmentioned in the book, which may well be because Obama's main interactions with Sanders came during the Vermont senator's clashes with the administration over its attempts to cut Social Security[144] and the US Postal Service.[145] In Obama's telling of the Copenhagen climate summit, he burst in to save talks that were going nowhere, pressuring intransigent countries like China and India to agree to crucial emissions reductions. In fact, the United States is widely blamed for being the reason that the Copenhagen talks produced no binding commitments, and instead resulted in a completely toothless aspirational pledge.

The Limits of Empathy

Early in the book, Obama says he has deliberately attempted to give the reader a vivid first-person description of what it *feels* like to be the president, what it's like to walk down the West Colonnade past the Rose Garden each morning on the commute from the residence to the office, what it's like to find yourself being saluted, give a soaring speech to a huge crowd, what it's like to feel the weight of people's expectations and know that your decisions have life or death consequences, what it's like to accidentally fumble your words and then see your "gaffe" earn a four-day news cycle. A recurring theme of the memoir is "putting oneself in others' shoes"—Obama is constantly putting himself in the shoes of the uninsured, of foreign leaders, even of Somali pirates—and he, in turn, puts the reader in his shoes.

One of Obama's core convictions is that a lack of empathy is one of the root problems in politics. If we just learned to imagine ourselves in each other's places—if the Israelis could understand the Palestinians and vice versa, if Republicans could understand Democrats and vice versa—we would learn that each of us, deep down, wants roughly the same things, and we could figure out compromises that would prevent division and hostility. In *A Promised Land*, as in his political career, Obama wants to be a bridge between antagonistic interests and groups: his centrism granting that Republicans are right about some things and Democrats right about others; his multiracial identity allowing him to be proudly Black while seeing where White people, even racist ones, are coming from (his famous "race speech" tries to sympathetically contextualize his own grandmother's bigotry).

But the more one scrutinizes *A Promised Land*, the more one feels manipulated. Obama powerfully *performs* empathy and modesty and conviction, but when one steps back and asks, "Empathy for whom?" or "Conviction about what?" the whole thing begins to look shallow. His empathy is also selective. He speaks about understanding all points of view, but then is weirdly soft on George W. Bush, whom he likes on an interpersonal level. (And he cites George H.W. Bush as an example of a president whose foreign policy he finds admirable.) He condemns "the arrogance of men like Dick Cheney and Donald Rumsfeld" in starting the Iraq War, but strangely leaves Bush himself off. Those protesters committed an unseemly violation of the norms of civility and decorum by going after Bush. But, one might ask, what about the hundreds of thousands of people who died violent deaths because of George Bush's criminality and lieş? Why would Obama be more concerned for Bush's feelings than about justice? Does Obama *disagree* with the protesters' case that Bush committed war crimes? If not, why does he believe that politeness should mean we decline to mention a powerful person's unprosecuted atrocities?

In fact, Obama is ultimately nicer to George W. Bush than he is to Jeremiah Wright, the pastor whose fiery political sermons caused a PR problem on the 2008 campaign trail (and whose services Obama attended for years). After first trying to contextualize Wright in a widely praised speech on race, Obama subsequently disavowed and broke ties with him completely. What Obama never did, and still does not do, is explain that the sermons for which Rev. Wright was criticized were wholly stripped of their context. Clips circulated repeatedly of Wright shouting, "God damn America," and Obama repeats the snippet without reproducing the passage from which it is drawn:

> And the United States of America government, when it came to treating her citizens of Indian descent fairly, she failed. She put them on reservations. When it came to treating her citizens of Japanese descent fairly, she failed. She put them in internment prison camps. When it came to treating her citizens of African descent fairly, America failed. She put them in chains, the government put them on slave quarters, put them on auction blocks, put them in cotton fields, put them in inferior schools, put them in substandard housing, put them in scientific experiments, put them in the lowest paying jobs, put them outside the equal

protection of the law, kept them out of their racist bastions of higher education and locked them into positions of hopelessness and helplessness. The government gives them the drugs, builds bigger prisons, passes a three-strike law and then wants us to sing "God Bless America." No, no, no, not God Bless America. God damn America—that's in the Bible—for killing innocent people. God damn America, for treating our citizens as less than human. God damn America, as long as she tries to act like she is God, and she is supreme. The United States government has failed the vast majority of her citizens of African descent. [146]

Wright was arguing that those who commit sin receive damnation, and that America believes it deserves to be blessed without reckoning with its sins. It is an important and defensible point. In fact, it is almost an *inarguable* point, and the only way you can get around the fact that 90 percent of Wright's indictment is true beyond a reasonable doubt is to air only three seconds of it, which is what the news media did.

Obama is now out of office, and there is nothing to stop him from giving Wright's side of the story forcefully and honestly. Instead, he says that he felt the reverend's sermons were inappropriate, in part because Wright used to discuss racism and militarism in front of a "prosperous" congregation.

There were times when I found Reverend Wright's sermons a little over the top. In the middle of a scholarly explication of the Book of Matthew or Luke, he might insert a scathing critique of America's drug war, American militarism, capitalist greed, or the intractability of American racism, rants were usually grounded in fact but bereft of context. Often, they sounded dated, as if he were channeling a college teach-in from 1968 rather than leading a prosperous congregation that included

police commanders, celebrities, wealthy businesspeople, and
the Chicago school superintendent.[147]

God forbid police commanders or the school superintendent should have
to hear "a scathing critique of America's drug war"! (Obama's treatment
of Wright is especially galling when one considers that it was Wright who
inspired Obama's "audacity of hope" phrase. Obama lifted the words but
left out Wright's meaning, for which he has obvious contempt.)

One can acknowledge that the Wright affair put Obama in a genuine
bind: stick by his reverend and risk being destroyed in the press, or throw
him under the bus and achieve an important landmark for Black Americans
by becoming president. Any critical account of Obama needs to acknowledge the fact that he *was* under a unique set of constraints. The racism
directed toward him was extreme. For Fox News, a fist bump became a
"terrorist fist jab."[148] The right treated him as if he were Malcolm X for noting that if he had had a son, that son would be Black.[149] When Obama correctly pointed out that the Cambridge police department had acted "stu-
pidly" in arresting Harvard professor Henry Louis Gates for breaking into
his own home, Obama was immediately faced with demands to apologize,
and felt the need to backpedal by inviting Gates and the arresting officer to
the White House for a "beer summit." And then there was birtherism, the
disgusting, transparently racist conspiracy theory that helped to propel the
current president to his position of political prominence.

It is the case, then, that Obama may not have had as much room
to maneuver simply by virtue of the fact that in a racist country, he was
under an impossible level of scrutiny. But this doesn't explain why after
leaving office, when he is free to speak his mind, Obama appears to partly
blame Gates for his own arrest.[150] It does not explain why he declines the
opportunity to fully expose the racist attacks on Wright for what they
were. As we have written before,[151] Obama's *post*-presidency can resolve
definitively the question of who he really is and what he wants, because

the constraints that were on him as a president have been removed. When Obama looks back proudly, then, on having stood up to the teachers' unions, appointing a neocon to head his defense department, or not intervening forcefully to protect people during the financial crisis because he held the sanctity of the market to be an inviolable shibboleth, we can be fairly certain he is honestly communicating his real beliefs.

From its outset to its conclusion, *A Promised Land* makes clear that Obama sees himself like one of the workmen in Norman Rockwell's *Working on the Statue of Liberty*—the guardian of a good and solemn order. But he also makes clear what kind of order he seeks to protect, as when he explicitly says that prosecuting bankers or taking more aggressive measures during the financial crisis would have done *violence to the social order*. This is perhaps the most telling sentence in the whole book, because it makes so explicit where (and on whose side) Obama ultimately stands. Unless we believe that the criminal laws should simply not apply to the rich, it would be outrageous *not* to prosecute those who dressed up bad mortgages as good ones. For Obama, aggressive government intervention during a national economic catastrophe constitutes unthinkable "violence to the social order." The single greatest liquidation of middle-class wealth since the Great Depression[152]—a direct result of the economic failures that produced the crisis and the administration's subsequent refusal to intervene—apparently does not.

The social order Obama commits himself to protecting, in other words, is the status quo. Reverend Wright's sermons, by making bourgeois parishioners uncomfortable, ultimately threatened that status quo. The protesters calling Bush a war criminal threatened it, too. Providing massive mortgage relief would have threatened it. Nationalizing the banks would have threatened it. Scrapping the filibuster would have threatened it. Obama is congenitally incapable of doing or saying anything he thinks will rock the boat too much or appear "unreasonable."

Thus even now, though he must surely know better, Obama says that it "doesn't make sense" for Joe Biden to assume that Republicans "are going to try to obstruct, stonewall, lie, and do everything they can to defeat my proposals" and perhaps instead will "consider it in their interest at least early on to cooperate."[153] His presidency provides eight years of evidence that Republicans do not consider it in their interest to cooperate, and that they are probably *right* about that. But if Obama were to admit that Republicans do not have an incentive to cooperate, and that Democratic naivete about this is politically suicidal, his entire kumbaya posture about the "bridging of divides" would become impossible to maintain.

Barack Obama is not stupid. He understands the world better than any previous American president. As a Black man, he has seen too much to accept the country's most galling lies about itself. In a recent interview, Obama was relatively honest about the Democratic Party's lurch to the right, pointing out the effect of "free market ideology" on "unraveling the social compact."[154] But Obama is, as always, the prisoner of etiquette and norms. He knows what the Iraq War was, but cannot call his predecessor a criminal. He knew the CIA tortured people, but would not prosecute its malefactors. He knew the financial crisis would destroy millions of livelihoods and make the rich even richer, but rejected popular demands for activist government. Being the kind of president some progressives hoped and believed he would be would have required him to militate against an order he committed to defend decades ago. It also would have required the abandonment of his "everything to everyone" aspiration and necessitated the discarding of his own carefully crafted universalist identity.

In political life, interests inevitably diverge and cannot be harmonized. The short-term financial interests of fossil fuel companies are in tension with the long-term survival interests of human civilization. You cannot make a playlist for everybody. You have to make choices, and those choices will express value judgments. Do you stand with the oil company polluting the town's water supply or with its residents? Do you stand with the workers striking for better wages or with the CEO? Will you maintain Bush's foreign policy or will you reject it? Are you with Rahm, Larry, and Hillary, or with average Americans at risk of losing their homes? Health insurance companies or sick people whose premiums prevent them from seeing a doctor? *Which side are you on?* Obama still insists he is with everyone, that his team is America. But there is no such thing as not taking sides.

Obama's failures and blind spots, of course, were not ultimately borne of good faith errors or misunderstanding—but of something much worse. He was not just naive about human conflicts of interest. By picking a side, but pretending there were no sides, Obama mobilized the hopes and idealism of millions only to betray them. He encouraged people to see his candidacy as the embodiment of their own aspirations for a better future and, having stuffed his cabinet with Beltway veterans who were never going to deliver, now insists that anyone who objects simply does not share in his deep understanding of political reality. He gave "idealism" a bad name by intoning that ideals and platitudes are the same thing, and "pragmatism" a bad rap by suggesting that being unwilling to fight is the same as being conscious of one's limitations. If a generation of angry young people are now becoming socialists, it is in part because Obama's hypocrisy and vacuity have radicalized them. We can and should appreciate Obama's achievement in breaking a civil rights barrier by becoming the first Black president. But the main lesson to take from *A Promised Land* is that Obama's politics did not, and cannot, provide a viable blueprint for the future. The "good and solemn order" of which he sees himself the "guardian" must be defeated rather than defended. The road to the "promised land" lies beyond the fraudulent universalism of Barack Obama.

—*A version of this essay first appeared in* Current Affairs, *December 2020.*

Justin Trudeau and the Politics of Spectacle

On October 19, 2015, Canada's historically dominant political party was returned to power, almost exactly reestablishing the dynamic that had reigned in the country throughout most of the twentieth century. The relative banality of this event was belied by the positively rapturous commentary that ensued in the weeks and months that followed. Historic! Stunning! A new dawn! Canada is back! So laden with inaccuracies, hyperbole, and unrestrained gushing was Trudeau's media reception at home and abroad that any casual observer could have been forgiven for thinking the country had undergone a seismic political transformation and elected radical new leadership rather than the son of a former prime minister at the head of an inveterately centrist brokerage party.

"Canada lurches to the left," proclaimed David Frum in *The Atlantic*, equating Trudeau with the likes of Jeremy Corbyn and Bernie Sanders. The UK's *Express* called him "Canada's new leftwing PM." Trudeau's pledge to run modest budget deficits even earned him an "anti-austerity" label, and *The Independent*'s Hannah Fearn declared that his government was "shaping up to be one of the most ambitious liberal premierships in modern history."

Trudeau-themed clickbait burst forth in a mighty stream, with an unrelenting deluge of schmaltzy profiles of the new Dauphine of Davos. Trudeau's particular brand of social media harlotry quickly took the internet by storm thanks to a series of Candid™ moments showcasing the adorable statesman in *Star Wars* regalia, Spontaneously™ "photobombing" weddings, and Accidentally™ losing his shirt in all kinds of places where professional photographers seemed readily available to immortalize the mishap. Social media swooned at his yoga poses and his diverse collection of colorful socks. Even in an age that has elevated online cringe to an art form, the resulting headlines read like a burlesque satire of the internet at its most embarrassing:

Ryan Gosling Knows Justin Trudeau Is Also Your Boyfriend

Trudeau does jazz hands at G20

Justin Trudeau's 7 Secrets to Being Extraordinarily Charming

Canada's New Prime Minister, Justin Trudeau, Is a Smoking-Hot Syrupy Fox: See Twitter Go Nuts!

Meet the prime minister of Canada, our new man crush

Canadian PM Justin Trudeau is really really ridiculously good-looking. And, yes, it matters.

****

It is impossible to understand the Trudeau phenomenon independently of the national and international contexts that produced it. Like any brand or commodity, it has grown by appealing to people's tastes and capitalizing on their desires. Canada had experienced almost ten years of right-wing rule under the iron hand of authoritarian hockey dad Stephen Harper. As in America after two terms of Bush, there was a genuine hunger for change—any change—and an inclination to give anyone peddling it, whoever they turned out to be, a warm reception and the subsequent benefit of the doubt. (For a variety of reasons, the social democratic NDP was unable to capitalize on this feeling and blew an early election lead to the Liberals.)

Internationally, the current of liberalism Trudeau represents—
one closely aligned[155] with senior figures in the Clinton wing of the
Democratic Party—finds itself uniquely challenged from both the left and
right. As such, some have clearly found comfort in the idea that good
old-fashioned liberal reformism is thriving north of the forty-ninth parallel, standing defiant against the fascistic carnival of Trumpism (a recent
cover of *Rolling Stone*, boasting a beaming portrait of Trudeau, asked:
"Why can't he be our president?").[156] To global elites, Trudeau's success
is reassurance that the disastrous order they have spent the past several
decades presiding over has life in it yet and can be salvaged from obliv-
ion, one superficial gesture or viral video at a time. To many ordinary
people, particularly in the liberally minded middle classes, he offers up
a comforting image of rational, well-intentioned, progressive leadership.

Like many a painstakingly manicured brand, of course, the reality of
Trudeau is altogether different from the airbrushed version that appears
on the label or company website. Nearly two years on from his election, some have begun to seize upon Trudeau's broken promises—and
certainly, there have been many. There was the pledge to end Canada's
combat mission in Iraq and Syria—a mission that was almost immediately expanded and continues to involve a conspicuous amount of fighting. And the explicit commitment that 2015 would mark the last election
under the country's anachronistic, nineteenth-century voting system,
cynically abandoned when it became clear neither experts nor public
opinion aligned with Trudeau's personal preferences.[157]

Then there was the promise to implement "fully [and] without qualification" the UN Declaration on the Rights of Indigenous Peoples such
that, among other things, indigenous First Nations would have full veto
over natural resource development in their territories. Not only has
Trudeau's government since approved two major pipeline projects, but
it almost immediately walked back its commitment to implementing

the declaration, glibly dismissing it as "unworkable" and stating that it wouldn't be adopted into Canadian law after all.[158] Equally repugnant is the $15 billion arms deal with the Kingdom of Saudi Arabia, vigorously opposed by the Liberals while they were in opposition, before they implemented it in government as part of a larger plan to make Canada a major player in the Middle East arms export market.[159]

Pushing all the right rhetorical buttons, Trudeau generated tremendous buzz by promising to raise taxes on "the 1 percent" (while cutting them for the "middle class") and run deficits to pay for unspecified "social infrastructure." While liberal commentators gushed about this supposedly radical break from economic orthodoxy, conservative pundits warned of a return to the bad old days of tax-and-spend activist government—thus continuing a familiar trend in which both wings of the commentariat (there continues to be a dearth of genuinely leftist media in Canada) symbiotically reinforce Liberal messaging. Upon delivery, as it turned out, the much-heralded deficit spending became in effect a massive shouldering of risk by the public to mostly private gain[160] and the tax plan a costly giveaway to the top 10 percent of earners.[161] Far, then, from resurrecting Keynes or channeling Occupy Wall Street, Trudeau offered a harmless, focus-grouped populism that carefully avoided alienating the interests of corporations and the well-off.

The cycle has since repeated itself. In a speech to an elite audience at the St. Matthew's Day Banquet in Hamburg earlier this year, Trudeau again gestured in a softly populist direction. When "companies post record profits on the backs of workers consistently refused full-time work," he declared, "people get defeated . . . When governments serve special interests instead of the citizens' interests who elected them, people lose faith."[162] The press responded with fevered speculation about a renewed "left turn" in Ottawa ahead of the upcoming federal budget. Inevitably, though, the budget delivered nothing of the kind, promising only to "build stronger communities," "lead globally and create jobs for Canadians," and "a government that puts people first." Trudeau's progressive halo was shining brighter than ever, and he'd barely even lifted a finger.

All the obvious charges of hypocrisy, apt as they may be in many cases, risk obscuring Trudeauism's actual project, which is one more palpably cynical than that implied by conventional political promise-breaking. Trudeau's own talent, such as it is, has always consisted in an ability to sound politically ambidextrous while lending an affirmative sheen to the insipid technocrat-speak of the boardroom, state bureaucracy, or industry conference luncheon. (Before entering politics, incidentally, Trudeau spent time on the public-speaking circuit giving lavishly paid talks to these very luncheons.)

Trudeau's speeches are full of vague and uplifting bromides. Once, summing up his political ethos, he declared: "History shows that this country works best when we all work together to solve the problems that matter most to Canadians."[163] Closing a televised election debate, he proclaimed: "We are who we are and Canada is what it is because in our hearts we've always known that better is always possible."[164] And during a 2015 stump speech, he announced: "We're proposing a strong and real plan. We can grow the economy not from the top down . . . but from the heart outwards."[165] In a 2014 speech he explained the Liberal Party's economic philosophy as follows:

> Too much government is an enemy of freedom and opportunity, but so too is too little. Governments can't do everything, nor should they try. But the things it does [sic], it must do well. As Larry Summers reminded us on Thursday, fiscal discipline is important, but sustained growth is the only route to balanced budgets over the long-term. To create that growth, we have to get the big things right. [166]

Here we see the Trudeau style in full form: blandly reassuring, managerial, and entirely devoid of ideological specificity or commitment. Anyone can find a nod to her political proclivities—for a more or less activist government; for higher or lower taxes; for a larger or smaller welfare state—buried somewhere between the lines. Government shouldn't be too big, and it shouldn't be too small. Canada is great because of the things that make it great. When you speak in tautologies, nobody can disagree with you.

It's easy, of course, to mock vacuous talk about growing the economy "from the heart outwards." But Trudeau's politics are not actually "empty" and he has, at times, been quite explicit about his actual function. In a 2013 essay addressed to Canadian elites entitled "Why It's Vital We Support the Middle Class," he wrote:

> National business leaders and other wealthy Canadians should draw the following conclusion, and do so urgently: If we do not solve [the problems facing the middle class and low-income earners], Canadians will eventually withdraw their support for a growth agenda. We will all be worse off as a consequence . . . Deepening anxiety yields deepening divisions in every society, and we are not immune to that vicious cycle here in Canada. We will begin to vote for leaders who offer comforting stories about who to blame for our problems, rather than how to solve them. [167]

Trudeau's turns of phrase seemed to pass by unnoticed, but in retrospect their subtext was all too clear: inequality, understood by some as a moral or structural problem, risks making the less well-off "anxious" such that they might "withdraw their support for a growth agenda." They may even (it seems to follow) elect new leadership with the audacity to point its dirty fingers squarely at elites. Taking measures to alleviate the worst effects of inequality, in other words, is a route to preserving the present system of wealth distribution, not dismantling it. Sure enough, once in office Trudeau was swiftly embroiled in a cash-for-access scandal, as it became clear that wealthy donors at Liberal fundraisers could purchase his attention.

On the one-year anniversary of his election, Trudeau once again let the mask slip, this time in response to a question about how his government was navigating the unpopularity of neoliberal globalization at the present political moment:

> We were able to sign a free trade agreement with Europe at a time when people tend to be closing off. We're actually able to approve pipelines at a time when everyone wants protection of the environment. We're being able to show that we get people's fears and there are constructive ways of allaying them—and not just ways to lash out and give a big kick to the system. [168]

It was a bizarre but revealing comment: Trudeau, the would-be progressive savior, effectively boasting about his government's success in perpetuating a widely disliked status quo—not by actually changing anything, but rather by "allaying people's fears" so that the cogs of the global economy could continue to spin without interruption.

Despite all the fanfare it has generated, the Justin Trudeau phenomenon is in many ways thoroughly unremarkable. This is because, stripped of its pretensions, it represents something all too familiar in Canada and elsewhere. Armed with platitudes, marketing savvy, cultural nostalgia, and the assistance of a generally compliant media, the party most synonymous with the country's social and economic elite successfully positioned itself, not for the first time, as the standard bearer of progressive change.

In this respect, Charles Taylor's observation about the elder Trudeau, penned nearly a half century ago, strikes an eerily familiar chord:

> Trudeaumania provided the ideal psychological compromise between [two] . . . contradictory drives. The Trudeau image offered all the excitement of change . . . while offering the reassurance which the average man could read in the benign reactions of power and privilege—that no serious challenge would be offered to the way things are. The act looked terrific, but everyone knew that no crockery was going to be broken. Everyone could relax and indulge the yearning for change without arousing the fear of novelty. [169]

American progressives remember well the frenetic euphoria of 2008 and the almost transcendent rhetoric that accompanied the election of Barack Obama, another figure who happily accepted that his values are malleable and respond to political circumstance.

Electoral considerations have also weighed heavily in determining Trudeau's principles. In response to questions from students at the University of British Columbia in 2015 about why he was voting in favor of a draconian Conservative bill widely seen as an assault on basic civil liberties, he responded as follows:

> We know that, tactically, this government would be perfectly happy if the opposition completely voted against this bill because it fits into their fear narrative and [their desire to] . . . bash people on security. I do not want this government making political hay out of an issue . . . or trying to, out of an issue as important as security for Canadians.

Then followed the kicker: "This conversation might be different if we weren't months from an election campaign, but we are."[170]

As with Obama, Trudeau's meticulously groomed, post-political brand is pure artifice: a place where the professionalized, marketing-obsessed business of modern campaigning converges with contemporary culture's preference for the personal over the political in elevating form over content.

Put simply, it is a politics that offers the ephemeral sensation of change rather than the actual thing. In place of a coherent program, it offers chirpy sound bites and superficially progressive language designed to tranquilize and comfort rather than mobilize or transform. Scratching its surface, we find not the youthful energy, dynamism, or innovation it claims for itself, but rather an all-too conventional and elitist style of leadership.

Practitioners of technocratic personality politics are, of course, nothing new. But Trudeau potentially represents a new model for conducting them. More efficiently than any other current Western leader, he has successfully fused elite liberalism with progressive rhetoric and new communications tools to produce a quintessentially twenty-first century politics of spectacle.

In the absence of a vibrant left-wing alternative—in Canada and around the world—this may turn out to be the fate awaiting all democratic politics in the decades ahead.

—*A version of this essay first appeared* in Current Affairs, *November 2017.*

Fear and LARPing on the Campaign Trail

It's still early going, but the basic dynamic of the 2020 Democratic primaries seems to be set and is likely to crystallize in the weeks and months ahead. Faced with a restless party base and an insurgent Bernie Sanders candidacy that appears worryingly viable, party elites and donors will continue to look to anything—and anyone—they believe might push the reset button and restore a sense of normalcy.

Indeed, there's every reason to believe that the coming primary contest will end up resembling the GOP's chaotic and disorienting 2016 race, in which Republican elites scrambled to find the secret formula that could arrest Donald Trump's momentum, cycling awkwardly through donor-friendly suits like Jeb Bush, Marco Rubio, and John Kasich before finally settling on the widely loathed (and spectacularly unsuccessful) Ted Cruz.

In similar fashion, Democratic power brokers and consultants have already auditioned several Anything But Bernie vehicles and are likely to test-drive a few more before any votes are cast. Even at this early stage, the primaries have become a kind of phony war in which an array of functionally indistinguishable establishment candidates compete to make the contest about something, anything, other than a decisive break with the political and economic status quo.

First out of the gate was Beto O'Rourke, fresh from his own unsuccessful Senate run against none other than Ted Cruz. Arriving to a chorus of effusive praise from pundits intent on proclaiming him The Most Exciting Candidate In A Generation, O'Rourke fast inherited the mantle of a Serious Contender, securing a high-profile interview with Oprah

Winfrey in Times Square and becoming the subject of a breathless 8,500-word *Vanity Fair* cover story[171] timed perfectly for his official campaign launch. Drawing on a familiar arsenal of political clichés and performing a painfully contrived rendering of what professional-class Gen-Xers think young people find cool, O'Rourke's campaign thus far has been like an extended meditation on the true meaning of emptiness—with few policy positions to speak of and little of substance to say about what its leading man actually believes or where he intends to take the country.

Betomania, at least in its first incarnation, proved short-lived—arguably cresting shortly before O'Rourke's official entry into the race and quickly being eclipsed by another dizzying media ascendency: that of Pete Buttigieg, a figure virtually no one had heard of mere months ago. Boasting an impeccable resume, boyishly unctuous grin, and no discernible agenda or program to speak of, the mayor of South Bend, Indiana was suddenly everywhere. From magazine covers to clickbait documenting his dogs' personalities and the candidate's taste in various consumer products (with Amazon links embedded for good measure) the Buttigieg brand swiftly established itself as institutional liberalism's flavor of the month.

Just like O'Rourke before him, the Democratic Party's latest rising star has succeeded in generating tremendous media buzz despite articulating his beliefs and goals in only the vaguest and most abstract of terms. As Nathan Robinson points out,[172] the Mayor Pete phenomenon has mostly been about Mayor Pete himself: his background, his temperament, and his credentials which, taken together, admittedly have strong brand potential.

Like O'Rourke, Buttigieg is a conventional Democrat from a less-than-blue state who is well-liked inside the Beltway—making him ideally situated to posture as if he's bringing the rugged, frontier wisdom from the hinterland to Washington while ensuring he never causes anyone there even a modicum of discomfort. He's the Democratic mayor of a small city in Indiana (a state convincingly won by Donald Trump in 2016) who is a veteran and a Christian, but also a gay man—certainly a more interesting and sympathetic background than O'Rourke's. Buttigieg's candidacy is thus a dream for the kinds of consultants and strategists who see politics as the art of ticking off various cultural and demographic boxes and then building a compelling story arc around them. Buttigieg, in fact, recently hinted at this himself when asked what sets him apart from his fellow candidates:

> You have a handful of candidates from the middle of the coun-
> try, but very few of them are young. You have a handful of young
> candidates, but very few of them are executives. We have a
> handful of executives but none of them are veterans, and so it's
> a question of: what **alignment of attributes** [my emphasis] do
> you want to have?[173]

Given his brand potential (not to mention his reported presence at secretive meetings with donors and party elites plotting to stop Sanders), no one should count Mayor Pete out just yet. But for the moment, the long-anticipated return of another figure on the Democratic scene has somewhat cooled the media's Buttigieg-induced delirium.

Unlike a failed Texas Senate candidate or the mayor of South Bend, a former vice president cannot even superficially claim to be an outsider. Joe Biden surely knows this and wouldn't feel comfortable in the role anyway, which is why he isn't even pretending to be something he's not. His Washington is one of elite camaraderie and locker room fraternity far exceeding anything ever dreamt up by Aaron Sorkin: an ancien régime to be preserved through endless backroom handshakes and magnanimous compromises between fundamentally decent people, be they milquetoast liberals, right-wing conservatives, or former segregationists. As far as the official narrative is concerned, Biden boasts strong appeal with the real America of hard-working, blue-collar Joes—the sort who toil in the mines and factories by day and toast bipartisanship with Comcast executives at gold-plated fundraisers by night.

More accurately, Biden's potential appeal is to a broad swath of voters who felt reasonably comfortable and secure during the Obama presidency and simply want to restore something resembling it. Far from being a hawkish corporate Democrat and one of the principal architects of mass incarceration, their Biden is the one of early 2010s internet memes and late-night comedy fodder: an avuncular, slightly potty-mouthed but ultimately loveable good guy who wants things to get better in a non-threatening sort of way. (Perhaps to a lesser extent, he also appeals to some older or more conservative Democrats simply because he reflects their beliefs.) Cashing in on Obama nostalgia—and presumably hoping his association with the still-popular former president will inoculate him against criticism—Biden has become the third figure to emerge from the party establishment's ongoing Anything But Bernie cavalcade and he may not be the last (get ready for the Klobuchar breakout).

From a pundit perspective, all three candidates no doubt seem quite disparate. For one, they all belong to different decades, the first two being forty-six and thirty-seven respectively and the former vice-president seventy-six. They're all white men but hail from different regions and are said to have divergent appeals: Beto to the young (he skateboards, after all, just like Steve Buscemi in *30 Rock*); Buttigieg to those who prize intelligence and sophistication (he's read James Joyce and is, like the very best among us, often called a "wonk"); Biden to erstwhile coal miners in Pennsylvania and West Virginia whose love of faith, flag, and family is exceeded only by an insatiable hunger for means-tested tax credits and a fondness for soaring oratory about deficit reduction and the inherent nobility of the nation's billionaires.

The Three Bs do indeed boast different sources of appeal, tick different demographic boxes, and will strike somewhat different cadences with their political messaging. Nonetheless, the candidacies of Beto, Buttigieg, and Biden ultimately all follow from the same template.

All three enjoy big political and media constituencies, both in the Beltway and its adjacent bases of power and influence; all three have been boosted by party mandarins as potential antidotes to the insurgent populist current represented by (among other things) the surging candidacy of Bernie Sanders; all three have been the subject of tremendous media buzz despite saying very little of substance. Each is campaigning based on personal signifiers rather than any actual program they hope to realize in office, appealing above all else to people's desire for a return to normalcy during the Trump era.

Beto, Buttigieg, and Biden—their variations notwithstanding—are all different reflections of the same, largely postpolitical strand of liberalism, one that has so thoroughly acceded to the logic of the market that it no longer recognizes the difference between branding and campaigning and is stubbornly uninterested in having it explained.

That's the unifying theme here, as the current trifecta of consultancy-hatched Anything But Bernie candidates auditions for the coveted role of National Savior. Having given up on the idea of leveraging political power for genuinely reformist ends, all that remains for centrist Democrats is to market aspiring leaders like brands to be consumed by potential buyers in the electoral bazaar. Not accidentally, this model of politics has increasingly drawn on a vast army of marketing executives, advertising professionals, and other technocrats who specialize in selling politicians the way Pepsi, Coke, and Frito-Lay periodically push exciting new twists on their classic flavors.

The recasting of politics as an exercise in marketing has a further corollary, namely the transfiguration of ordinary voters from complex people with material needs and political values into shallow market niches with buttons to be pushed and pleasure centers to be stimulated; from human citizens into consumers. The underlying assumption here, shared with the world of advertising and cloying sales pitches, is that all people want to see something about themselves represented in the products they purchase and consume. Envisioned this way, politics quickly becomes an exercise in pure spectacle: a contest of broad personal narratives to be manufactured and affected by politicians qua brands campaigning on the basis of this or that reductive cultural taxonomy they supposedly embody—their own "alignment of attributes" to borrow the arid phraseology of Mayor Pete.

Taking the notion still further, Buttigieg has openly embraced a "storytelling first, policy details later" ethos premised on the idea that voters don't actually want to hear much about policy at all, remarking recently: "The story that we tell, not just about government but about ourselves, and the story we tell people about themselves and how they fit in, really grounds our politics."[174] Here Buttigieg is at least partly correct. The average person probably doesn't have the time or the inclination to study the mundane details of a politician's agenda and every candidate must necessarily tell some kind of story. But the content of that story, and its grounding in something other than sand, ultimately matters a whole lot more than whether it ticks the right boxes for pundits, party elites, and marketing gurus.

Sanders himself has a story, featured in every stump speech and similar to the one he's been telling for decades. He is not the protagonist but merely a supporting character in a long-standing struggle against inequality and exploitation, fought between ordinary people and an entrenched class of political and economic elites—Democratic and Republican alike—bent on maintaining the status quo and its many injustices at all costs. It's a story that has the virtue of being grounded in material reality and it includes both a tangible policy program and a plan of action for bringing it about.

The oft-cited dichotomy between policy and storytelling—the former substantive but esoteric, the latter compelling but shallow—is as much a mirage as the range of choice represented by the Three Bs: each one a conventional, donor-friendly Democrat born of a political and media environment intent on treating politicians as brands and voters as consumers.

As the phony war rages on, expect the focus groups at Liberalism Inc. to serve up a few more flavors between now and New Hampshire—every one of them vanilla and caffeine-free.

—A version of this essay first appeared in Jacobin, *May 2019.*

Farewell to Betomania

It is customary to begin a campaign obituary with some kind of cliché. If the candidate in question enjoyed some success before the fall, a hypothetical retrospective will probably commence on a downbeat but defiantly optimistic note ("While not securing the ultimate prize, there can be little doubt that Candidate X has made their mark," etc.). Less successful politicians, meanwhile, are liable to generate still more inane platitudes that could mean practically anything (e.g., "a campaign that ended much as it began," "never really found its footing," "couldn't ultimately attract enough support to win by getting more votes than its competitors," etc.).

In truth, it's difficult to find the right cliché with which to describe the demise of Beto O'Rourke: a figure whose campaign was at once so utterly generic in its politics and so unbearably awkward in its execution that it belongs in a museum alongside other 2019 oddities that will probably prove indecipherable to future generations. Even for those of us who lived through the failed Texas Senate candidate's Icarus-like ascent and subsequent fall, the pace of events makes his candidacy a dizzying one to unpack.

In less than six months, O'Rourke successfully made the journey from national celebrity to forgettable also-ran: a breathtaking trajectory typically reserved for erstwhile YouTube stars and former reality-show contestants. Such comparisons are only too fitting for a candidate who initially shot to fame thanks to a series of viral, off-the-cuff videos before arguably being undone by the same transitory environment that had enabled his rise in the first place. The kind of ephemeral political commodity that is only possible in the social media age, O'Rourke's campaign began with comparisons to Bobby Kennedy and ended only months later in a flourish of increasingly desperate, almost pitiable attempts to generate clicks at any cost.

Coming down from a near miss against the loathsome Ted Cruz, the congressman from El Paso seemed primed, at least to some, to be a serious contender for the Democratic presidential nomination. Young, photogenic, and viral, O'Rourke's reliably conservative voting record in the House and knack for speaking in glittering generalities made him ideally suited to capture the mantle of dynamic progressive without making donors or corporate interests too uncomfortable—the veritable Holy Trinity of Beltway political scripture.

Many of the nation's pundits evidently agreed and, ever on the hunt for something shiny that might momentarily cause the youngsters to forget about socialism, they hastily inaugurated Betomania as the season's most captivating electoral earthquake-in-waiting. Comparing O'Rourke to Alexandria Ocasio-Cortez, the *New York Times'* Sydney Ember confidently pronounced Bernie Sanders a relic.[175] The *Washington Post's* Jennifer Rubin declared "Beto fundraising number suggests Bernie [is] now officially yesterday's news, faces stiff competition for [the] youth vote."[176] Jonathan Chait, meanwhile, dismissed left-wing criticisms of O'Rourke[177] as the splenetic outbursts of a handful of cultists too puritanically minded to get on board with a candidate well on his way to becoming the next Barack Obama.

Such hyperbole inarguably reached its zenith with an eight-thousand-word profile published by *Vanity Fair*[178] to coincide with O'Rourke's official launch and brimming with passages meant to showcase his ostensibly irresistible hipness ("Beto O'Rourke is quintessentially Generation X, weaned on *Star Wars* and punk rock and priding himself on authenticity over showmanship and a healthy skepticism of the mainstream"). Though the piece's now infamous final grafs ("The more he talks, the more he likes the sound of what he's saying. 'I want to be in it,' he says, now leaning forward. 'Man, I'm just born to be in it ...'") have only grown more cringeworthy with the passage of time, they were nonetheless an accurate reflection of a real, if fleeting, media zeitgeist that sought to make the triumph of O'Rourke's candidacy seem so inevitable it would be useless to resist.

From this euphoric beginning, O'Rourke's descent into irrelevance was swift and unforgiving, his momentary presence in a few national polls evaporating and his initially solid fundraising numbers plummeting. In hindsight, the limitations of his embarrassingly try-hard schtick should have been difficult to miss. Preceding both the *Vanity Fair* profile and a now-famous live broadcast of his gums, O'Rourke sought to lay the groundwork for his presidential bid with a series of strange blog posts penned in a minimalist style that read like a mashup of Jack Kerouac and Aaron Sorkin:

> I walked over to the north wall and read Lincoln's second inaugural address. My body warm, blood flowing through me, moving my legs as I read, the words so present in a way that I can't describe or explain except that I'm so much more alive in the middle of a run, and so are the words I was reading.
>
> The words, describing the country in the midst of Civil War. The reasons for the war. Slavery. The masterful, humble invocation of God. Acknowledging that both sides invoke his name and saying of the South: "It may seem strange that any men should dare to ask a just God's assistance in wringing their bread from the sweat of other men's faces, but let us judge not, that we be not judged." That he could pronounce this judgement and then remind himself and us that we should not judge . . ."[179]

Obviously hoping to replicate the supposedly shoot-from-the-hip style he had popularized in Texas, O'Rourke's quixotic quest for the Democratic nomination fast became a series of similarly strained attempts to translate his initial celebrity into viral content and thus popular support—all of which failed spectacularly. Though a horrific mass shooting in El Paso briefly gave his flailing candidacy a renewed focus, O'Rourke's attacks on the NRA, phony war with fellow centrist cipher Pete Buttigieg, and newfound fondness for swearing[180] nevertheless mostly seemed like extensions of this same initial strategy: designed to punch through an oversaturated media environment by grabbing attention and creating the appearance of novelty wherever possible.

The launch and ultimate failure of Betomania is instructive of many things: the continued significance of celebrity in the elite liberal imagination and its declining currency among the electorate at large; the limits of ephemeral personality politics in an age of widespread economic hardship and looming climate catastrophe; the appalling superficiality of influential Democratic power brokers who allowed themselves to believe the country would fall head over heels for yet another photogenic white guy marrying vague uplift with familiar centrist timidity; the unforgivably patronizing attitude toward the young that still predominates in American politics.

Most reassuring, O'Rourke's resounding failure to catch fire (let alone even hang on until Iowa) suggests that the once impregnable grip of the usual pundits and consultants is showing real signs of waning. Like Marco Rubio in 2016, another candidate whose ostensibly broad national appeal was in practice mostly limited to a handful of area codes, Betomania was a naked, if uncannily bizarre, attempt at political astroturfing—and it crashed in similarly spectacular fashion.

Adios, Beto. We hardly knew you.

—*A version of this essay first appeared in* Jacobin, *November 2019.*

Amy Klobuchar and the Electability Hustle

As the Democratic nomination race nears Iowa at long last, Amy Klobuchar sits with a resounding 2.4 percent in the RCP average of presidential primary polls. Like several other candidates who have received lavish praise and momentum stories from the pundit gallery, the Minnesota senator's press attention has palpably failed to crystallize into significant or lasting popular support—with one extremely amusing difference: ephemeral and contrived as they may have been, the breathless, effusive media campaigns that accompanied the momentary surges of figures like Kamala Harris and Beto O'Rourke were at least accompanied by a noticeable uptick in a handful of polls.

Klobuchar, by contrast, has been an also-ran from the moment she entered the race, having failed to crack even the mid–single digits since announcing her candidacy in February. She is a distant ninth in quarterly fundraising—behind the likes of Cory Booker, Andrew Yang, and Kamala Harris (who suspended her campaign this week)—and unless America's liberal establishment somehow burns through its seemingly inexhaustible reserve of focus-tested centrists and billionaires before the polls close in Iowa, her position seems unlikely to shift.

None of this would matter in the slightest if elite pundits and marquee op-ed writers hadn't been taking it upon themselves to tell us, again and again, that Klobuchar is both incredibly impressive and eminently electable. Indeed, perusing the coverage of the Minnesota senator's perpetually flailing campaign, the casual reader might easily conclude that

America is currently in the throes of Amy Mania or, at any rate, that an insurgent Klobuchar breakthrough is mere days or weeks away.

Poll a representative sample of the nation's leading pundits and you'll discover that Klobuchar is an able and charismatic debater whom ordinary voters adore for her folksy charm, down-home affect, cuttingly dry sense of humor, and doggedly realist political outlook. Her debate performances invariably receive wide acclaim from the martini-soaked galleries at press viewing parties, and her campaign is currently receiving its fifth or sixth second look from a primary electorate that pundits still insist is crying out for a Plainspoken Moderate whose biggest offering is expanded personal savings accounts.

So why, exactly, do elite pundits love Amy Klobuchar so much? The simplest explanation is that many are more or less glorified sports commentators who revel in the kind of speculative, horse-racey meta-commentary that now comprises the vast majority of campaign coverage. Viewed in this way, electoral contests are mostly an infotainment spectacle wherein various candidates compete on the basis of neatly taxonimizable personal attributes—like professional athletes or fantasy characters digitally rendered with +7 Electability and +15 Midwesternness for the latest release by EA Games. This was evidently the thinking behind a February analysis penned by pollster qua soothsayer Nate Silver entitled "How Amy Klobuchar Could Win the Democratic Nomination," brimming with observations like the following:

> The beer track ... without the baggage? Klobuchar's campaign
> is likely to emphasize her working-class Midwestern roots, her
> staff said; you'll hear stuff about how her grandfather worked
> as an iron-ore miner, for instance. It will also pitch her to voters
> on candor, honesty, pragmatism, an ability to "get stuff done,"
> work ethic and so forth. It's going to lean pretty heavily into

her Midwesternness, in other words. The idea is to draw a contrast—probably softly at first, and maybe more explicitly if the campaign grows more combative—between Klobuchar and more left-wing candidates from the coasts, particularly Harris, Warren, Sanders and perhaps Booker. In some ways, this will recall the old distinction between "beer-track" ("flyover-state" moderates) and "wine-track" (coastal liberals) Democrats.[181]

The preceding, of course, would make a bit more sense in a world where it was somehow possible to abstract a candidate's "electability" from their popularity among actual people who cast votes. Given the obvious disconnect between her ostensible electability and her cavernous numbers, a bewildered Silver was thus forced to conclude of a recent poll unfavorable to Klobuchar: "[She] probably has one of the best electability arguments in the field, so the fact that she's tied for last here is a sign that voters don't really think about electability in the same way that political analysts do."[182] (Let that one marinate for a moment.)

However bleak her polling among the wider population might be, the Minnesota senator can at any rate rest easy knowing she's doing well within the Pundit Track—a kind of special electorate for which elections are pure pageantry and political appeal has nothing to do with a politician's ability to attract actual votes from real people. In this respect, Klobuchar is the quintessential Beltway phenomenon: a Highly Electable Candidate with virtually no popular support. Satire hasn't been this obsolete since Henry Kissinger won the Nobel Peace Prize.

Nonetheless, there's a bit more at work in Klobuchar's narrow appeal than the superficial crushes she's induced in a handful of pundits made giddy by her canned one-liners and tiresome, "aw-shucks" Midwesterner schtick. Run through the most effusive coverage her campaign has received, and you'll repeatedly find something else in the mix: namely, that Klobuchar is a darling of the pundit class because her principal political message involves telling people wracked by angst and economic insecurity that they can't and shouldn't expect anything better.

Asked by a reporter to comment on the twin ideas of free college and the elimination of student debt a few weeks ago, for example, the candidate had this to say: "I just don't agree with these policies and I also think that they know they most likely won't go through because they don't make any sense when you really take down the veneer and get them off a bumper sticker ... but they just keep promising it."[183]

Taken in isolation, such a comment would merely be emblematic of the narrow way centrist liberals tend to conceive of what's possible. But Klobuchar's follow-up when asked why anyone would dare to promise free college or the elimination of student debt in the first place offered the real kicker: "Because people like it. They like to hear that they're going to get everything free. Right?" Watch the clip for yourself, and you'll hear Klobuchar's voice oozing a kind of paternalistic relish reminiscent of imperious substitute teachers and conservative members of the clergy.

Some of the nation's leading pundits evidently hear much the same thing when Klobuchar speaks, only they've decided it's this very quality that makes her worthy of praise and admiration. Read through the most fawning coverage of the senator's campaign, and you'll find a cavalcade of well-heeled pundits telling us more or less explicitly that her tendency to reject ambitious and popular policies is precisely what makes her so appealing:

Perhaps the most important figure on the stage was Amy Klobuchar, by which I mean that she most readily accepted and aggressively played the necessary role of suggesting that the most progressive proposals—namely, Medicare for All, backed by both Warren and Bernie Sanders—existed in the realm not of the doable but of the dream-able, and that they weren't going to fix needy Americans' lives anytime soon. (Frank Bruni)

In the 2020 field, two Democrats have the strongest track record of running as middle-class fighters: Amy Klobuchar and Sherrod Brown ... Both have also smartly avoided some ideas that play better with liberal Twitter than swing voters, like the fever dream of eliminating private health insurance ... If I were Trump, I would fear Klobuchar. (David Leonhardt)

Before last week, Beth Kundel Vogel was undecided when it came to the Democratic presidential hopefuls. But in the debate on Tuesday, Senator Amy Klobuchar of Minnesota impressed her by calling out Senator Elizabeth Warren of Massachusetts for offering voters a "pipe dream" rather than a plan to pay for universal health care. (Trip Gabriel)

As Senator Elizabeth Warren promised "big, structural change," and Senator Bernie Sanders offered his brand of "political revolution," Ms. Klobuchar was steadily reminding voters of the factors that have long mattered in national politics, at least before the election of a certain current president: expense, experience and electability. Now, as the moderate wing of the party reasserts itself in the primary campaign, her message of plain-spoken politics is drawing greater attention. (Lisa Lerer)

Klobuchar has embraced her no-nonsense image of someone willing to tell constituents "no." She has developed an unusual signature move, namely debunk the pie-in-the-sky proposals of the staunch progressives, undaunted by their arguments that she is not thinking "big enough." If Warren and Sen. Bernie Sanders (I-Vt.) do not win the nomination, much of the credit should go to Klobuchar, who has effectively grabbed the party by the lapels and told its members to "Snap out of it!" (Jennifer Rubin)

In an alternate timeline with a less hierarchical culture suffusing both media and politics, it would be difficult to imagine a candidate like Amy Klobuchar receiving such fulsome treatment from democracy's so-called fourth estate. Most likely, her well-established reputation as one of Capitol Hill's worst bosses would be considered instantly disqualifying, and she wouldn't be running for president at all.

Boasting the highest rate of staff turnover for any member of the Senate last year, Klobuchar's fondness for mistreating subordinates (which in 2015 even earned her a rebuke by Democratic Senate leader Harry Reid) has been widely reported—with former staffers describing "a workplace controlled by fear, anger, and shame" according to an investigation by *BuzzFeed* earlier this year.[184] Among other things, Klobuchar has allegedly engaged in multiple efforts to shut down prospective job opportunities for members of her staff; thrown objects such as binders and phones in their direction; forced low-level employees "to perform duties they described as demeaning, like washing her dishes or other cleaning"; and emailed staff "at all hours of the day and night" with appraisals of their perceived incompetence. Her reputation as a boss is so bad it reportedly drove several people away from the opportunity to manage her presidential bid. As a February report from the *Huffington Post* described it, Klobuchar "defended her office as a 'tough' workplace that molds her employees for even greater challenges."[185]

If Klobuchar is well-liked among elite members of the media for her ability to affect a folksy charm while talking down to constituents, her reputation as the Hill's most tyrannical boss certainly hasn't proven any kind of hindrance—if anything, it has evinced an eerily parallel appeal. Reacting to a *New York Times* report entitled "How Amy Klobuchar Treats

Her Staff" detailing (among other things) an occasion when the Minnesota senator is said to have told a subordinate "I would trade three of you for a bottle of water," *New York* magazine's Jonathan Chait chuckled: "This line makes me want to vote for Klobuchar."[186]

To which the *Washington Post*'s Jennifer Rubin replied: "Exactly."[187]

—A version of this essay first appeared in Jacobin, *December 2019.*

Variations in B-Flat Minor

Review of Trust: America's Best Chance *by Pete Buttigieg (Liveright, 2020)*

There's a famous aphorism often attributed to Miles Davis which says that the notes you don't play in jazz are more important than the ones you do. Much the same can be said of political memoirs and, indeed, most books written by politicians or professional apparatchiks, particularly if published during an election year. Being a genre largely concerned with PR and brand-building, they tend to be heavy on pablum and feather-light when it comes to substance: glorified press releases masquerading as earnest reflections or honest tales of personal triumph in the face of adversity. To any but the most credulous reviewer, they therefore present something of a dilemma. How exactly, after all, are you supposed to write about what isn't there?

Apocryphal though they may be, this is where the words ascribed to America's great jazz innovator really come in handy. In my experience as a regular (and almost always reluctant) appraiser of books and speeches by liberal and centrist politicians, identifying the blank space—the things left unsaid, the issues unaddressed, the possibilities elided, the questions unanswered, the past events ignored, the facts omitted, etc.—can often get you quite a long way.

David Plouffe's *A Citizen's Guide to Beating Donald Trump*, for example, spends just over 250 pages telling readers to canvass, phone bank, and write approving social media posts about a generic and entirely hypothetical Democratic nominee. Tasked with reviewing it, I was initially stumped about what, if anything, to say—an ostensible handbook for fighting the right with scant reference to ideology, program, or social vision not exactly offering up a lot of raw material with which to work. My writer's block persisted until I realized that Plouffe's omissions were precisely the point, his vision of liberalism being one that either treats most real political questions as settled or considers them none of the average person's business (the permissible kind of rank-and-file activism in the modern Democratic Party being about deference to party elites and not much else).

Anyone attempting a critical reading of Barack Obama's (admittedly far superior) *A Promised Land* must similarly spend hours navigating lush thickets of prose and literary adornment to discover what really is and, more importantly, isn't there—the author's style being so coldly elegant and his perspective so ethereal that the conservatism of his worldview can easily escape notice. In stunningly brazen fashion, the paperback edition of Hillary Clinton's *Hard Choices*—the memoir originally published in 2014—scrubbed a section that effusively detailed her role in promoting the Trans-Pacific Partnership (just in time for the former secretary of state's election season rebrand as a free-trade skeptic).

Finding the blank space in a mass-market political book or memoir is therefore a useful way of stripping away its artifice. And, since most entries into the genre by mainstream politicians feature far more artifice than they do genuine insight, whatever remains tends to be the key to understanding their authors' actual beliefs, commitments, or intentions.

Which brings us to Pete Buttigieg and his recently published *Trust: America's Best Chance*, released last fall just ahead of November's presidential election. As an uninteresting book written by a ravenously ambitious and brand-conscious politician, plenty about *Trust* barely merits comment. Running less than two hundred pages if you don't count its appendices (the first being an excerpt from a Pew Research study on the subject of, you guessed it, trust; the second a transcript of Buttigieg's Sorkinesque 2020 campaign concession address), it is mostly just as

you'd expect: a quick read that is part politics and part autobiography—
the sort of book that counts the likes of Edmund Burke, Thomas Jefferson,
Hannah Arendt, David Axelrod, and Nate Silver among its citations. The
sort to prominently feature the word "trenchant" on its back cover.

As its title suggests, the content of Buttigieg's *Trust* mostly riffs on
the same simple and central conceit, and, here again, I think Miles Davis
can be of some help. Davis's 1959 masterwork *Kind of Blue* famously rev-
olutionized jazz by replacing bebop's emphasis on complex chord structures with modalities, permitting boundless melodic improvisation using
only simple scales. In much the same way, Buttigieg's book takes a very
basic concept (that of trust, in case you've forgotten) and blows it up into
one epic solo showcasing endless variations on a theme.

Though he's certainly no Davis-esque pioneer (just as *Kind of Blue*
influenced much of what came after it, almost every liberal politician
since 2008 has in some way imitated Barack Obama, who remains the
undisputed virtuoso of centrist storytelling) Buttigieg can reasonably
claim to be a skilled practitioner of the genre. For what it's worth, the
average politician could not produce a half-decent sentence if their life
depended on it and, on a basic technical level, *Trust* reads better than
many of its obviously ghostwritten equivalents.

This isn't to say that Buttigieg's latest literary effort refrains from
indulging in the extraneous. On the contrary, true to the basic form of
a mass-market political memoir, there are more than a few passages of
padding to be found throughout—the worst culprit probably being the
author's painstakingly detailed description of what it looked and sounded
like when a modem connected to the internet:

> After coming to rely on Internet connections at the university
> where they worked, my parents finally agreed we should get
> it at home, sometime in the mid-nineties, around when I was
> entering middle school. A miraculous modem appeared, wired

into the phone jack next to the big gray Mac in the front room, with a sequence of about ten little LED lights from top to bottom. To dial up was like watching a rocket launch: first the top light was on, then the second . . . then came the sound of the modem talking to whatever it was talking to . . . sounding like an Atari game's parody of birdsong or of a clarinet solo, pinging and ponging as more and more of the little lights came on, blinking and then steady, orange and then green . . . the sound building to a crescendo that recalled the noise of TV static, as machines confided who-knows-what secret binary handshakes between them while I listened. Then came a key change. Then the pitch of the static pulse tweaked, now higher, now lower, and then, gloriously, the final light went to green and I was online, in orbit: cyberspace.

Though Buttigieg inevitably spins the preceding into a series of observations about the ups and downs of living in an increasingly interconnected world, it seems to exist for no real reason other than to fill out his word count and assure us he is a bona fide Millennial™ (Buttigieg's generational affiliation having done noticeably little to win over young voters in last year's Democratic primaries).

Still, the biggest issue with *Trust* stems from the broadness and therefore ultimate thinness of its central conceit. To be fair to Buttigieg, his stated aims for the book are quite narrow. "*Trust*," as he writes in its introduction, "is not a sweeping account of how we got here, or a full assessment of what it is to be alive and American in 2020 ... Rather [it] is written in the spirit of what must come next." The problem is that, in Buttigieg's hands, the idea of "trust" comes to apply to so much that it works more as a crude framing device than a vehicle for genuine insight.

Trust, as we learn, is necessary for an army to work together effectively (something impressed upon the author during his brief tour in

Afghanistan). A community relies on trust between its members to function. So does the economy. The US Constitution? That was also an act of trust. The delivery of vaccines during a pandemic, it turns out, similarly requires the ethereal presence of the t-word in question. Old Faithful, Yellowstone's venerable and famously punctual geyser, too, embodies the concept (which, by its very nature, implies predictability). Elections, voting, and the daily functioning of American democracy? Folks . . .

Nuance, however, requires us to understand that trust, though generally laudable, isn't always good. Donald Trump's supporters often trusted him to their detriment, particularly when the coronavirus struck. A cruel huckster who once cheated a young Buttigieg out of some baseball cards was abusing a child's trust in the goodness of adults. Trust, in other words, is ultimately a land of contrasts.

Which isn't to say that Buttigieg's various riffs on the concept are exactly incorrect. The issue is that when you've cleaved the fat off a medium-rare thesis like "democracy requires trust" or "a wide array of factors has reduced the overall level of trust in various institutions, imperiling the overall functioning of society," very little meat remains, and most of what's left tends to be banal or anecdotal.

A handful of genuine propositions suggest themselves here and there, and most are perfectly fine. Buttigieg floats, for example, the idea of "moving beyond the electoral college." (He road tested the idea early in the Democratic primaries before growing rather quiet about it.) He also suggests that a Truth and Reconciliation Commission on America's history of racial injustice might help repair its frayed social contract. Nordic levels of taxation and public spending also receive favorable mention, though feel more than a little disingenuous coming from a politician who spent his most recent campaign courting the nation's billionaires and defending their right to pour money into elections. In the book's introduction, the author even makes hopeful noises about the prospects for "a new American social democracy." (Buttigieg can be accused of many things but, having actively helped to crush the single greatest hope for American social democracy in living memory, no one can accuse him of lacking in chutzpah.)

The book's most dishonest and cynical section concerns Buttigieg's retelling of the events surrounding the 2020 Iowa caucuses and the ensuing criticisms directed at his campaign. Recounting his own, now-infamous declaration of victory before any results had actually been reported, the former mayor of South Bend offers a decidedly slippery account of what transpired. "Thrilled with our internal numbers and the fact that one way or another our placement in Iowa had been a spectacular triumph," he writes, "I stood in front of my supporters to thank them for their work and congratulate them ... It felt good to join them and share the one thing we did know, by any reckoning of the results: 'We are going to New Hampshire victorious!' That much was clearly true."

Ambiguous by design as this passage so clearly is, it nevertheless appears to suggest that Buttigieg's declaration wasn't meant to be taken literally (a decidedly creative interpretation that closely resembles the spin he attempted last year). The author might have found this a harder premise to sustain if he had included just a few more of his own words, an expanded version of the quotation in question reading as follows: "So we don't know all the results, but we know by the time it's all said and done ... Iowa you have shocked the nation. Because by all indications, we are going on to New Hampshire victorious." Viewed in its full context, the intended meaning of Buttigieg's declaration remains as clear as it did the day he uttered it. (If this sounds pedantic or nitpicky, revisit the clip and see for yourself).[188]

For that very reason, plenty of perfectly justified questions emerged about the legitimacy of the caucus results and a mysterious app created by a company with ties to Buttigieg's campaign—a development the author cynically dismisses as tinfoil hat conspiracism boosted by "Russia-linked accounts." "With surprisingly little effort," he writes, "conspiracists had convinced sixty percent of the population that it was at least possible that something had gone maliciously wrong in Iowa." Gee, whatever could have given them that idea?

In a noticeable break from Buttigieg's 2019 memoir *Shortest Way Home*, the author's background in management consulting barely appears in *Trust*—his corporate alma mater McKinsey (which formed a major part of his political brand until it became inconvenient during last year's primaries) is mentioned exactly once, and only in passing. In a review of that book soon after its publication, Nathan Robinson remarked on how readily Buttigieg seemed to adapt his branding and rhetoric to new circumstances:

> In the last five minutes of his political life, Buttigieg has started making some radical noises, as is necessary to compete in a Sanders-dominated primary. Buttigieg is smart, and I think people should be warned: He's probably going to say a lot of good stuff. He's probably going to sign on to major left initiatives ... But here's a fact about Pete Buttigieg: He picks up languages quickly. He already speaks seven of them, and you can find stories online of him dazzling people by dropping some Arabic or Norwegian on them. The lingo of Millennial Leftism will be a cinch for Pete. He will begin to use all the correct phrases, with perfect grammar. The question you should ask is: What language has he been speaking up until now?[189]

That question is very much worth posing in relation to *Trust* which, like any half-decent product relaunch, updates the Buttigieg brand to one more in keeping with the zeitgeist of early Biden-era liberalism. *Shortest Way Home* found the author positively giddy about the prospect of turning Indiana into a "Silicon Prairie," remaking South Bend into "College Town 2.0," and filling the "once-moribund Studebaker corridor with data centers and start-ups." Heavy on grating marketspeak as it was, the book was astonishingly light on discussions of poverty, the racial wealth divide, homelessness, mass evictions, or opioid overdoses—all of them serious problems in the city Buttigieg governed.

Trust, by contrast, sees him ditch the lingos of Silicon Valley and management consultancy for the liberal rhetoric of social justice. In the roughly twenty-one months separating its release and the February 2019 publication of *Shortest Way Home*, Buttigieg has clearly read his Robin DiAngelo. Unlike its predecessor, the book thus devotes more than a few pages to race and finds the author reflecting on his own whiteness. It even finds him adopting a pro-labor stance and criticizing the Reagan era offensive against unions.

At first glance, there's nothing wrong with either posture—the obvious, charitable interpretation being that Buttigieg's outlook has simply evolved, albeit in an amazingly brief span of time. But, as with so much of what he writes and says, his newfound outlooks are difficult to square with previous, even very recent incarnations of his political brand. During his work for McKinsey in 2010, for example, Buttigieg belonged to a team of consultants that pushed cuts and privatization at the US Postal Service, recommending, among other things, the replacement of unionized workers with nonunionized retail staff. During the 2020 primaries, he was a vocal opponent of Medicare for All, despite having explicitly endorsed it in 2018. (The issue of health care, incidentally, is mostly absent from *Trust* apart from a single vague reference to "delivering health care for all Americans.") *Trust* finds the author endorsing social democracy, Nordic levels of taxation, and renewed public investment, none of which seemed to be at the front of his mind during his first run for public office just over a decade ago—when he courted the Tea Party.

When a politician appears to constantly reconfigure their rhetoric, posture, and public persona, it is perfectly reasonable to wonder how seriously their words can ever be taken. Trust, as the author himself so ceaselessly reminds us, requires consistency by definition. Which brings us back to the idea of blank space. The Democratic primaries yielded a greater than usual volume of flash-in-the-pan political personalities in the mold of Beto O'Rourke, whose Teflon brand ultimately had less cultural staying power than Netflix's *Tiger King*. Buttigieg, to his credit, created one more durable than most and, unlike many of his rivals, has successfully parlayed it into a cabinet position (Buttigieg was sworn in as Secretary for Transportation earlier this month). What exactly that brand consists of has seemed to evolve with remarkable speed, Buttigieg having made the journey from progressive-minded outsider™ to sensible moderate™ and back again in less than two years (to say nothing of his various pre-2019 incarnations).

As a freestanding work, *Trust* is a par-for-the-course affair perhaps a notch or two above similar contributions to the genre: not particularly bad, but mostly uneventful; a series of technically proficient improvisations around a single, simple theme. Viewed in a wider context, it can be taken as the latest update to the constantly mutating Buttigieg discography: an already sweeping body of rhetorical modes to be riffed on as the political zeitgeist demands. As a relatively short work, plenty of notes go unplayed. But, knowing the artist, it probably won't be long before the next album drops and we get to hear him solo in an entirely different register.

—A version of this essay first appeared in Jacobin, *February 2021.*

Blairism Undead

Faced with an absolutely disastrous set of results in last week's local elections, Keir Starmer waited a few hours to emerge from the shadows and answer questions from the media. When he finally did appear, the leader of the Labour Party had nothing to offer beyond a series of verbal circumlocutions so meaningless he might as well have stayed silent. Asked by the BBC about his catastrophic election performance—which saw Labour hemorrhage council seats throughout the country, but also the County Durham constituency of Hartlepool, a solid Labour seat since its creation in 1947—Starmer proved so unable to say anything of substance that he was ultimately forced to regurgitate the same stock answers for several minutes straight.

STARMER: This is not a question of left or right. It's a question of whether we're facing the country. We have changed as a party, but we've not made a strong enough case to the country. We've lost that connection, that trust, and I intended to rebuild that and do whatever is necessary to rebuild that trust.

BBC: But what does change mean in, say, policy terms?

STARMER: It means stopping, as a party, quarreling amongst ourselves, looking internally, and facing the country, and setting out that bold vision for a better Britain . . .

BBC: Sorry, Sir Keir, what is that vision?

STARMER: . . . changing the things that need changing, and that is the change that I will bring about.

Pressed again and again by his interviewer, Starmer's evasions only grew more absurd—his solitary brush with anything even approaching a political vision being a momentary reference to ending "the injustice and inequality that millions of people face every day." Encouraged to develop the idea further, however, he again defaulted to the same vague language about learning lessons, facing the country, and rebuilding trust:

> BBC: What are you going to change over the next few days? What are you referring to?
>
> STARMER: I will set out what we need to do to reconnect the Labour Party to the voters that have cast their verdict on us last night, particularly in places like Hartlepool. We have changed as a party. We have changed as a party. But we need to go further, and we need to set out that strong case to the country. We have not done that.
>
> BBC: So you're going to set out a new policy agenda? Is that what you're saying?
>
> STARMER: I am going to set out a strong case to the country, learn the lessons of the elections that have come in so far, and accept that we must reconnect and rebuild trust with working people, particularly in places like Hartlepool.

The most sympathetic reading of this car crash is that some combination of stress and poor sleep caused an embattled politician to bungle an interview. Both may be applicable in Starmer's case, but they hardly negate the more obvious interpretation that he was ultimately unable to articulate a vision or policy agenda because he doesn't really have them. Paul Williams, Labour's candidate in Hartlepool, could do little better when asked by Owen Jones to articulate his party's vision for Britain earlier this month:

JONES: Don't use any platitudes when you answer this: What is Labour's vision for the country now? What does Labour stand for? Don't say "fairness" and everything being nice . . . What, concretely, is the vision?

WILLIAMS: People in this election aren't talking, though, about Labour's vision for the country. They're talking about Labour's vision for Hartlepool.

JONES: Okay, what is Labour's vision for Hartlepool that is unique and different and distinct?

WILLIAMS: Yeah, so . . . the best companies come to Hartlepool to provide the best jobs because we have the best trained people . . .

JONES: Do the Tories disagree with that?

WILLIAMS: . . . because we've invested in people right from the start of life. And you make that difference to children, so by the time they start school, they're able . . . they're not behind their peers, they can read . . . they can . . . you then have small class sizes and really, um, you know . . . You help people get to a point where they can be . . . have really great skills, really great training, and then employers come to you not because you've got the lowest taxes [but] because you've got the best people.

****

Even for those unsympathetic to him, it can be difficult to fathom how a politician like Keir Starmer, capable of rising to the leadership of a major political party, has proven quite so unable to offer anything resembling a coherent political vision or statement of purpose after more than a year on the job. Whatever its original pretensions may have been about offering a more digestible and electable version of the program championed by Labour under its previous leadership, Starmerism has been a vapid farce from its outset: a Westminster-centric project with no discernable agenda or policy offerings, unwilling to fulfill even the most rudimentary obligations of a parliamentary opposition during a period of crisis, and so wedded to branding as an organizing principle that its adherents seem to think they can reverse structural political decline simply by bludgeoning erstwhile Labour heartlands with patronizing slogans and empty flag-waving.

Under Starmer's leadership, the party has bled more than one hundred thousand members, been outflanked by the Tories from the left on corporation taxes, and, as of last week, can add electoral catastrophe to its ignominious roster of political achievements. If nothing else, it's a somewhat ironic outcome for a leadership whose entire modus operandi was supposedly about offering a veneer of professional "competence" that its predecessor lacked.

Having followed up last week's electoral disaster with a botched reshuffle that has further inflamed internal tensions and will ultimately see Labour's front bench become even more right-wing, Starmer will presumably spend the coming weeks attempting to craft answers to the questions he so spectacularly failed to answer on the BBC. Whatever sound bites he and his besieged team of advisers do manage to assemble, it's decidedly unlikely they will amount to much beyond a more polished (or perhaps a more explicitly conservative) version of what Starmerism has offered already.

Though it is invariably tempting to put the failures and vacuousness of a political project down to individual leadership, centrist hollowness of the kind reflected in a figure like Keir Starmer is not ultimately about the personal flaws or deficiencies of a single person at the top. Starmer might have proven a better retail politician or someone quick enough on his feet to avoid cringeworthy phrasings like "changing the things that need changing," and he would still have been ill-equipped to offer a coherent vision or meaningful contrast with the government he is charged with opposing.

Revisit the Labour leadership hustings from 2015, and you'll similarly find the coterie of mostly interchangeable centrist automatons who dominated its earliest stages struggling to articulate anything resembling a positive political vision beyond a handful of buzzwords. From the vaguely center-right figures (Chuka Umunna, Tristram Hunt, Liz Kendall) to the vaguely center-left ones (Yvette Cooper, Andy Burnham), there seemed little of substance to debate beyond how a warmed-over version of New Labour–era triangulation was going to be packaged. In Starmer's leadership, we have finally gotten a glimpse of what the Labour Party might have looked like between 2015 and 2019 had any of the various alternatives to Jeremy Corbyn succeeded, and the result has been every bit as politically nebulous as the early race to succeed Ed Miliband.

Once again, it is tempting to ascribe this lack of dynamism to the individual calibers of the current cohort of centrist politicians. And, true enough, there has been a marked decline in talent among those who broadly embrace the New Labour consensus since it was first inaugurated nearly a quarter century ago. It's next to impossible, for example, to imagine a Liz Kendall or a Keir Starmer laying out their political vision with the clarity, rhetorical skill, and ideological zeal possessed by Tony Blair in 1998:

> My vision for the 21st century is of a popular politics reconciling themes which in the past have wrongly been regarded as antagonistic—patriotism and internationalism; rights and responsibilities; the promotion of enterprise and the attack on poverty and discrimination . . . Human nature is cooperative as well as competitive, selfless as well as self-interested; and society

could not function if it was otherwise. The grievous 20th century error of the fundamentalist left was the belief that the state could replace civil society and thereby advance freedom. The new right veers to the other extreme, advocating wholesale dismantling of core state activity in the cause of "freedom". The truth is that freedom for the many requires strong government. A key challenge of progressive politics is to use the state as an enabling force, protecting effective communities and voluntary organisations and encouraging their growth to tackle new needs, in partnership as appropriate. These are the values of the Third Way.[190]

Blair's vision could be articulated more lucidly not just because he was a more talented politician, but because it gave real expression to the zeitgeist of the late 1990s. In 1997, the neoliberal consensus (whatever else one might say about it) was still relatively new and untested in its post-Thatcherite incarnation, and there remained plenty for the apparatchiks of New Labour to do when it came to sweeping away the old order. If the neoliberal center today seems unable to communicate any substantive vision beyond the inane language of focus groups, a major reason is that the project that originally animated it has, by and large, already succeeded.

Blair's revolution has come and gone, and with it a world where anything about its core tenets might be seen as dynamic or modern. With neoliberalism now firmly embedded as the lingua franca of British politics, there remains little for its present-day adherents on the center right and center left to do beyond try to put lipstick on the proverbial pig of an order to which they have already surrendered. (The only other course available is to fall back on old slogans, reflexes, and habits—a fact which explains why the Starmer leadership has found its few moments of genuine energy in fighting or smearing the left.) To this end, they debate empty

PART III

catchphrases and microscopic differences of policy, trading in vague narratives about how British capitalism might be rebranded to seem ever so slightly less cruel.

With a Conservative Party dexterous enough to reinvent itself every few years, this effort will come to nothing in nine elections out of ten. Large sections of the British media, and even larger sections of British capital, will invariably prefer a Tory government over even the most neutered Labour opposition. Labour's structural decline will continue as long as its leaders preclude the kind of radical critique and mass membership strategy that enabled Corbyn's near-victory in 2017—the sole exception to two decades of hemorrhaged votes and professionally managed political ossification.

Keir Starmer's spluttering inability to respond to even basic questions about the contours of his vision was thus about much more than the ineptitude of a single, sleep-deprived centrist out of his depth and suddenly worried about his job after a year of kid-gloves treatment from the media. The terror in the Labour leader's eyes was that of a man not only unwilling to offer answers but congenitally unable to even imagine what they would be. A less mediocre figure than Starmer might have possessed the skills necessary to avoid the disastrous press tour and subsequent near-toppling that accompanied last week's election results. But anyone waiting for a more politically savvy leader to draw a substantive political vision from the atrophied corpse of Britain's neoliberal center will find themselves just as empty-handed as his bemused interviewer on the BBC.

—*A version of this essay first appeared in* Jacobin, *May 2021.*

Joe Biden Is Not a Radical

As Joe Biden delivered his first address to Congress last week,[191] it was obvious that something had shifted. In place of the rhetoric of deficit hawks, Biden touted spending and economic expansion. Where the first Democratic president of the neoliberal age had lauded small government, he instead spoke of jobs, public infrastructure, and invoked the spirit of activist states during the Second World War. He spoke of cutting child poverty, raising the minimum wage, and the specter of climate change. With a cursory and characteristic nod to the personal virtue of people on Wall Street, he talked of blue-collar workers, unions, and the middle class, even calling on Congress to send the potentially transformative Protect the Right to Organize (PRO) Act to his desk.

In at least some respects, the speech represented a marked break from the language of the liberal consensus in the post-Reagan era—and also the rhetoric that has defined Biden's own career at the vanguard of the Democratic center-right. What does it signify? What did it mean? And what does it tell us about the state of American liberalism as the Trump presidency, and the very worst of the deadly virus that ultimately defined its catastrophic final months, recede into memory?

Across partisan lines, swathes of the media have been quick to settle on an answer to these questions. The consensus (expressed with varying degrees of approval, caution, or disapproval, depending on the source) is that Joe Biden is, if somewhat improbably, a radically inclined figure, intent on bringing about lasting changes in the tenor of American life and swerving sharply from the ideological shibboleths that have defined politics since the Reagan revolution. It's a tidy, compelling and, for many, an understandably comforting story in the aftermath of a presidency experienced by virtually all but its own committed zealots as a singular national trauma. It is also, at best, a cart-before-the-horse exercise in preemptive political wish fulfillment; at worst, a case study in the way intoxicating media narratives can overtake reality and inaugurate a new age before anything resembling one has actually arrived.

Even before he had won the presidency, Joe Biden's stated policy agenda was already drawing comparisons to LBJ and FDR. Since January, such analogies have only increased in volume as commentators and media outlets respond to the earliest days of his administration: "Is Biden Really the Second Coming of F.D.R. and L.B.J.?" (the *New Yorker*); "Will Joe Biden Take His Place Alongside FDR and LBJ?" (CNN); "Can Biden Achieve an FDR-Style Presidency? A Historian Sees Surprising Parallels" (the *Washington Post*). Some, particularly the more effusive, have even eschewed the pretense of a question mark in favor of straightforward proclamation: "Four Ways of Looking at the Radicalism of Joe Biden" (Ezra Klein); "Joe Biden Is a Transformational President" (David Brooks); "Welcome to the New Progressive Era" (Anand Giridharadas). (A third, more sycophantic genre, meanwhile, has effectively fused both formats to ask how exactly it is that Joe Biden is so awesome.)

Taken together, pieces like these—wildly varied as they are in terms of breadth, thoughtfulness, and perspective—constitute a decently representative sample of the media consensus throughout Biden's first hundred days. Putting the conclusions most offer (or at any rate suggest) aside, the many analogies to LBJ and FDR do give us a useful metric for evaluating the Biden presidency, and in particular the claims made about its radical impetus and transformative ambition. Both presidents, albeit in different ways, presided over eras which saw the reconfiguration of American institutions but also a partial redefinition of the terms through which they were collectively understood.

The New Deal, to take the most obvious example, produced a durable political consensus, but also a new and lasting framework for thinking about rights, welfare, and the role of the state. The programs and legislation that made up the Great Society, meanwhile, similarly yielded the foundations of a new social contract when it came to health care, housing, and Civil Rights, and reordered America's political imaginary in the process. In a radically different spirit, the Reagan revolution successfully embedded conservative ideas about taxation, public spending, and culture while ushering in reforms that would be embraced by subsequent administrations.

Rupture with the past, durability into the future, and an imprint at once institutional and ideological: these are the basic hallmarks of any political era that can in retrospect be called transformative or radical.

While it's certainly easier to pronounce upon presidencies past than one barely four months old, the first hundred days of the Biden era have not given us particularly strong indication that the new administration is animated by this sort of reformist zeal. On immigration and foreign policy—two files which attracted special attention among liberals during the Trump presidency—it has thus far maintained a lamentable continuity with its predecessor.

With some notable exceptions, it has refrained from exercising the tremendous discretionary power at its disposal to maximize the potential of executive orders. On what is arguably the single most important moral question facing global politics today—the potential waiver of intellectual property rights around vaccines for COVID-19—it also needlessly dragged its feet on an explicit campaign promise and had to be shamed by activists into putting the interests of pandemic victims in the developing world ahead of pharmaceutical companies.

In at least one other significant area, namely health care, Biden has also been characteristically conservative. Though unsurprising given many of his statements on the campaign trail, the context is nonetheless instructive. Some of America's most significant reforms, after all, have been born as much out of crisis as straightforward political intent, and a president unwilling to use a once-in-a-generation pandemic to push structural change to the way health care is delivered has a less than convincing claim to radical élan. While Biden's recent speech to Congress did include a liturgical recitation of the mantra that "Health care should be a right, not a privilege," any reference to his once-touted (and supposedly feasible Public Option), let alone an actually universal model, was nowhere to be found—as sure a clue as any that the Democratic leadership has no plans to alter its mostly amicable relationship with insurance companies.

The obvious exception, of course, is the recently passed $1.9-trillion American Rescue Plan—a package that, among other things, includes several social policy provisions experts believe will cut child poverty in half by mid-summer. In size and scope, the plan is undeniably a major improvement on its Obama-era equivalent (the 2009 stimulus bill being considerably smaller). A whiff of fiscal heterodoxy, however, does not imply transformation or political realignment, less still when it has direct precedent in the not-so-distant past. The $2.2-trillion Trump-era CARES Act passed just over a year ago, after all, was in fact slightly larger and its anti-poverty impact was roughly the same. As *Jacobin*'s Seth Ackerman pointed out in March, the key anti-poverty measures contained in Biden's stimulus are also only temporary, which is surely a relevant detail given how they have sometimes been framed:

> Intoxicating vistas notwithstanding, the bill's poverty-fighting measures, as written, provide for a series of checks to be mailed out for twelve months and then they shut down . . . In other words, Biden's COVID relief plan is what you would have expected a President Joe Biden to pass in an emergency. Like

the 2020 vintage, it's a collection of temporary expedients to dampen hardship during a crisis. What it's not—by itself, anyway—is any kind of paradigm shift. Nor does it transform anything in particular, at least not past 2021.[192]

The suite of policies contained in the American Rescue Plan represent a much-needed injection of public investment during a historic crisis, but they do not constitute a social democratic program (his yet to be passed American Families Plan, for what it's worth, does propose to extend measures like the enhanced Child Tax Credit to 2025). As the pandemic has so cruelly underscored, the nation's social and economic infrastructure is cripplingly frail, and Biden's stimulus will go some way toward patching it up. But, as the plan's widespread buy-in from big business suggests, there is an important distinction to be made between utilitarian public spending during a crisis and FDR-esque ambition for an egalitarian renegotiation of the social contract.

As Matt Karp recently put it:

> For all the huzzahs about progress toward American social democracy, it is hard to see how anything here even begins to alter the social relations between worker and boss, citizen and state, labor and capital. There is a reason why 170 business leaders, including the CEOs of Goldman Sachs, Google, Lyft, Siemens, Visa, and Zillow released a letter supporting the package. The one provision in the House bill that did challenge the preferences of some business leaders, the $15 minimum wage, was dispatched in the Senate without any countervailing pressure from top Democrats.[193]

Biden's tax plan, meanwhile, proposes to fund spending by restoring George W. Bush–era rates for the top tax bracket (rather than Roosevelt levels of 94 percent or even pre-Reaganite levels of 70 percent), and Biden has recently appeared to resurrect his conventional hostility to deficit spending.

Both the PRO Act and, potentially, the landmark voting rights bill HR 1, currently sitting in the Senate after passage through the House, on the other hand, would be genuinely transformative if realized. But it's unclear, as of yet, what the Democratic strategy for them is given the continued presence of the filibuster (or indeed if the White House will stick its neck out for them at all, the recent debate around the minimum wage setting a somewhat less than encouraging precedent).

All told, the thrust of Biden's domestic agenda thus falls far short of anything worthy of comparisons to the Great Society or New Deal in either scale or scope. As distinct from 2009 and with a smaller congressional majority on its side, the new administration has at least provisionally opted to break from the conservative rhetoric and—with business approval—the instinct toward fiscal restraint that hamstrung Barack Obama's first term. But it has not, as sometimes insinuated over the past few months, declared a crusade against injustice nor shown a particular willingness to antagonize private industry in the manner necessary to achieve lasting political realignment or democratic renewal.

The story of Joe Biden's first hundred days is ultimately one of a liberalism compelled by a mixture of circumstance and necessity to be less cautious and more activist than its analogues in recent memory. But it has also been a tale of centrist meliorism mistaken for radicalism and restorative intent conflated with transformative ambition. If lasting change does emerge from the next four years, it will be because popular mobilization successfully extracts concessions from those in power they do not want to concede—not because a conventional liberal delivered it from above.

—A version of this essay first appeared in Jacobin, *May 2021.*

PART IV

On the Media

The beauty of the system, however, is that . . . dissent and inconvenient information are kept within bounds and at the margins, so that while their presence shows that the system is not monolithic, they are not large enough to interfere unduly with the domination of the official agenda.[194]

    —Noam Chomsky and Edward Herman

History does not repeat itself. Nor does it unfold in cycles. The real future is contingent, rich beyond imagining, a perennial gobsmack, tragic and glorious in equal measure; the pundits' future, spun of "conventional wisdom," is only a sucker punch to that common-sense fact.[195]

    —Rick Perlstein

Manufacturing Consent One Chyron at a Time

Review of Hate Inc.: Why Today's Media Makes Us Despise One Another *by Matt Taibbi (OR Books, 2019)*

No single incident can holistically sum up the sheer derangement and utter absurdity that has characterized cable news punditry during the Trump era. But in pondering the phenomenon, one especially emblematic moment comes to mind: namely a December 2015 appearance on Tucker Carlson by *Newsweek* journalist Kurt Eichenwald.[196]

Eichenwald, who is probably best known to the Twitterverse for accidentally tweeting out his own tentacle-themed search history,[197] was then a highly visible member of the burgeoning anti-Trump pundit brigade and had recently made the rather incendiary claim that the Republican frontrunner had been "institutionalized in a mental hospital for a nervous breakdown in 1990." The actual details of said claim (Eichenwald, as far as I can tell, never offered even a shred of evidence that it was true) are ultimately beside the point.

Challenged repeatedly by Carlson, whose own agenda was obviously to pantomime a paint-by-the-numbers conservative complaint about liberal media bias, Eichenwald obfuscated for over seven minutes while insisting with increasing absurdity that he was being prevented by the host from substantiating his claim—in the process making use of a prop he had prepared in advance (a large binder emblazoned with the words "Tucker Carlson Falsehoods" printed in oversized Arial font). Several minutes in, Eichenwald's filibustering act had become so blatant that a

.lighted Carlson would gush: "This is performance art! I've never
. interview like this in my life!"

Somehow, what came next was even more absurd. Challenged
.rectly, yet again, to provide corroborating evidence for his claim that
Donald Trump had been institutionalized in 1990, *Newsweek*'s intrepid
truth-teller decided to make a bizarre appeal to the personal sacrifice of
the individuals who staff America's espionage apparatus while seeming
to imply he was also the bearer of a message on their behalf intended for
both Carlson and Trump:

> Eichenwald: Ok, I will say this, cause it's a message I've got from
> people at the CIA. I know a lot of officers, I know a lot of agents.
> I've been in their homes, and they're really delivering this to you
> and to Donald Trump. These are people who have sacrificed a
> lot for this country. They go through into the CIA every day, they
> walk past that wall with 117 Black stars.
>
> Carlson: What's the message?
>
> Eichenwald: If you're going to say we can't talk about the fact
> that there are 117 patriots whose lives have been lost serving this
> country, that's fine. Right now we have people in Russia who
> are putting their lives on the line to be sources of information
> for the CIA. That information is coming in. That information is
> then being put together by analysts who are not well paid, and
> they do very hard work, and they do it because they are patriots.

Its theatrical quality aside, off the charts even by the standards of cable
news, there is nothing particularly remarkable about the incident. Any
number of others could just as easily stand in to demonstrate the frenetic inanity of the medium through which tens of millions of Americans
unfortunately get their news and formulate their opinions about politics.

Nevertheless, the roughly nine-minute Carlson vs. Eichenwald train wreck offers us a decent checklist when it comes to parsing the worst themes of mainstream media coverage in the Trump era: a notoriously partisan news anchor hosting a segment to decry the scourge of media partisanship; a fact-free claim about a presidential candidate from a guy LARPing as a hybrid of Watergate-era Woodward and Bernstein; the foregrounding of props and empty spectacle over any pretense to objectivity or truth; a reflexive appeal to the CIA made in conspiratorial undertones; an obligatory reference to the Red Menace and the thin blue line of iron-hearted patriots standing in its way. Between all this and (of course) a whole lot of shouting, it's pretty much all here.

Notable also is that, despite their adversarial back and forth, Carlson and Eichenwald were less interacting with each other than they were performing for their respective audiences: one which despises the godless liberal media in all its smugness and coastal elitism; the other which loathes Trump and sees him as a potential agent of foreign subversion.

Too dumb for words, but somehow absolutely par for the course on American network TV.

****

Matt Taibbi's *Hate Inc.* is a seething, if amusing, indictment of American political media in the Trump era. More importantly, it is a systematic account of the sources of media derangement and the ways in which particular patterns of behavior are now hardwired into the news.

Those unfamiliar with Taibbi's past work in media criticism, invariably skewering, may get a misleading impression of the book's content from both its title and cover. Subtitled "Why Today's Media Makes Us Despise One Another" and featuring ominous profile shots of both Rachel Maddow and Sean Hannity, *Hate Inc.* at a casual glance looks like it might be yet another generic screed leveled against partisanship or lamenting the descent of the once-proud enterprise of journalism into adversarial bickering. The American political class and its media proxies have been pumping out versions of this story for decades, bemoaning the sorry state of a politics where no one gets along, leaders won't work together to find bipartisan "solutions" (invariably assumed to be centrist hobbyhorses like conquering the almighty deficit or gutting Social Security), and the discourse is confrontational rather than conciliatory.

That narrative has long been nestled in the public imagination as well, particularly among liberals, and ultimately became one of the defining impulses of the Obama era. Amid the rise of the Tea Party, Jon Stewart and Stephen Colbert famously held a kind of ironic opposition rally whose basic MO was to issue a giant plea for Americans to start using their indoor voices (the meanest, least conciliatory people imaginable would recapture the House of Representatives a few days later). During the Trump era, the popular front coalition of establishment liberals and so-called Never Trump conservatives has appealed in similar fashion to the idea of restoring sanity and friendly cooperation as a bulwark against the nasty extremes of both right and left.

In this all-too-popular conception of what ails American politics, the issue is mainly one of aesthetics and tone rather than substance, structure, or ideology. Vacuous shouting matches a la Eichenwald vs. Carlson are source rather than symptom, and media rancor is largely about the moral decline of a once noble institution. Given the ubiquity of these narratives, we certainly do not need a further contribution to the tired "American politics are excessively partisan and the media is to blame" genre so beloved by centrists, nor another paint-by-the-numbers attempt to blame Fox News for everything ailing America.

Thankfully, *Hate Inc.* is neither. Instead, Taibbi offers us a necessary and timely update to the theories advanced by Noam Chomsky and Edward Herman in their landmark 1988 book *Manufacturing Consent* and a series of illustrative case studies drawing on his own frustrations with contemporary journalism. The basic thesis advanced by Chomsky and Herman was that management of public opinion in capitalist democracies rarely takes the form of overt propaganda or censorship but is instead achieved through vigorous policing of what constitutes acceptable opinion such that, as Taibbi puts it, "the range of argument has been artificially narrowed long before you get to hear it."

The classic illustration is how the American media covered the Vietnam War by presenting the spectrum of support or opposition as one running from "hawks" to "doves," with the former group holding the war to be noble and winnable and the latter noble but unwinnable. One polarity being pro and the other at least nominally con, the average news consumer got the impression that a vigorous debate was underway. Missing entirely from the equation was genuine dissent about the war's actual prosecution or any hint that it might be less an idealistic enterprise that failed than a murderous one that should never have been undertaken to begin with.

While the same basic epistemology is undoubtedly still at play in today's media landscape, Taibbi makes the case that three significant changes since the late 1980s necessitate an update of the thesis pioneered in *Manufacturing Consent*. The first is the rise of conservative talk radio and Fox News, which triggered the partisanization of news so familiar to today. "Using a point of view rather than 'objectivity' as commercial strategies," Taibbi writes, "these stations presaged an atomization of the news landscape under which each consumer had an outlet somewhere to match his or her political beliefs." The second major change is the advent of the twenty-four-hour news cycle, which the author says trained reporters to "value breaking news, immediacy, and visual potential over import" while creating "a new kind of anxiety and addictive dependency" among consumers. Finally, the rise of the internet and social media exacerbated the general atmosphere of frenzied and atomized content consumption that today structures the news business.

Much of the book is taken up with case studies showing the modern media model in action and underscoring how its basic structures contribute to a toxic, often deranged ethos that systematically fails to hold powerful people and institutions to account. A particular highlight is the chapter on Russiagate, which forensically deconstructs the hyper-politicized stylization of information that gave us the Trump era's equivalent of Iraq's nonexistent weapons of mass destruction. Another notable chapter concerns what Taibbi calls "the media's great factual loophole," which deals with the way bogus national security and law enforcement stories can effectively be laundered through sourcing to "unnamed officials"—a tactic that often succeeds thanks to media class's default posture of deference toward the military and State Department.

The chapter on the transformation of the news business into one dominated by affluent professionals is also a highlight thanks to Taibbi's discussion of the way class biases have led some media figures to view the powerful more as "cultural soulmates" to be celebrated than subjects to be challenged. One of his anecdotes is particularly illustrative of the "courtier culture" that now inflects much of political journalism:

> By the 1990s and 2000s, the new model for political reporting was found in books like *Primary Colors* and *Game Change*, which celebrated politicians and their aides, and looked at things from their point of view . . . I remember stepping onto Obama's campaign plane for the first time and seeing the press section plastered with photos. It looked like a high school yearbook office at the end of a semester. Apparently, there was a tradition of reporters taking pictures of themselves covering Obama. They often posed with the candidate and pasted the pics on the plane walls.

Again and again, *Hate Inc.* returns to its central insight that the media is first and foremost a business driven by the pressures and imperatives of large-scale private enterprise. Though this will probably sound like a truism to many on the left, it is still a usefully materialist explanation for why the media tends to operate within discrete partisan silos: not, as is so often suggested, because the country suffers from some vaguely defined culture of "divisiveness," but because it's what the current business model both necessitates and demands. With audiences cordoned off into partisan niches, the media can more easily commodify resentment and its leading talking heads can always get a ratings boost by stoking outrage, engaging in conspiracy, or just plain making stuff up.

It is unclear what the solution is, or to what extent Taibbi even believes there is one. The preceding era of the news business, taken on by Chomsky and Herman in *Manufacturing Consent*, was arguably preferable to today's media in that its ranks were more working-class and its leading voices a bit less shrill. But the ethos of objectivity it projected was still the function of a business model driven first and foremost by the profit imperative and ridden through with deference to corporate and national security interests.

Hate Inc. ultimately makes a forceful case that the American media is broken by design. Though no one will find this a particularly comforting thought, it's nonetheless a liberating insight for those of us who would sooner suffer a hundred hours of sensory deprivation than sit through three minutes of Rachel Maddow talking about Donald Trump's tax returns—or watch Kurt Eichenwald and Tucker Carlson do performance art on national TV.

—A version of this essay first appeared in Jacobin, *April 2020.*

The Agony and the Ecstasy of Chris Matthews

Amid herculean competition, Saturday, February 22, 2020, will probably go down in history as one of the strangest and most embarrassing dates in the history of cable news. Though the symptoms of a full-blown media crackup have undoubtedly been festering for weeks, Bernie Sanders's overwhelming victory in the Nevada caucuses turned out to be the proverbial levee-breaking moment for the talking heads who populate what is supposedly America's most liberal cable network.

In a medium not exactly renowned for offering wisdom or insight, MSNBC's marathon coverage felt like a broadcast from another dimension; a parallel reality with a peculiar metaphysics of its own. At once painful, hilarious, and appalling, the network's unhinged response to Sanders's win doubled as a master class in everything wrong with cable news—from reflexive deference to the corporatist center to instinctive hostility toward populist candidates who refuse to accede to the arbitrary rules set down by elite politicians and media executives.

Over the course of a single afternoon, or so it seemed, the self-serving narratives and rhetorical shibboleths that have sustained an entire era of liberalism were successively burst, leaving many of MSNBC's star personalities to respond with a mixture of denial, anger, and fear. As *Rising*'s Krystal Ball described it:

> Faced with a choice between the man they have loudly proclaimed to be a cross between Hitler, Mussolini, and Benedict Arnold and a man who threatens the very lifeblood of their access journalism, personal self-conception, and class interest,

what would they choose? . . . As caucus after caucus turned in overwhelming results in favor of Bernie Sanders, the flummoxed anchors were left to cope with this singularly myth-exploding event in their own ways.[198]

Thus, an incensed James Carville, somehow looking even more cadaverous than usual, came on to announce, "The happiest person right now . . . it's about 1:15, Moscow time? This thing is going very well for Vladimir Putin," before waving hysterically at the camera and barking, "How ya doin', Vlad?"[199] Reporter Chris Jansing could be heard audibly sighing as she reported with unconcealed frustration that the predominantly Latino voters caucusing at a location near the Bellagio were going overwhelmingly for Sanders. A furious Joy Reid, meanwhile, declared, "No one else is as hungry, angry, enraged, and determined as Sanders voters," before urging the Democratic establishment to "sober up" and figure out "what the hell they're gonna do about that."

In a rare moment of clarity that inadvertently seemed to sum up the whole afternoon, former George W. Bush communications hack Nicolle Wallace was finally forced to concede, "I have no idea what voters think about anything anymore." The day's undisputed champion, however, was MSNBC carnival-barker-in-residence Chris Matthews who, fresh from imagining an alternate reality involving his own execution by Cuban communists in Central Park a few weeks ago,[200] managed to outdo himself by equating Sanders's victory in Nevada to the Nazi blitzkrieg of France in 1940.

Justifiably under fire for the remarks, Matthews has since apologized. But the moment may nonetheless be symbolic of something larger than the deranged outburst of a septuagenarian TV host channeling warmed-over Cold War propaganda.

Matthews is in many ways a creature of cable news to his very bones—the product of a modern infotainment culture that has long prized received wisdom, empty provocation, and branded personality over any particular desire to enlighten or inform. A veteran of what is laughably called America's "national conversation," he's been a fixture of the Washington political scene since his days as a staffer for Jimmy Carter and Tip O'Neill.

Boorish, ill-tempered, and punctuated by a particularly repugnant streak of old-world misogyny, Matthews's schtick is virtually unwatchable unless you've already pickled your brain with a million or so hours of TV. Having been described by one profiler as "soothing like a blender," his voice sounds like a balloon perpetually stuck in the act of trying to deflate and never quite succeeding. The same writer would diplomatically call Matthews "a whip-tongued, name-dropping, self-promoting wise guy" of the sort "you often find in campaigns, and in the bigger offices on Capitol Hill or K Street"—that is, one who graces interlocutors with incandescent insights like, "Barack Obama is Mozart and Hillary Clinton is Salieri."[201]

His biggest intellectual contribution, such as it can be called one, has been to articulate the art of Beltway social climbing as a kind of public philosophy: breaking through with the best-selling 1988 book *Hardball* (described by *New York Times Magazine* as "a how-to guide to social and career climbing in Washington").[202] Though Matthews got his TV start courtesy of Roger Ailes, it would be the 1997 debut of his show on CNBC (which carried the same title) and the ensuing Clinton-Lewinsky scandal that put him firmly on the national cable news map. As MSNBC attached its brand and its business strategy to the rise of Obama—its prime-time audience would rise a whopping 63 percent in 2008—he would enter his heyday as a fixture of America's media establishment.

Though a long-form' profile published that same year tries its absolute darndest to find virtue in Matthews's loutishness and personal ambition ("There is a level of solipsism about Matthews that is oddly endearing in its self-conscious extreme, even by the standards of television vanity"),

PART IV

the portrait that emerges is largely that of a man obsessed with hollow
status-seeking and the pursuit of fame for its own sake:

> Matthews has an attuned sense of pecking order at MSNBC, at
> NBC, in Washington and in life. This is no great rarity among
> the fragile egos of TV or, for that matter, in the status-fixated
> world of politics. But Matthews is especially frontal about it.
> In an interview with *Playboy* a few years ago, he volunteered
> that he had made the list of the Top 50 journalists in DC in *The
> Washingtonian* magazine. "I'm like 36th, and Tim Russert is No.
> 1," Matthews told *Playboy*. "I would argue for a higher position
> for myself."[203]

None other than Jon Stewart exposed the moral vacuum at the core of
Matthews's personal philosophy in a 2007 grilling[204] of his book *Life's
a Campaign: What Politics Has Taught Me About Friendship, Rivalry,
Reputation, and Success* (which channeled similar themes to 1988's
Hardball). Catching Matthews off-guard, Stewart's opening challenge
was both pointed and lethal:

> What you are saying is people can use what politicians do in
> political campaigns to help their lives? It strikes me as funda-
> mentally wrong. It strikes me as a self-hurt book. Aren't cam-
> paigns fundamentally contrivances?

Matthews's response, justifiably met with a bemused stare, amounted to
a naked defense of amoral ladder-climbing coupled with the idea that
everything about life should be treated like a campaign qua sales pitch:

> Yeah, campaigns can be. But the way politicians get to the top
> is the real thing. They know what they're doing. I mean, you
> don't have to believe a word they say. But watch how far they
> got. How did Clinton get there? How did Hillary get there? How

181

did Reagan get there? They have methods to get to the top, and you can learn from those methods ... Do you wanna succeed? Do you wanna have friends? ... Everything about getting jobs is about convincing someone to hire you, right? It's about getting promotions. It's about selling products. It's always a campaign. It's a campaign to get the girl of your dreams. It's a campaign to do everything you want to do in life.

"This strikes me as artifice," replied Stewart. "If you live this book, your life will be strategy."

In a striking way, Matthews's personal philosophy mirrors the acquisitive, market-centric ethos of the modern Democratic Party with which he's become so intimately aligned: one which values personal striving over solidarity and embraces the idols of wealth and celebrity as its lodestars.

In Bernie Sanders, this ecosystem and the apparatchiks who populate its gilded ranks have met their first real nemesis in decades: a figure whose support owes itself to explicit rejection of the politics of triangulation and craven self-interest they have so voraciously embraced. Thanks to a social and ideological base outside the clutches of the elite media, Sanders and the millions of people who comprise his movement may be totally alien to Chris Matthews and the culture that has produced him, but they also represent an existential threat to its primordial rites and sacraments.

Ever partisan for personalities rather than policies or principles, the Democratic Party and its media surrogates plainly expected a traditional primary contest auditioning competing centrist brands ahead of November's scheduled season finale. In Nevada, both collided suddenly and violently with the realization that their world may in fact be coming to an end; that huge numbers of Americans find their self-serving narratives unconvincing; and that their expectations of deference are now largely being ignored.

The cable news crack-up that crescendoed in Matthews's splenetic outburst was thus about something more than the frustration of conservative Democrats at the prospect of a socialist insurgent winning his third electoral contest in a row. Beneath the layers of ugliness in the *Hardball* host's execrable analogy could be heard the anguished cry of an elite culture jarringly coming to terms with its increasing isolation and utter remove from the people for whom it has long claimed to speak. In the weeks and months ahead, expect it to reach a fever pitch.

—A version of this essay first appeared in Jacobin, *February 2020.*

All the President's Tweets

Roughly a third of the way into the first of her three 2016 debates with Donald Trump, an exasperated Hillary Clinton appealed to moderator Lester Holt, who had just signaled his desire to end the segment and move on. "That can't—that can't be left to stand," said Clinton, who was referring to a series of claims about tax cuts and regulations made by her Republican opponent a few moments earlier. Granted thirty seconds to respond, Clinton proceeded to direct the audience to a fact-checking section on her official campaign website (incidentally given the cringe-worthy name "Literally Trump")—something she would do several more times in the debate that followed a few weeks later.

Whatever exactly these appeals to Literally Trump were supposed to achieve, we can safely call them a failure. Trump surprised everyone, most of all the Clinton campaign, a few weeks later by winning the election against all odds: plenty of voters evidently not knowing or not caring about his well-established proclivity for falsehood (or, at any rate, failed to spend adequate time on the Literally Trump section of HillaryClinton.com before pulling the lever in their local polling station).

With virtually the entire weight of the US media and political establishments against him, Trump lied, hectored, and bullied his way into the most powerful executive office in the world. It seemed 2016 had been a referendum on The Facts and The Facts had suffered a humiliating defeat.

****

Earlier this week, following a series of patently false tweets about mail-in balloting, the Twitter corporation took the unprecedented step of labelling Donald Trump's statements incorrect—the offending tweets now coming with a tag which invites users to "get the facts" and links to a page with articles from outlets like CNN and the *Washington Post* that subject the president's claims to fact-checking.

The spread of online misinformation has been a major concern since 2016, in large part thanks to Trump himself, whose tweets fast became a chief antagonist in the wider panic surrounding Fake News. Fact-checking has consequently become a huge preoccupation for the media in a way it arguably never was in a pre-2016 world. As a result, whole teams of journalists are now assigned to patrol the corridors of Twitter and other social media services looking for misleading information and nascent conspiracy theories with a view to putting the facts straight.

Many of the anxieties prompting this trend are perfectly warranted. The internet, more than any other medium in human history, is uniquely well-suited to the creation and rapid spread of claims that are completely untrue and potentially dangerous. Each of us, at one time or another, has probably fallen victim to a forged tweet or been a bit too hasty in believing an incorrect claim that happens to validate our existing preferences or partisan commitments. Misinformation is also routinely spread on purpose by private interests, political campaigns, national governments, and others trying to bend public perceptions for one reason or another—a reality that may well result in real world harm. A basic commitment to factual accuracy and something that at least aspires to objective reality is necessary for any even partly democratic media ecosystem to function. Anyone who wants to call themselves a journalist should do their utmost to cleave to it.

Since 2016, however, this truism has taken on an entirely new weight: the spread of misinformation now perceived by some as the animating force of our entire era. Transformative global events and political outcomes—Brexit, France's *gilet jaunes* and, of course, Trump's election—can now be said to owe themselves to a general dearth of facts (or, alternatively, the successful incursion of falsehood). As one *Huffington Post* contributor put it in the wake of Trump's shock 2016 victory: "The greatest problem of our future is not political; it is not economic; it is not even rational. It's the battle of fact versus fiction. Sadly, a Trump victory illustrates that we are no longer able to distinguish between the two."[205]

The supposed demise of truth, and the urgent need for regular interventions by Big Fact Check, has unsurprisingly become a significant preoccupation for liberals during the Trump era—"misinformation gave us Trump" being a central premise of the Russiagate boondoggle. (Spend enough time looking into it, and you'll quickly discover that virtually any significant development in global politics can now be said to find its origin in the vague menace of "Russian bots.")

Though the generalized stream of falsehoods found on Trump's Twitter feed has not occupied quite the same perch in the liberal political imagination post-2016, it has arguably been a close second to Russia and Putin—Democratic debates regularly making reference to Trump tweets and presidential hopefuls like Michael Bloomberg offering somber pledges not to tweet from the august space of the Oval Office. In what certainly counts among the most impotent and toothless gestures of the entire Democratic primary season, Senator Kamala Harris even sought to score a viral moment by dramatically calling on the mods at Twitter HQ to delete the president's account.

Falling flat as it did, many will probably be celebrating Twitter's recent decision to tag Trump's tweets with hyperlinked fact-checks as some kind of genuine political win. But the obsession with Trump's Twitter habits and the wider preoccupation with fact-checking that his 2016 victory has helped inspire fundamentally misunderstands the currency of truth and lies in determining the course of human events— particularly when it comes to social media and the causal role it now supposedly plays in determining major political outcomes.

Most obviously, it tends to reduce the complexities of politics to defective public epistemology: assuming that unwanted events (particularly electoral ones) occur primarily because people lack the correct information, i.e., The Facts. It is probably for this reason that many self-identified Democrats now place so much of their trust in several of the country's largest media institutions—their reporting and fact-checking seen as a bulwark against Trumpian misinformation and therefore as a stopper on all its damaging implications. Given the concentration of ownership in the American media, the biases inherent in the dominant corporate model, the partisan nature of the media landscape, and the issues inherent in entrusting the truth to huge, for-profit conglomerates, this reflex has plenty of problems on its own.

On a more basic level, the fact-checking zeitgeist misinterprets the role facts actually play in shaping people's worldviews and drastically exaggerates the limits of fact-checking as an effective countermeasure against deception. Fact-checking, after all, is ultimately an empirical exercise: one that can be useful in correcting a bogus statistic or misleading statement but is completely impotent when it comes to the master narratives against which all of us tend to actually structure our beliefs.

A politician who lies once about a past vote in the House of Representatives or overstates the size of the federal deficit during a debate is easily corrected because the fib is small and quantifiable. The most insidious deceptions, however, rarely if ever take this form. Instead, they conscript facts or some approximation of them into the service of a larger story that may be entirely untrue but remains politically impervious to fact-checking. As Rune Møler Stahl and Bue Rübner Hansen explain:

> Fact-checking only has power over only simple lies—statements the speaker knows not to be true . . . Fact-checking does nothing to disabuse people of the myths that structure their worldviews, which are neither factual nor completely fictional. Myths play a

central role in people's moral orientation, because they reduce
reality's murky struggles into simplified stories of good and
evil, greatness and failure.[206]

It should be abundantly clear by now that Trump's appeal lies firmly
outside the realm of empirical truth and that a person already inclined
to "believe" the kinds of things that appear on the president's Twitter
feed is about as likely to be swayed by a hyperlinked fact-check from
the *Washington Post* as a red state uncle was to visit a section of
HillaryClinton.com called "Literally Trump" in September 2016.

Though fact-checking will always be a necessary and important
task for any democratic media, it is also an inherently limited one—and,
almost four years into the Trump era, far too many liberals and partisan
Democrats are still confusing it with politics.

—May 2020

Erasing the Working Class

Review of No Longer Newsworthy *by Christopher R. Martin (Cornell University Press, 2019)*

A particular image of the worker—generally white, male, and employed in the manual trades—has been a recurring idiom of Americana for at least a century. It is revealing, given this ubiquity, that since 2016 the White male worker has also become a persistent object of media fascination and puzzlement: the central character in a seemingly endless deluge of newspaper reports and longform essays in which metropolitan journalists depart their coastal havens for exotic safaris into the hinterland, intent on discovering and investigating "working-class Americans" (who are often, incorrectly, depicted as universally white and male) in their natural habitats.

As the University of Iowa's Christopher R. Martin notes at the outset of *No Longer Newsworthy*, "Who are these people?" fast became the anguished cry of major media outlets in the wake of Donald Trump's shock 2016 election victory—and the subject of a whole genre aimed at providing a heavily upper-crust readership with a neat and compelling answer. Such attention, Martin argues, should neither be taken for earnest concern nor a renewed interest in the working class as such. The really existing working class—vast and diverse—remains largely invisible, except as a reductive caricature opportunistically invoked by politicians and media elites. This is the thesis of Martin's effort in media criticism, which charts the press' persistent erasure and misrepresentation of America's working-class majority and the gradual transformation of the journalistic lexicon into one virtually indistinguishable from the language of management, capital, and the bipartisan neoliberal consensus.

Central to this story is the decline of labor reporting, once a mainstay of major dailies. Today, by contrast, as Martin puts it: "A conference gathering of labor/workforce beat reporters from the country's leading newspapers could fit into a single booth at an Applebee's." Of the country's top twenty-five newspapers, he notes, a majority no longer covers the workplace/labor beat on a full-time basis, and the landscape for such reporting appears to be even bleaker on television. One 2013 survey cited by Martin, for example, reveals that only 0.3 percent of network TV news in the years 2008, 2009, and 2011 covered labor issues.

Much of the book is concerned with accounting for this decline, which, for the author, is both the result of conscious political effort and a myopic shift in the business model embraced by major newspapers. The former argument is fairly non-controversial, though illustrated in great detail via (among other things) a careful examination of the rhetoric around workers and labor used by various presidents, and the news media's increasingly pro-corporate framing of jobs and economic issues. As to how a changing business model has served to disempower and erase the American working class, Martin posits that a shift in the 1960s and 1970s toward an advertising model aimed at an upscale middle-class readership is the primary culprit. With the rise of television, the newspaper industry grew ever more consolidated and concerned with addressing and reflecting the interests and lifestyles of a predominantly middle-class audience. In Martin's words:

> [In] this new vision of how a newspaper should serve its community, the newspapers and their corporate owners only wanted the right kind of readers, those who were "well-to-do," "affluent moderns," "influentials," and people with plenty of "effective buying power" and "giant-sized household incomes." Nearly

every newspaper began publicizing their readership as if they were the children of Garrison Keillor's fictional Lake Wobegon: all above average.

As a consequence, he argues, the entire language of the news media began to shift: the labor beat gave way to lifestyle and consumer-oriented content; workers became "employees," engaged not in collective action but in the individualized aspirational culture of neoliberal capitalism— no longer participating in economic affairs as active subjects but instead "hailed" (in the author's words) as "passive objects" in a system of private enterprise directed by entrepreneurs and CEOs.

The erasure and disempowerment of workers as a class contributed to another significant development in the American media landscape explored in Martin's narrative, namely the rise of populist conservative outlets able to capture the market niche vacated by major newspapers by trading in faux anti-elitism and cultural politics. This is not, he stresses, to be mistaken for actual representation of the working class, which is considerably more diverse (in both the ideological and demographic senses) than implied by the white, male, conservative caricature generally invoked by the right-wing media.

Some of the book's most interesting moments involve detailed case studies showing the media's treatment of the working class at its best and worst: a 1941 New York transit strike, for example, during which the *New York Times* largely centered the contract dispute between workers and their employer in its reporting—contrasted with examples from decades later showcasing the way newspapers now tend to focus on how labor actions affect consumers and cause inconvenience for members of the middle class.

Another important case study involves the media's treatment of then President-elect Trump's visit to a Carrier facility in Indiana, which mostly overlooked the diversity of the plant's workforce and the efforts of United

Steelworkers Local 1999 to prevent jobs from being outsourced. As Martin puts it:

> The national news organizations that covered the Carrier story did so mainly from a political perspective. These Carrier workers were the working class, blue collar, Middle America, white male breadwinners who were Trump's voter base . . . The news media's general focus on white male Carrier workers as subjects denied the fact that the Carrier workers were far more diverse in terms of gender, race, and politics than the role they were given in the story (as white, male, ardent Trump supporters).

Even when supposedly receiving media attention, then, workers were essentially reduced to the level of caricature: invoked primarily to bolster a post-election narrative favored by political and media elites.

As with any history so vast and detailed, parts of Martin's story beg irritating (and, given the book's scope, largely semantic) questions of cause and effect. How much weight, for example, do we afford the print media's commercial turn in the 1970s versus the decades-long march to the right in American politics and culture that took off under Reagan? How much of a role did the growing invisibility of the working class play in enabling the wider political shift, or was it itself more a consequence of politics and shifting material conditions (such as the decline of union density or the outsourcing of manufacturing jobs)?

These may be questions worth investigating, but they need not distract from the insightful commentary offered in *No Longer Newsworthy*— at once an important work of Trump-era criticism and an urgently needed condemnation of a media culture that persistently erases and misrepresents the lives and concerns of America's diverse working-class majority.

—*A version of this essay first appeared in* Jacobin, *March 2019.*

James Carville, Cajun Clausewitz

J. R. R. Tolkien famously christened "cellar door" as the most aesthetically pleasing phrase available in the English language. By way of contrast, I submit that it's nearly impossible to conjure a less euphonious sequence of words than "James Carville interviewed by Chris Cuomo." It is similarly difficult, even by the lowly standards of cable news, to imagine a program description that sounds less appetizing. Whatever your politics, I think we can all agree that the prospect of hearing Andrew Cuomo's brother pick the brains of a Clinton-era apparatchik mainly known for yapping received centrist wisdom in a Louisiana accent doesn't exactly scream "good vibes."

Not counting myself among the dozen or so millennials who regularly watch network primetime shows, I hasten to add that I discovered the interview in question[207] while scrolling through Twitter—that is, without the intercession of paid agitprop from personal injury lawyers, insurance companies, or miracle weight loss scams. And so it was that I happened to stumble upon the iconically cadaverous face of a man who has not had the flicker of an original political insight or purchased a skincare product since 1992.

At a glance, very little about the segment was actually notable. With a few assists from a sympathetic Cuomo, Carville essentially regurgitated a version of the same narrative centrist Democrats have been peddling since they barely won last November, the crux of it being that a "noisy" and pronoun-obsessed "identity left," representing about 15 percent of the party, has become an albatross round the necks of those in the sensible middle—imperiling their prospects with voters who are turned off by rhetoric about defunding the police.

Nuance and careful analysis, for what it's worth, have never exactly been Carville's strong suits. As the *New Republic*'s Osita Nwanevu pointed out,[208] 15 percent is actually a less than negligible chunk of the Democratic base—barely smaller than the African American share of the electorate and in fact more sizable than Hispanics, which seems somewhat beside the point that Carville was, with characteristic hyperbole and imprecision, attempting to make.

What struck me, though, was how tiresomely familiar it all sounded. Interminable debates about November's election notwithstanding, Third Way liberals like Carville really have been performing the same basic schtick for decades—its thrust being that Democrats win by scolding and/or disciplining a portion of their own base and lose whenever said portion is allowed to become too vocal.

Whatever the era, whatever the actual debates at hand, and however many cultural and political realignments occur, there is somehow always said to be a segment of liberal voters or activists whose crank enthusiasms are alienating the good people of the hardworking, reasonable middle. The exact contours of the caricature, of course, can be amended as needed. Thus, in one fell swoop, the same cadre of Dem hacks who so cynically wielded identity politics as a cudgel against Bernie Sanders can now just as easily blame a phantom version of them for their own lackluster election results.

South Carolina's Jim Clyburn, among the originators of the spin presently being wielded by the likes of Carville (and one of the biggest recipients of Big Pharma money in Congress),[209] can casually collapse Medicare For All supporters and slogans about defunding the police into the same, hazily defined scapegoat constituency.[210] Last year's feral pinko "cult"[211] can become this year's cop-hating pronoun brigade.

Triangulation may come in many forms, but the basic political cosmology embraced by centrist liberals really hasn't changed since the early

PART IV

1990s when Bill Clinton consolidated the shunning of Jesse Jackson's Rainbow Coalition and made antagonizing the left a formal part of the Democrats' national political repertoire.

For Carville and many others involved, Clinton's 43 percent victory in 1992 was less a conventional electoral event than it was an act of providence. As far as electoral tactics were concerned, it was also taken to represent a formula that could be repeated more or less indefinitely. Since this was so obviously not the case (two years after Carville's would-be Machiavellian genius helped build the indomitable Clinton coalition, the Democrats lost control of the House for the first time in forty years), it followed that the same logic could also be applied in instances of failure—even, and especially, when centrists themselves had defined, planned, and executed a campaign.

Talking to Chris Cuomo, Carville's warmed-over bash-the-fringe routine thus had all the vitality and dynamism of a flash-in-the-pan pop star performing a one-hit wonder decades after its disappearance from the charts. In the nearly thirty intervening years spanning today and 1992—years which have seen dynasties rise and fall, the global economy collapse, orthodoxies dissolve, and American culture undergo innumerable seismic shifts—his political outlook does not seem to have evolved one iota. To give the Ragin' Cajun due credit, consistency is hard to come by in the political mainstream and, for what it's worth, the man has never wavered from his steadfast determination to be wrong as often as humanly possible.

The Carville mythos, such as it is, owes heavily to 1993's *The War Room*, codirected by the legend of documentary cinema D. A. Pennebaker. Its stylistic flair notwithstanding, the film has aged about as poorly as the Third Way consensus itself, it now being a kind of monument to the final conquest of American politics by backroom hacks whose air of impenetrable wizardry has at least as much to do with playing savvy operatives on TV as it does with actually being them.

195

"He's become a commodity of himself by design . . . a walking conglomerate," a Washington insider once said of Carville in an apparent attempt at a compliment.[212] The remark wasn't exactly wrong. In fact, Carville's rather dubious billing as a kind of ur-political impresario has earned him astonishing sums in the form of book deals, media appearances, and corporate ad campaigns (the beneficiaries ranging from Heineken and American Express to Nike).

For a guy whose original billing was as a "strategist," however, it must be said that he is hardly a modern-day Sun Tzu. Animated by a hall monitor–like desire to defeat Bernie Sanders in 2020, Carville's finely tuned political instincts led him to go all in with Colorado Senator Michael Bennet, who fetched a whopping 952 votes, or roughly 0.3 percent of the total, in the New Hampshire primary[213] and ultimately finished behind several write-ins (one of whom was quite literally Donald Trump).[214]

Last year, he brazenly boasted that November's contest would swing so decisively in Joe Biden's favor that its outcome would be known by 10 p.m. on election night, a crystal ball divination so eerily prophetic it would later be included by *Politico* on a list of "the most audacious, confident and spectacularly incorrect prognostications about the year."[215] No matter. In the sclerotic culture of the Beltway, the reheated bilge of triangulations past can be forever packaged as hardheaded political wisdom; the hacks of neoliberal yesteryear as electoral grandmasters of Clausewitzian insight.

James Carville will never stop being wrong. But, God help us all, he'll never stop being on TV.

—A version of this essay first appeared in Jacobin, *July 2021.*

The Progressive Era That Wasn't

Just ahead of his inauguration, Joe Biden released the details of a stimulus package that is almost certain to represent the most consequential legislative item of his first year in office. On its face at least, the plan is clearly more ambitious than the one that emerged in the early days of the Obama presidency. Coming in at nearly $2 trillion, today's bill, if passed as written, would be more than a third larger than its 2009 equivalent—representing not only a break with decades of fiscal orthodoxy but also with Biden's own past as an especially vocal deficit hawk.

As Paul Heideman recently explained in *Jacobin*,[216] Biden's newfound boldness reflects a wider shift in the business consensus around public deficits (the US Chamber of Commerce, for example, has actually endorsed Biden's COVID rescue bill in spite of its $1.9 trillion price tag). True to form, Biden has also indicated that he wants to seek bipartisan support for the deal. Still, his apparently unabashed embrace of large-scale public spending certainly leaves the impression of a president preparing to govern to the left of the last two Democratic administrations, at least on the domestic policy front. As the *Huffington Post*'s Zach Carter put it: "Despite [the] oddities and disappointments in Biden's proposal, there is simply no denying that his program is more ambitious and progressive than the economic agenda of former President Barack Obama."[217]

We will know soon enough whether these initial impressions, encouraging as they seem, are borne out in practice. For the time being, however, they have added fuel to a narrative some pundits have been pushing since the Democratic primaries ended last spring: that Biden is positioned to become a transformative president in the mold of FDR or

Lyndon B. Johnson (the latter being, like Biden, an especially unlikely figure to assume such a role).

For what it's worth, there remain plenty of good reasons for skepticism: FDR and Johnson both presided over permanent structural shifts in national policy and state institutions, whereas Biden's stimulus bill—even if it were to pass in its present form—contains nothing of comparable weight or permanence. In other areas, notably health care reform, there is little evidence his administration is planning a meaningful break with the status quo—notwithstanding its advocacy, on paper at least, for a public option.

We don't, of course, know what the future will hold. But a look back at the media consensus that prevailed around this time during the very first months of the previous Democratic administration underscores the danger of making bold predictions of a new dawning era of liberalism.

No two political moments are identical, and there are many important differences between the period surrounding Barack Obama's January 2009 inauguration and the present. Nonetheless, there are also plenty of obvious similarities: the presence of a major national crisis, the departure of a deeply unpopular Republican president, a historic surge in general election turnout resulting in a Democratic presidential victory, to name just a few.

Biden, like Obama, enters office courtesy of an ideologically diverse voter coalition—one that includes both young progressives and affluent suburban conservatives. Biden, like Obama, has also sent decidedly mixed signals about how he actually intends to govern: formally embracing some priorities held by the progressive wing of the Democratic Party while also quite vocally courting Republicans and championing bipartisan compromise.

While a similar ambiguity existed twelve years ago, there seemed to be widespread agreement, spanning from center-left to center-right, that a new liberalism had arrived and that a progressive ideological consensus was in the making. Some, like former Reagan speechwriter Peggy Noonan, felt confident enough to announce it even before the ballots had been cast. "Whoever is elected Tuesday, his freedom in office will be limited," Noonan reassured readers in the *Wall Street Journal* less than a week before the 2008 presidential election. "But let's be frank. Something new is happening in America. It is the imminent arrival of a new liberal moment. History happens, it makes its turns, you hold on for dear life. Life moves."[218]

The *Journal* itself was far less sanguine about the ramifications of an Obama victory, publishing an ominously worded editorial about the dangers of unified Democratic control of the federal government. "Though we doubt most Americans realize it," the editorial read, "this would be one of the most profound political and ideological shifts in US history." It continued:

> Liberals would dominate the entire government in a way they haven't since 1965, or 1933. In other words, the election would mark the restoration of the activist government that fell out of public favor in the 1970s. If the US really is entering a period of unchecked left-wing ascendancy, Americans at least ought to understand what they will be getting, especially with the media cheering it all on."

What would they be getting after Obama's all-but-inevitable victory? According to the *Journal*'s editorial board, a new policy consensus defined, among other things, by institutional animus toward business, newly empowered trade unions, a green revolution, DC statehood, and the ineluctable march toward fully socialized medicine. "Mr. Obama wants to build a public insurance program, modeled after Medicare and open to everyone of any income," it warned. "Single payer is the inevitable next step."[219]

The same general impression of what an Obama presidency signified continued to prevail in conservative precincts into the administration's early months. "Those of us who consider ourselves moderates, moderate-conservative, in my case, are forced to confront the reality that Barack Obama is not who we thought he was," David Brooks would lament in a March 2, 2009 op-ed for the *New York Times*. "His words are responsible; his character is inspiring. But his actions betray a transformational liberalism that should put every centrist on notice."[220] Animating Brooks's alarm was a piece by Clive Crook in the *Financial Times*, which had written favorably of Obama's budget legislation—legislation which, as Crook then wrote "contains no trace of compromise. It makes no gesture, however small, however costless to its larger agenda, of a bipartisan approach to the great questions it addresses. It is a liberal's dream of a new New Deal."[221]

This also proved to be the consensus among influential liberal voices—even those, like Paul Krugman, who had previously been critical of Obama. "Will the election mark a turning point in the actual substance of policy? Can Barack Obama really usher in a new era of progressive policies?" Krugman wrote a few days after Obama's landslide victory. "Yes, he can . . . Anyone who doubts that we've had a major political realignment should look at what's happened to Congress."[222] A few days later, the columnist had grown even more buoyant, opening a piece titled "Franklin Delano Obama?" with the words "Suddenly, everything old is New Deal again. Reagan is out; FDR is in."[223]

As the *Times'* Edward Rothstein observed, FDR comparisons were all the rage during the Obama transition, arguing in a December 2008 piece that the scale of the incoming president's crisis-inspired ambitions appeared to echo those of the New Deal era:

Since Mr. Obama's election, references to Roosevelt have become even more plentiful. Caricatures of the president-elect with a cigarette holder and an insouciant Roosevelt grin have appeared in major publications. Mr. Obama has implicitly invoked Roosevelt's approach to what was the worst financial crisis of the 20th century, saying he would enact the largest public-works program since the building of the federal highway system in the 1950s. And he has made clear (conceptually echoing Roosevelt) that his attention to the welfare of the citizenry would be inseparable from his attention to the health of the economy.[224]

Channeling this zeitgeist, the November 2008 cover of *Time* magazine would depict Obama in FDR-inspired caricature, the president-elect appearing with Roosevelt's trademark eyeglasses while smoking a cigarette against a Black-and-White backdrop accompanied by the words "A New New Deal." (A June 2020 issue of *Newsweek*, incidentally, featured a cover showing Biden alongside FDR.)[225]

The most intellectually fleshed-out and well-articulated argument that a new political consensus had dawned was probably found in a November 9, 2008, *New Yorker* essay by George Packer appropriately titled "The New Liberalism."[226] While eschewing some of the triumphalism found elsewhere and accounting for various possibilities—"Reagan couldn't cancel Roosevelt's legacy; Obama won't be able to obliterate Reagan's"—Packer was nonetheless bullish about what the election would herald for liberalism and the forthcoming return of activist government:

> Barack Obama's decisive defeat of John McCain is the most important victory of a Democratic candidate since 1932. It brings to a close another conservative era, one that rose amid the ashes of the New Deal coalition in the late sixties, consolidated its

power with the election of Ronald Reagan, in 1980, and immolated itself during the Presidency of George W. Bush . . . For the first time since the Johnson Administration, the idea that government should take bold action to create equal opportunity for all citizens doesn't have to explain itself in a defensive mumble . . . By the end of the campaign, Obama wasn't just running against broken politics, or even against the Bush Presidency. He had the anti-government philosophy of the entire Age of Reagan in his sights.

Whatever ultimately came next, Packer argued, there lay ahead a new era concerned with "public [rather than] private goods." "The meal will be smaller, and have less interesting flavors," he concluded, "but it will be shared more fairly."

In fairness to Packer, it's easy to be clairvoyant in hindsight. But to put it bluntly, very little about the media consensus at the time of Obama's victory, and continuing for a while following his inauguration, was borne out in practice. Most obviously, Republicans would recapture the House only two years later in what became the worst electoral defeat for congressional Democrats in decades. Wealth inequality dramatically increased during the Obama presidency, with the average wealth of the bottom 99 percent dropping by $4,500 and the average wealth of the top 1 percent rising by $4.9 million between 2007 and 2016.

Far from bringing back vigorous activist government, the administration would forgo a large scale overhaul of the financial sector in favor of perfunctory leak-plugging that left the basic contours of Clinton-era deregulation intact. Its signature domestic policy achievement, the Affordable Care Act, did expand Medicaid coverage for the poor and near-poor, but found its primary inspiration in market-based ideas originating from a conservative think tank rather than New Deal or Great Society liberalism.

Though buzz about an epoch-defining political realignment would take some time to dissipate, the administration's overall direction of travel was made clear a few weeks after inauguration day. Alarmed by David Brooks's March 2 op-ed (which had predicted a "transformational liberalism" and warned that the hallowed institution of political centrism was now under threat), senior figures in the Obama White House reached out to the columnist to offer reassurance. Brooks would devote his next column to summarizing this response.

"In the first place," he would write, "they do not see themselves as a group of liberal crusaders. They see themselves as pragmatists who inherited a government and an economy that have been thrown out of whack. They're not engaged in an ideological project to overturn the Reagan Revolution, a fight that was over long ago." Despite his own dire predictions a few days earlier, the columnist, visibly more relaxed than in his previous op-ed, would go on to write:

> The budget . . . isn't some grand transformation of America . . .
> It raises taxes on the rich to a level slightly above where they
> were in the Clinton years and then uses the money as a down
> payment on health care reform . . . It's not the Russian Revolution.
> Second [the Obama White House contends], the administration
> will not usher in an era of big government . . . they aim to bring
> spending down to 22 percent of GDP in a few years . . . Third,
> they say, Republicans should welcome the budget's health care
> ideas. The Medicare reform represents a big cut in entitlement
> spending. It amounts to means-testing the system. It introduces
> more competition and cuts corporate welfare. These are all
> Republican ideas . . . [The president] is extremely committed to
> entitlement reform and is plotting politically feasible ways to
> reduce Social Security as well as health spending.

Furthermore, Brooks continued, "the Obama folks feel they spend as much time resisting liberal ideas as enacting them."[227]

So far, on the issue of deficits at least, Joe Biden's rhetoric has diverged from the fiscal hawkishness Obama's team promised Brooks nearly twelve years ago. But even a cursory look back at the narratives that prevailed in the wake of the last Democratic presidential election victory nonetheless underscores the danger of making bold predictions about the return of activist governance or a political realignment-in-the-making.

In what became a wave election that handed Democrats unified control of the federal government, Barack Obama rode into office channeling liberal evangelism while simultaneously promising unity and bipartisan compromise. As Joe Biden follows in the former president's footsteps, it's difficult not to see the parallels between the present moment and its analogue in 2009. History, to paraphrase Mark Twain, may not be repeating itself, but it very well might be about to rhyme.

—*A version of this essay first appeared in* Jacobin, *January 2021.*

PART V

All That's Solid . . .

Notes on Neoliberalism

Neoliberalism should not . . . be identified with laissez-faire, but rather with permanent vigilance, activity, and intervention.[228]
—Michel Foucault

What we have been living for three decades is frontier capitalism, with the frontier constantly shifting location from crisis to crisis, moving on as soon as the law catches up.[229]
—Naomi Klein

Economics are the method; the object is to change the heart and soul.[230]
—Margaret Thatcher

"It is not that nothing happened in the period when the slow cancellation of the future set in. On the contrary, those 30 years have been a time of massive, traumatic change . . . The shift into so-called Post-Fordism—with globalization, ubiquitous computerisation and the casualisation of labor—resulted in a complete transformation in the way that work and leisure were organized. In the last 10 to 15 years, meanwhile, the internet and mobile telecommunications technology have altered the texture of everyday experience beyond all recognition. Yet, perhaps because of all this, there's an increasing sense that culture has lost the ability to grasp and articulate the present. Or it could be that, in one very important sense, there is no present to grasp and articulate any more."[231]
—Mark Fisher

Savory Snacks for Social Justice

In April 2017 the corporate overlords at PepsiCo rolled out a nearly three-minute video clip evoking a formless idea of solidarity toward no one in particular.[232] Featuring a diverse cast of telegenic young people and starring none other than superstar Kendall Jenner, the segment foregrounds a gathering vaguely encoded as a protest march thanks to a few raised fists and a handful of signs showcasing a series of not exactly firebrand slogans such as "Join the Conversation."

At video's end, the glamorous Jenner glides toward a phalanx of uniformed police to share a cold can of Pepsi with an officer, to general approval from everyone involved. As the camera fades to the tune of Skip Marley's "Lions," the Pepsi logo appears and viewers are invited to Live For Now®.

Virtually everything about the ad, from premise to staging to sheer existence, was absurd from start to finish. As corporate self-parody, it was nothing short of an Olympic-level performance that the finest satirists at *Clickhole* or *The Onion* couldn't match if they tried. Tone-deaf and painful to watch even by the lowly standards of social justice–themed corporate cringe, and rather shamelessly appropriating imagery from Black Lives Matter, it elicited a fierce enough backlash to be taken down in record time, but continues to live on in the popular memory as a kind of gold standard for capitalist wokeness gone awry.

That may well change in the coming days as crowds of ordinary Americans courageously take to the streets in a series of increasingly assertive protests against police brutality while a chorus of corporate brands offers up vague displays of support on social media. Running the gamut from well-meaning-but-absurd to downright sociopathic, the comms teams at various corporate HQs are already working overtime to align themselves with the wider cause of racial justice and make known their general commitment to inclusion.

Pringles Chips went dark on Twitter for #BlackOutTuesday. The official *Star Wars* account released a short statement in support of Black employees and artists. @Barbie pledged to champion diversity and declared her solidarity with the entire Black community. Toronto-based restaurant GarfieldEATS, meanwhile, tweeted an image of the eponymous cat's sullen eyeballs accompanied by the hashtag #BlackLivesMatter, as if to suggest that the infamously lazy and glutinous feline dislikes discrimination almost as much as he hates Mondays.

To give the brands their due, some of these efforts seem well-intentioned (commercial enterprises offering even nominal endorsement of anti-racism, after all, is obviously preferable to the alternative). The burlesque absurdity of reading vague messages of inclusion drafted by the branding specialists at *Call of Duty: Warzone* and Frito-Lay aside, there's something altogether less innocuous about the way companies inevitably seize on anything social justice–tinged as an opportunity for the most transparently cynical exercises in PR.

This includes corporate leviathans like Amazon, which proudly touts its commitment to diversity and opposition to discrimination while underpaying its workers and treating many people of color in its employ like less than garbage.[233] It includes McKinsey, which (among other things) eagerly offered its services to the Trump administration's brutal immigration agenda and advised Immigration and Customs Enforcement (ICE) to restrict the caloric intake of migrants held in detention camps[234] while earlier this week issuing a statement that condemned "racism, hatred, and prejudice" in every form. It includes NFL Commissioner Roger Goodell, who has evidently developed a severe case of amnesia about his contemptible response when San Francisco 49ers quarterback Colin Kaepernick decided to take a knee for civil rights.

Whether hypocritical, sinister, or simply absurd, the apparently irresistible reflex of corporate brands to insert themselves into popular causes raises a real issue about the commodification of social justice and the way everything from poverty to racial discrimination is now assumed to have a market solution—even, or especially, when the companies themselves are directly complicit in the problem.

Patently ridiculous though it was, the now infamous Pepsi video was a kind of extreme case study in what happens when market forces spend the better part of four decades cannibalizing everything in their path, from entitlements and trade union rights to the conceptual repertoires of social justice and intersectionality. When the very idea of society has been corroded in the name of market efficiency, the available lexicon to authentically express anything inevitably shrinks—to the point that virtually everything can and must be bent around the soulless logic of money and corporate brands. It is thanks to this takeover that even the most patently evil companies on earth can display floats at LGBTQ Pride and that big corporate blockbusters are now seen as a central terrain of cultural struggle while genuine or programmatic resistance to inequality and racism is marginalized and ignored.

More acutely than anything else to date, Pepsi's risible effort in social justice commodification perfectly encapsulated the market ethos that now so inescapably pervades American society—wherein even the iconography of dissent and inclusion is seamlessly slid in right next to the logo of your favorite carbonated beverage, ecommerce app, hookup service, or laser-guided munitions manufacturer.

In this Pepsified rendering of America, heavily armed police, Black Lives Matter activists, celebrities, and ordinary citizens alike coalesce around airbrushed imagery of social harmony and frictionless protest, all of it facilitated by a profitable sugary soft drink made by a multibillion-dollar corporation. In the real America, meanwhile, the combined forces of market capitalism and systemic racism conspire to sustain inequality and prejudice while repressing activists and ordinary citizens alike.

Big companies discriminate, union-bust, underpay their employees, and generally treat America's vast and diverse working class like complete shit. Behind the woke smokescreens of Big Philanthropy and intersectional HR pablum, their corporate political action committees pour contribution after contribution into the coffers of establishment politicians, Democratic and Republican alike, who uphold a morally indefensible status quo, while their armies of lobbyists and consultants ensure that no one's need for health care, housing, or basic dignity ever transgresses against the bottom line.

This is why, as cops brutalize marginalized Americans and they collectively resist, there will be plenty of nebulous calls for inclusion from corporate PR departments but comparatively few threats to claw back political contributions or demands on political leadership to carry out necessary measures like the defunding of city police departments gorged on *Rambo*-esque arsenals of military hardware.

The ubiquity of a single commodity in any marketplace inevitably brings down its value—and, as the past week has shown, social justice of the brand-washed and trademarked variety is both a cheap and omnipresent product in the hyper-marketized, hyper-carceral version of America that exists today. It is hardly incidental that, amid this deluge, the real kind continues to be in such dangerously short supply.

—A version of this essay first appeared in Jacobin, *June 2020.*

Fall of the House of Windsor

In the unforgettable opening passage of his 2009 book *Capitalist Realism*,[235] the late Mark Fisher recalls a scene from Alfonso Cuarón's *Children of Men* in which the film's hero, Theo (played by Clive Owen), visits London's Battersea Power Station—best known in the popular imagination for its appearance on the cover of Pink Floyd's 1977 album *Animals*. In the building, which seems to be at once a private and a government facility, Owen's character encounters a number of famous cultural treasures, among them Picasso's *Guernica*, Michelangelo's *David*, and the famous inflatable pig from Floyd front man Roger Waters's 1977 cover design.

The subtle power of the scene, for Fisher, lay in its depiction of iconic artworks desacralized by the commodifying pressures of late capitalism: *David*, now missing part of a leg, looks on as King Crimson's "In the Court of the Crimson King" plays in the background and the owner's pets play at its feet; *Guernica*, "once a howl of anguish and outrage against fascist atrocities," sits with little fanfare as mise-en-scène in the dining area of an antiseptic bourgeois loft while guests are serenaded by a Handel aria; the iconic pig has returned to Battersea, though has been clunkily repositioned so that it will be visible from the dining room window. The sculpture of Florentine Italy, '70s prog rock, the Spanish Civil War, and baroque music alike: all are on equal footing amid the atmosphere of bleak patrician decadence.

As Fisher observes, the building housing the treasures is itself an object of the same process: the once-functioning coal-fired power station (in real life partly decommissioned two years before its appearance on the cover of *Animals*) having been turned into a kind of "refurbished heritage artifact" in *Children of Men*'s imagined, though uncomfortably plausible London of the near future. (Fisher will regrettably never know quite how prophetic his interpretation was. In 2018, Battersea was purchased[236] by the Malaysia-based sovereign wealth fund Permodalan Nasional Berhad and will soon house a mixture of luxury lofts, restaurants, retail outlets, a "Chimney Lift" tourist attraction,[237] and a five-hundred-thousand-square-foot "campus" owned by Apple Inc.) That process, says Fisher (with an assist from Marx and Engels), amounts to the "transformation of culture into museum pieces" by the inexorable forces of global capitalism. "The power of capitalist realism," he elaborates:

> . . . derives in part from the way that capitalism subsumes and consumes all of previous history: one effect of its "system of equivalence" which can assign all cultural objects, whether religious iconography, pornography, or *Das Kapital*, a monetary value . . . . In the conversion of practices and rituals into merely aesthetic objects, the beliefs of previous cultures are objectively ironized, transformed into artifacts. . . . Capitalism is what is left when beliefs have collapsed at the level of ritual or symbolic elaboration and all that is left is the consumer-spectator, trudging through the ruins and the relics.

****

As royal events go, this month's sit-down between Oprah Winfrey, Prince Harry, and Meghan Markle was about as consequential as they come—and by all appearances, it has provoked quite genuine fear in pro-monarchist circles about the future of the institution. Over the course of roughly ninety minutes, the couple offered an account of their mistreatment inside the palace that even many hardened skeptics of televised celebrity events seemed to find authentic and convincing.

Indeed, taken on its own terms, it is both easy to see why so many found the story compelling, and why pro-royal partisans found it so threatening: the precise details aside, Markle's experience of racism in particular was bound to resonate with plenty outside of her own luxurious income bracket. As a pure news event, the Oprah sit-down has therefore proven quite the headache for a Windsor PR machine still reeling from the Jeffrey Epstein episode—one likely to carry on in one way or another for years to come.

The more subtle and real threat to the aura and reputation of the institution, however, probably has less to do with the specifics disclosed than what the interview ultimately suggested about the couple's ongoing cultural reinscription. The monarchy, by definition, is not something you are supposed to leave. More importantly, when removed from their regal context and interviewed by Oprah, Harry and Meghan looked more or less exactly like the Californian nouveau riche with whom they now share an area code.

Propelled by their sympathetic roles in a global news event, the former royals have since been busy relaunching themselves in the most quintessentially American ways: signing big media deals with Netflix and Spotify and, in Harry's case, taking up the causes of mental health and "self-optimization" at Silicon Valley–based company BetterUp in the newly created role of "Chief Impact Officer."

In real time, we are seeing the British royal aura refurbished to suit the needs and affectations of West Coast American wealth and the assimilation of one kind of celebrity by another. More than anything else, this is probably why royal partisans and ideologues for hereditary monarchy alike have viewed *l'affaire* Oprah as such an existential threat: whatever fictive transcendence that supposedly still lingers behind the facade of Buckingham Palace seems unlikely to weather the process.

In the twenty-first century, royalty will be a commodity like everything else—an especially lucrative lacquer in the era of personal brands and neoliberal selfhood, but a lacquer nonetheless. For the monarchy and its members, the choice will thus be between absorption by the seductions of bourgeois personal autonomy on the one hand or demotion to the status of kitsch tourist attraction on the other, both options ultimately being subordinate to the dictates of exchange value rather than high symbol.

In many ways, this transformation has already occurred. The Obamas, in their post-2016 incarnation, have already provided a template for the twenty-first-century fusion of regal prestige, secular celebrity, and grotesque wealth that Harry and Meghan look destined to follow. Visit famous sites in central London today, meanwhile, and you'll see as much gaudy spectacle as you will ancient splendor—from self-described "British pubs" that exclusively serve the most credulous breed of American tourist to Guard Mountings outside of Buckingham Palace that look like twee cosplay rather than living culture.

Over many centuries the monarchy has been gradually stripped of its active constitutional functions—reduced to the status of spectral symbol in a country whose ruling class still gorges itself on a diet of imperial nostalgia. In the coming decades, even this residual symbolic power seems likely to wither away as the institution makes further concessions to a world of pluralist liberal democracy and consequently completes its final transformation into a heritage artifact.

This is not to say that the monarchy itself, or the order it represents, will literally disappear. The morbid genius of British conservatism has always been its capacity to fuse the iconography of "tradition"—the crown, the country estate, the public school, the grouse hunt—with the dynamism of liberal modernity. From the Victorian era to the present day, England's landed aristocrats and their cultural courtiers have proven astonishingly adept at embracing bourgeois affectations without being fully swallowed by them. Absent a political realignment or social revolution, that seems unlikely to change.

But, like the precious artworks in the Battersea Power Station of Cuarón's *Children of Men* (to say nothing of the soon-to-be-opened suites in the real-life version) the idea of royalty will be reduced to a purely aesthetic concept, its dejected inheritors left to trudge through the ruins and the relics—or, failing that, travel further afield in search of self-optimization, a Spotify contract, or a gig in Silicon Valley.

—A version of this essay first appeared in Jacobin, *March 2021.*

Barons of the Valley

Though most often applied to the plutocrats and monopolists of America's Gilded Age, the phrase "robber baron" has a much earlier derivation. During the reign of Holy Roman Emperor Frederick III in the mid-thirteenth century, feudal landowners in the Rhine Valley were awarded lucrative rights to a series of strategic toll points along the river, then one of Europe's most critical highways for transport and trade. When the Emperor died without a successor in 1250, the ensuing power vacuum afforded landowners the latitude to gain even more from their monopoly.

The robber barons of thirteenth-century Germany lived under feudalism, but their operating ethic was identical to that of their capitalist equivalents hundreds of years later: to maximize profit with minimal expenditure while extracting rents through control of a vital piece of infrastructure. This was what Henry J. Raymond had in mind when he issued a salvo against Cornelius Vanderbilt in the February 9, 1859, edition of the *New York Times*, comparing the shipping magnate to "those old German barons who . . . swooped down upon the commerce of the noble river and wrung tribute." "Mr Vanderbilt," wrote Raymond, "has devoted himself to the study of steam navigation of his country—not with the object of extending its development, but for the purpose of making every prosperous enterprise of the kind in turn his tributary or his victim."[238]

Mark Twain would similarly write an open letter to Vanderbilt in 1869, denouncing among other things the public idolatry he inspired: "You seem to be the idol of only a crawling swarm of small souls, who love to glorify your most flagrant unworthiness in print or praise your vast possessions worshippingly; or sing of your unimportant private habits and sayings and doings, as if your millions gave them dignity."[239]

It would be many decades—arguably not until the Great Depression—before an equally jaundiced perception of the Gilded Age's so-called "captains of industry" would become the norm in American culture. A few years after his death in 1877, an official biographer would write that without Cornelius Vanderbilt (or "the Commodore" as he was affectionately called) there would be "no railroads or steamships or telegraphs; no cities, no leisure class, no schools, no colleges, literature, art; in short no civilization."[240] The totemic institutions of American life itself, it seemed, were owed to a single wealthy benefactor.

By contrast, as historian Steve Fraser notes, biographies of later industrialists like Carnegie and Rockefeller "were often laced with moral censure, warning that 'tories of industry' were a threat to democracy and that parasitism, aristocratic pretension and tyranny have always trailed in the wake of concentrated wealth."[241] Ask the average person today to describe a robber baron and there's a good chance they'll proffer a similar depiction grounded in the same historical idioms. Which is to say: a greedy capitalist synonymous with the obscene inequality of America's early industrial period.

Despite a concerted effort at revisionism since the 1960s, the classical image of the robber baron—an avaricious tycoon in a suit, quite possibly brandishing a cigar and boasting a portly gut—largely maintains itself today. Perhaps attuned to this reality, the multibillionaires of big tech who now populate lists of the globe's wealthiest people have deliberately sought to cut a very different image.

****

Today, the greedy robber baron qua monopolist is said to be no more, having given way to a more enlightened class of entrepreneur who uses their wealth for the betterment of the human race and serves at once as both innovator and role model: Bill Gates is known as the world's most generous philanthropist, Mark Zuckerberg and Priscilla Chan as some of its most philanthropically minded millennials. Twitter CEO Jack Dorsey (worth over $3 billion) projects a monk-like existence characterized by dogged work ethic, fastidious routine, and personal asceticism. Elon Musk, meanwhile, presents as an affably nerdy guy who invents flamethrowers in his spare time. Alongside Virgin's Richard Branson, both he and the planet's wealthiest person (Jeff Bezos of Amazon) claim to be working toward no less than the colonization of the universe.

Officially, today's tech overlords are exceptional, eccentric geniuses whose wealth and power we reign in at our collective peril. Contra the robber barons of nineteenth-century America, theirs is said to be a benign class that works to educate, innovate, and give back. Even supposedly reform-minded liberal politicians like Elizabeth Warren, who last year pledged a modest tax on billionaire wealth, basically agree. Strip away the aesthetic differences owed to the passage of time, the evolution of technology, and the rise of global society, however, and you'll find very little daylight between the gilded tycoons of America's first industrial age and the would-be prometheans who today adorn the cover of *Forbes* magazine.

Most obviously, all are people of extreme wealth. Adjusted for inflation, Standard Oil's John D. Rockefeller's fortune hit $257.3 billion in 2018 dollars—one sixty-fifth of American GDP. Today, even after history's most costly divorce, Jeff Bezos is worth around $139 billion—making three times what the median US worker makes in a year every second.

Perhaps more significantly, the explosion in their wealth has followed on the heels of a major economic transformation. Just as the shift from agriculture to industry in the decades following the Civil War became the context for the vast fortunes of the Gilded Age, the contemporaries of Vanderbilt and Rockefeller—similarly lionized in their own times as great men of creativity and vision—have ridden an epochal technology boom and the expansion of information infrastructure and consumer goods that has come in its wake (upon his death in 1992, Walmart founder Sam Walton was likely America's richest man at $8 billion—a figure dwarfed by the tech fortunes of today).

PART V

Like the robber barons of the mid to late nineteenth century, today's tech tycoons preside over vast networks of commerce and communication, commodifying the basic infrastructure of social and economic activity and securing monopolistic control wherever they can. (This predictably extends to political activity much as it once did for the tycoons of steam and steel. In March 1881, Henry Demarest Lloyd wrote of Rockefeller's efforts to buy politicians that his oil company had "done everything with the Pennsylvania legislature, except refine it";[242] in 2015 Facebook's political action committee poured more into campaigns than even Goldman Sachs.) Notwithstanding the careful cultivation of an image that suggests otherwise, the resulting wealth no more owes itself to invention or innovation than Standard Oil's balance sheets did during the 1880s.

Virtually everything that makes the iPhone a successful consumer product—from GPS to touchscreen technology, not to mention the existence of the internet itself—is owed to state investment and public research, not the personal toil of an individual genius. Vanderbilt didn't invent rail transport any more than Musk invented electronic transactions or Bezos home postal delivery.

Substitute fiber optic cable for railways, personal computers for steam-powered locomotion, or app startups for oil refineries and the average tech billionaire starts to look less like a modern promethean than a reincarnated Rockefeller in a black turtleneck. As their contemporaries in the Gilded Age once did, today's tycoons leverage philanthropy, social concern, and a mythos of personal exceptionalism to obscure their actual roles as capitalists. And, just like the thirteenth-century robber barons of the Rhine, the overlords of Silicon Valley jealously guard both their wealth and the means through which all wealth is produced.

Perhaps it's time to evict them from the riverbank.

—A version of this essay first appeared in Jacobin, *May 2020.*

From New Deal to Nudge

In February 2018, teachers in West Virginia staged a dramatic strike action in protest of low-wages and soaring health insurance premiums. Among the worst paid educators in the United States, the situation had become so bleak that some had even been forced to turn to federal assistance. As art teacher Jacob Fertig informed the media: "There were a lot of times where we got to choose between groceries and health coverage for my family."[243] A professionally accredited instructor working not one job but two, Fertig himself made so little that he qualified for food stamps.

Among the surrounding issues which garnered less attention was a proposed change to the state's public worker health plan that would have encouraged teachers to download a mobile fitness app branded with the ominously cheery title "Go365." Generously offered by friendly neighborhood "wellness vendor" Humana Inc., a Kentucky-based, for-profit insurance provider with revenues in the tens of billions, the plan would have allowed users to earn points for various activities deemed to contribute to healthy living, ranging from a "Verified Workout" (up to 50 points per day!) to a dental examination (200 points!!) to a nicotine test (up to 800 points!!!).[244] As described in an official document outlining the program,[245] those who either refused to enroll or failed to rack up the required 3,000 points—measured by way of a Fitbit or similar monitoring device—would subsequently face a fine.

Employing a pastiche of Kafkaesque bureaucratic language ("You will need your Go365 Member ID #, DOB and zip code"), effervescent pep squad feel-goodism ("Be a part of culture change—WV on the move!"), and explicit threats of discipline ("Those who DIDN'T meet the Healthy Tomorrows goals for this year MUST submit bloodwork within range by

5/15/18 or pay $500 penalty deductible"), said document went on to market the program as both an exciting opportunity *and* an unfortunately necessary public health initiative—citing various statistics on West Virginia's low levels of physical activity and high instances of obesity and smoking. Complete with "recommended activities" personalized to each individual by way of information garnered from health assessments and biometric screenings, Go365 aimed to prod its users toward goals like lower blood pressure and a more nutritious diet. To complete this dizzyingly dystopian circle, the app even came with a built-in system of rewards in the form of "bonus bucks" to be tendered (by the sufficiently healthy and compliant) at participating locations including Apple, Nike, and Macy's.

Under fire, the plan was eventually scrapped and the strike, which concluded in a major victory for the teachers after nine days, will hopefully see it buried for good. Still, the mere existence of a private insurance company app designed to monitor workers' physical activities and mold their behaviors on behalf of employers is a terrifying illustration of the state-corporate complex at its most Orwellian. It is also a case study in the current of paternalism which today courses through all the vital organs of neoliberal society.

The New Victorians

Throughout the final decades of the twentieth century a sweeping political and cultural zeitgeist conquered the Anglo-American world, spreading outward amid the collapse of both Soviet communism and European social democracy. Like every counter-revolution in disguise, its gospel was one of liberation: in this case, from the arbitrary edicts of distant technocrats and the ideological crusaders of East and West who, in the twentieth century, had viewed centralized government as a vehicle to enact their grand plans. Declaring the state an intrusive menace, the progeny of Milton Friedman and Friedrich Hayek set out to roll back the institutions of "collectivism" wherever they identified them and quickly had the pillars of the postwar settlement—from Keynesian orthodoxy to welfarism—teetering on the brink of collapse.

As the new order's market individualists traded in various narratives of personal freedom and self-reliance, their animating rhetoric was avowedly anti-paternalist. This was the basis of Ronald Reagan's conservatism, which he summed up succinctly in 1975 as consisting of "a desire for less government interference . . . less centralized authority or more individual freedom."[246] Reagan's now famous declaration that "government is not the solution to our problem, government is the problem,"[247] would therefore go hand in hand with a libertarian language attacking indolence and advocating personal autarky. "It is now common knowledge," he would declare during a 1987 radio address, "that our welfare system has itself become a poverty trap—a creator and reinforcer of dependency."[248] The slogans of the Thatcherite insurgency, Reaganism's analogue across the Atlantic, had a similar thrust, valorizing "thrift" and "personal responsibility" while blaming the structures of British social democracy—specifically and revealingly "the nanny state"—for creating an "undisciplined, decadent society"[249] that institutionalized idleness as a cultural pathology.

The basic formulation—that the redistributive and welfarist functions of the state were inherently paternalistic and coercive—had an elegant populist simplicity: the government is an external force, distant yet authoritative; inscrutable but intrusive. Its retreat, or so it followed, therefore amounted to the removal of arbitrary constraints, the absence of which would give people more space in which to move. To this end, the market was to take on the role of both medium and facilitator: offering a space for endless voluntary exchange and satisfaction of individual desires while providing an impetus toward more virtuous forms of behavior among those deemed too dependency minded.

Contrary to what the rhetoric of rolling back and "laissez-faire" suggested, the spirit of this new market ideology was ultimately activist rather than passive in character. And though its language was that of modernist capitalism, its philosophical sinews ran deep into the past: its economics being neoclassical and its animating ethos neo-Victorian.

"Whatever is done for men or classes, to a certain extent takes away the stimulus and necessity of doing for themselves; and where men are subjected to over-guidance and over-government, the inevitable tendency is to render them comparatively helpless." Such were the words of Scottish self-help author Samuel Smiles in 1859, who would be quoted with approval by Margaret Thatcher more than a hundred years later. Much as Reagan's revolution expressed itself through the idioms of tradition, she would preach a "return to Victorian values" as an antidote to postwar economic and social malaise.[250]

Her chosen era of inspiration, whose memory brings to mind images of imperial opulence, bourgeois prosperity, and swelling industrial capitalism but also those of grotesque urban poverty, class hierarchy, and withering aristocratic disdain toward the lower orders, was hardly incidental. It also inevitably recalls the workhouse, established by Parliament as part of the Poor Law Amendment Act of 1834 and famously depicted in Charles Dickens's *Oliver Twist*. Inspired in part by Thomas Malthus's beliefs about population numbers and poverty, the act was a primitive piece of social policy created with the explicit purpose of molding particular behaviors and discouraging others among Britain's suffering industrial poor. To this end, it drew explicit distinction between those deserving and undeserving of relief. In turn said relief was designed to be so unpleasant and unpalatable that most would be deterred from ever seeking it out, nudged instead toward the manual and domestic labor the country's rulers and industrial barons needed to power the expanding capitalist economy. By casting poverty as both an individual failing and a cultural pathology to be corrected through a legislated system of deterrents and incentives, Victorian patricians achieved a remarkably creative fusion of the ancient and the modern: a new form of noblesse oblige bent around the individualist logic of liberal capitalism.

More than a century later, a distinctly similar synthesis would motivate partisans of the neoliberal revolution: combining market fervor with a paternalist streak open about its intention to discourage certain behaviors and stamp out the deviant, dependent, and degenerate alike. For all their libertarian rhetoric, both the conservatism of the 1980s and the liberalism of the 1990s were as much concerned with creating a particular kind of citizen and enforcing a particular way of living.

Thatcher's famous declaration that "There is no such thing as society" is widely remembered as a radical statement of purpose about the overthrow of the bureaucratic state built after 1945. Less well-remembered is how the statement concluded ("There are individual men and women *and there are families*."). Thatcher's new Victorianism thus extended to her broader conception of social relations, which were to be rigidly maintained by the state through legislation like Section 28—a law which sought to purge publicly-funded schools of anything that normalized homosexuality and banned them from teaching "the acceptability of homosexuality as a pretended family relationship."[251] Parents, in the words of Mrs. Thatcher's secretary of state for education Dr. Rhodes Boyson (himself a former school headmaster), "did not want their children to be taught deviant practices by proselytising homosexuals." Instead, they were "to learn discipline, self-discipline, order, punctuality and precision" and be "punished when they step out of line."[252]

It was no coincidence that Reagan's free enterprise schtick made common cause with the Moral Majority in allying right-wing cultural politics to the secular demigods of big business and unbound finance capital. In the new market society, social and fiscal conservatism would form a natural and mutually reinforcing symbiosis.

While the new Victorianism championed by Bill Clinton (and later Tony Blair) would strike a softer and more communitarian cadence, its broad contours were remarkably consistent with what had preceded it. It was therefore no coincidence that Clinton's famous censure of big government paired its exhalations of the market with a healthy dollop of moral prescription. Thus, the forty-second president's hailing of the end of "the era of big government" during the 1996 State of the Union address carried with it, among other things, calls for Congress to legislate V-chips in every TV set "so that parents can screen out programs they believe are inappropriate for their children," earnest pleas to media giants to produce more wholesome content, and a distinctly Reaganesque decree that "family is the foundation of American life." Repudiating the New Deal, Clinton would preach "a government that steers more than it rows; a government that is a catalyst for action by others; a government that is market-oriented, less bureaucratic, and more entrepreneurial."[253]

In true Victorian fashion, both the most zealous moral censure and the strictest institutional coercion were reserved for the underclass. The supposed end of intrusive statism, appropriately enough, would thus be accompanied by "the end of welfare as we know it" and the menacingly-named Personal Responsibility and Work Opportunity Reconciliation Act—necessary because, in Clinton's words, the welfare system was "undermining the values of family and work instead of supporting them."[254]

From the days of Reagan's Chicago "welfare queen" and well before, the politics of anti-welfarism had been communicated in the form of barely muted racial dog whistles, and Clinton's own efforts very much formed a part of this continuum. As historian Premilla Nadasen puts it, the bill "transformed welfare from an exclusive and unequal cash assistance system that stigmatized its recipients into one that actually criminalized them." To realize its intended purpose—forcing people off welfare programs and into the labor market—the new regime employed "multiple strategies to deter the needy from applying for aid" including "complicated and demeaning application procedures" which relied on invasive methods such as fingerprinting and drug-testing. Its revamped system of temporary grants (Temporary Assistance to Needy Families), meanwhile, included punitive measures targeting low-income single mothers and clauses that aimed to "bolster marriage" and offer parenting classes. As the size of the federal workforce was slashed, Clinton would invest billions in new carceral facilities and draconian law enforcement.[255]

On the cusp of a new millennium—the prisons overflowing, the poor forced into work, and the agoras of high finance spinning at dizzying velocities—the market and its logics reigned supreme, firmly ensconced as the bedrock of public policy and the reigning ideology of the new global elite.

Not With a Bang, But a Nudge

The collapse of Lehman Brothers—the global investment bank with some $600,000,000,000 in assets—in September of 2008 represented a real, albeit hastily sealed, crack in this foundation. As it and other financial giants toppled like dominos, breaking fortunes and the security of millions of ordinary lives unwittingly chained to them in the process, the unassailability of the market seemed briefly in peril. The Great Depression, after all, had once produced a crisis of faith in capitalism so severe its aftermath saw huge expansions of the social safety net and inspired a newly activist state. This time, however, something like the opposite occurred. The state indeed stepped in, but as capital's cavalry reserve rather than its antagonist. Amid huge bailouts and corporate subsidies, a global political class steeped in market fundamentalism soon expeditiously found another culprit in the form of bloated public spending and bureaucratic largesse.

Less a return to the 1940s or '50s than a redux of the 1980s and '90s, liberal and conservative politicians alike again talked endlessly of belt-tightening and the moral necessity of slashing taxes, deficits, and welfare budgets. Coming to power with a populist mandate in the thick of the crash, Barack Obama might have opted to put the markets and their corporate overlords on notice. But the guiding thinking of his presidency would instead resemble a synthesis of Reagan and Clinton: the former's dogmatic deference to markets fused with the latter's fierce conviction that the role of government is to inculcate the correct kinds of behavior among the citizenry.

The technocratic hemisphere of the liberal brain would thus find its ethical center in the new concept of "nudging," a supposedly revolutionary policy framework invented by behavioral theorists Richard Thaler and Cass Sunstein and favorably cited by the New Republic's Franklin Foer as the Obama presidency's ideological core during its breathlessly optimistic early days.[256] Imagining itself an enlightened fusion of the New Deal's activist tendencies and Clintonism's respect for markets, the basic principle of "nudging"—characterized by Sunstein as a series of "choice-preserving, low-cost tools"[257]—is intuitively simple to grasp: policymakers seek to produce a particular outcome but, since overt state intervention is anathema in a society where the market rules, carefully structured prods and incentives can instead be used to realize the designated objective. One illustration of nudging in action, as described by Foer:

> In addition to the retirement saving reform, which Obama later wrote into his budget, the campaign also warmed to a proposal called "intelligent assignment." The idea was a response to the fact that seniors enrolled in the Medicare prescription drug program are often overwhelmed by the dozens of plans they have to choose from, sometimes to the point of paralysis. The Obama wonks favored automatically enrolling many of them in the plan

that best suited their needs, based on their drug-buying histories, then allowing them to switch if they found one they liked better.[258]

The administration would apply the same concept in its approach to the financial crisis, directing the Treasury to "partner with hedge funds and private equity firms to relieve the banks of their toxic assets" thus making "banks more attractive to investors" (that is, in lieu of nationalization or breaking them up). Even in the field of health care, where Obama briefly pushed a public option—i.e., a thoroughgoing public insurance program— the desired outcome was still changing the behavior of private insurers by introducing new competition. (Revealingly, even the Obama era's momentary flirtation with a straightforwardly public sector approach was still ultimately concerned with nudging the market.)

By incorporating a degree of voluntarism in the form of opt-outs, nudgeocrats Sunstein and Thaler implied a harmonious resolution of the conflict between state and market—rather vaingloriously branding their philosophy "libertarian paternalism." Sunstein, who worked as a high-ranking official in the Obama administration's Office of Management and Budget, would even go on to push for the establishment of a Council of Psychological Advisers with a mandate to figure out "when people could benefit from a nudge."[259]

Like its analogues in the Reagan and Clinton eras, "nudging" promoted paternalism while simultaneously claiming to roll it back. For one thing, it implicitly assumed that enlightened technocrats already held the "correct" answers and solutions, knew the proper outcomes, and were fully equipped to diagnose the problems. For another, its ideologues clearly believed that the main obstacle to be overcome was people's misguided choices, individual deviations within a perfect system to be benignly nudged in a more virtuous direction by a brain trust of experts—not unlike a parent who dangles the prospect of after-dinner ice cream so that the kids will eat their asparagus.

As Thaler and Sunstein themselves describe it, the guiding principle of nudging "is that we should design policies that *help the least sophisticated* people in society *while imposing the smallest possible costs on the most sophisticated* [my emphasis]."[260] "Libertarian paternalism" is therefore quite an apt descriptor for nudging, though for different reasons than its architects intended: its libertarian component implying deference to the market from policymakers ("Fix your broken economy with these incredible, choice-preserving, low-cost tools, available at participating locations!"); its paternalist one in valuing the knowledge of well-credentialed experts recruited from the right schools.

Of Freedom and Fitbits

If the legacy of the neoliberal revolution consists of anything, it is the intrusive presence of the market—not only in our social safety nets, our governments, and our political imaginations—but also in our daily lives. Having once preached self-reliance, the market and its ideologues now simply refuse to get off our backs: their vision of radical liberty having reached its logical endpoint in technocratic theories of the state and panoptic surveillance apps that seek to reduce health-spending by forcing underpaid schoolteachers to do sit-ups.

By redefining greed as enlightened self-interest and conflating wealth with social value, all the while wielding the market's invisible hand to nudge the lower orders, the real goal of neoliberalism's would-be anti-paternalists has always been to reproduce a class society—its injustices obscured by a bogus ontology of individualism that legitimizes hierarchy and naturalizes plunder.

As it was for the patricians of the high Victorian era, paternalism is the governing ethos of this society: the subconscious logic of a self-replicating elite looking down from metropolitan spires and ivory towers and liturgically passing its judgements on the lower orders with the priggish moralism of a Dickensian aristocrat. Having inserted the market into every crevice of modern life, the wagging finger of libertarian paternalism now nudges us almost everywhere we go. Our only recourse is to take off the proverbial Fitbit and head to the nearest picket line.

—March 2019

Neoliberalism? Never Heard of It.

For the first time in decades, it has become possible to envision real alternatives to the prevailing political and economic order of the past forty years. Across Europe and the Americas, the neoliberal consensus is facing a deep crisis of moral, intellectual, and popular legitimacy: proving unable to deliver either the growth or the broad prosperity its ideologues once promised and facing robust electoral challenges from both the socialist left and the nationalist right.

Predictably enough, this turn of events has elicited a defensive response from neoliberalism's greatest partisans and those otherwise invested in its political and cultural hegemony. "Reminder: Liberalism Is Working, and Marxism Has Always Failed," asserts an anguished Jonathan Chait.[261] "It's Time for the Elites to Rise Up Against the Ignorant Masses," bellows an indignant James Traub.[262] "Not left, not right, but forward," meanwhile, has once again become the median posture among those seeking the Democratic nomination for president—with most candidates channeling the spirit of Tony Blair's famous 1998 call[263] to neoliberal technocracy and making familiar appeals to moderation and meliorism.

But the past several years have also given birth to a related, albeit more curious phenomenon: namely the regular insistence by prominent liberals and centrists that neoliberalism is either a phantom created by leftists or, alternatively, a term so ethereal it defies definition and therefore serves no useful purpose. In Britain and America especially—two of neoliberalism's most significant ideological beachheads in the 1980s and '90s—some commentators cannot seem to resist this strange line of argument, even as the contours of the neoliberal order become more visible amid its weakened political prospects and declining economic returns.

These arguments have come in several variations. The first, and most plainly superficial, caustically insists that neoliberalism doesn't exist or, at any rate, ceased to have a meaningful existence long ago. "Nobody has spotted a neoliberal in the wild since Gary Hart's 1984 presidential campaign," writes *Politico*'s Bill Scher, in his stunningly humorless review of *The Chapo Guide to Revolution*.[264] Or, to take the petulant words of prominent online Clinton sycophant Tom Watson: "There are no neoliberals in the US Congress—not one. Not one in any statehouses in the nation, either. Yet it's constantly bandied about by the white academic left as a functioning and present ideology."[265]

A second, though related, version holds that the word mainly exists as a term of abuse: that is, a reductive epithet hurled by leftist trolls looking to slander everyone in sight. This variation's most prominent adherent has to be the ever-aggrieved Chait who, in a July 2017 piece titled "How 'Neoliberalism' Became the Left's Favorite Insult of Liberals," insists that liberalism has remained largely consistent and unchanging (thus making "neo" an unnecessary and pejorative addendum). Chait's argument hinges on the breathtakingly ahistorical claim that liberal politicians had no hand in the generalized rightward shift that followed the 1970s and, furthermore, have not wavered in their basic commitments, particularly when it comes to economic policy, since the New Deal:

> The Democratic Party has evolved over the last half-century, as any party does over a long period of time. But the basic ideological cast of its economic policy has not changed dramatically since the New Deal ... Progressives are correct in their belief that something has changed for the worse in American politics. Larger forces in American life have stalled the seemingly

unstoppable progressive momentum of the postwar period . . .
All this forced Democrats more frequently into a defensive posture . . . Barack Obama's far more sweeping reforms still could
not win any support from a radicalized opposition. It is seductive
to attribute these frustrations to the tactical mistakes or devious
betrayals of party leaders. But it is the political climate that has
grown more hostile to Democratic Party economic liberalism.
The party's ideological orientation has barely changed.[266]

In this telling, both liberal writers like Chait and Democratic politicians like Clinton and Obama have remained largely consistent with
the liberalism of the mid-twentieth century. The "neoliberalism" charge
is therefore an abusive tactic invented by socialists and designed primarily to "bracket," as he puts it, "the center-left together with the right
as 'neoliberal' and then force progressives to choose between that and
socialism."

    This calls to mind a third and perhaps more emblematic variation
on the form, which says that the wide application of "neoliberal" renders
the term too vague and imprecise for it to retain any real value. In an
editorial for the *Independent*, for example, Ben Chu takes aim at the regular charge made by some on Labour's Corbynite left that the EU is a
neoliberal institution: a reflex he believes to be incoherent, conspiratorial,
and even mildly sinister.[267] Partly echoing Chait, Ed Conway (economics
editor for Britain's *Sky News*) asks: "What is neoliberalism and why is it
an insult?" While socialists and others on the left are fond of branding
everything they dislike "neoliberal," he writes, no one can actually agree
on the word's meaning:

> You could pick any one of [Jeremy Corbyn's] speeches over the
> past few years for . . . examples. The Grenfell Tower was a tragedy
> of neoliberalism . . . Austerity was a product of neoliberalism.

The City is neoliberal, the government is neoliberal, the press is neoliberal . . . Despite the fact that neoliberalism is frequently referred to as an ideology, it is oddly difficult to pin down. For one thing, it is a word that tends to be used almost exclusively by those who are criticizing it—not by its advocates, such as they are (in stark contrast to almost every other ideology, nearly no one self-describes as a neoliberal). In other words, it is not an ideology but an insult."[268]

A somewhat more earnest and coherent version of this argument can be found in a recent essay by *Vox*'s Ezra Klein,[269] which does at least grant the term neoliberalism some tangible meaning. "In its simplest form," Klein writes, "neoliberalism refers to a general preference for market mechanisms over state interventions." This, however, is where the problems begin:

> Since almost everyone sometimes prefers market mechanisms to state interventions, and sometimes prefer state interventions to market mechanisms, the conversation quickly gets confusing. Ronald Reagan and Margaret Thatcher were neoliberals. Bill Clinton is often seen as a neoliberal. Barack Obama is sometimes considered a neoliberal. Elizabeth Warren is occasionally called a neoliberal.

As such, Klein concludes, the label is often over-applied to the point of incoherence. "A label that can describe everyone," he argues, "doesn't usefully describe anyone." To his credit, Klein doesn't want us to abandon the term entirely. Nor does he pretend, as others do, that the phenomenon it describes is so nebulous it might as well not exist (to his earlier definition, he even adds: "Neoliberalism describes what happens when capitalism mutates from an economic system to a governing and even moral philosophy").

The primary purpose of the essay, however, is to argue that the Obama presidency fell short of progressive expectations because of an intransigent Congress rather than an attachment to neoliberalism. This is where Klein, his more nuanced and inquisitive posture notwithstanding, begins to sound a bit like Chait:

> In recent years, neoliberal has reemerged as political slander, meaning something like "corporatist sellout Democrat" . . . I've become more frustrated with the lazy ways the term is tossed around—and, particularly, how it becomes an all-purpose explanation for any political outcome someone doesn't like.

****

Despite their variations and varying degrees of good and bad faith, each of these arguments (and countless others in the same vein) share some certain common features. The first is a poor, or at any rate incomplete, telling of history.

Far from being abstract or immaterial, neoliberalism was the consciously pursued project of an initially small group of intelligentsia who, thanks to decades of well-funded organizing and adept political maneuvering—particularly during the various crises that afflicted Keynesian social democracy in the 1970s—gradually succeeded in taking their ideology from the fringes to the heights of institutional and cultural power. First capturing the old right (in Britain's Tory Party, the disappointments of the Heath era gave way to the more dynamic and confrontational ethos of Thatcherism, just as in America Nixon and Ford were succeeded by Reaganism), the neoliberal ascendency eventually secured a foothold in the center-left by way of figures like Bill Clinton and Tony Blair.

The new generation of ideologues who came to dominate Western liberalism in the 1990s was hardly dragged kicking and screaming into the embrace of its more market-zealous incarnation. On the contrary,

New Labour acolytes and Atari Democrats were some of neoliberalism's most enthusiastic converts and set out to realign their parties with the consensus already set in motion by the new right. Here's how the Democratic Party's shift away from postwar liberalism was described in 2013 by none other than Chait himself:

> [Various] magazines once critiqued Democrats from the right, advocating a policy loosely called "neoliberalism," and now stand in general ideological concord. Why? I'd say it's because the neoliberal project succeeded in weaning the Democrats of the wrong turn they took during the 1960s and 1970s. The Democrats under Bill Clinton—and Obama, whose domestic policy is crafted almost entirely by Clinton veterans—has internalized the neoliberal critique.[270]

Given these observable shifts, it is simply ahistorical to argue that liberalism has been ideologically stagnant, or that its transformation during the 1990s did not occur; equally so to suggest that liberal politicians like Clinton or Obama were simply the casualties of a generalized rightward drift, akin to a fierce weather event, rather than the conscious practitioners of an ideology. If neoliberalism is sometimes invoked as a pejorative term for today's liberal politicians, it is because the left opposes the consensus they seek to perpetuate and argues that a more humane alternative is both desirable and available.

Having dealt with the historical details, what about the second major component of the arguments at hand—i.e., that the moniker "neoliberalism" is either too widely applicable or too contested to be of any use?

This is the fulcrum of the reasoning offered in varying degrees by Klein, Conway, and Chu, and like many erroneous arguments, it contains at least a smidgeon of truth. There is indeed some ambiguity surrounding the term, but that's only because what it describes is now so multifaceted.

At face value, neoliberalism describes a mixture of classical liberal philosophy and neoclassical economics. Officially at least, its advocates champion an ethic of governance that sees individual freedom as maximized under conditions of limited state activity, favor private enterprise over public ownership, and are skeptical of centralized regulation.

But neoliberalism might also, variously, describe: an existing set of interconnected economic and political institutions; a conscious ideological offensive that transformed global politics in the 1980s and '90s and the frontiers of acceptable public policy since; a range of principles and pressures that exert influence on elected leaders whether they are conscious adherents to neoliberal philosophy or not; the near-totalizing reality of life under the pressures and logics of late capitalism.

For some, this is reason enough to abandon, dismiss, or severely limit the application of the term—in some cases to the point that it ceases to be a recognized feature of contemporary life. If a set of political ideas can be applied too widely, so this thinking runs, then continuing to identify or isolate them as a causal force becomes basically pointless. How, after all, can a label applicable to politicians as distinct as Ronald Reagan and Barack Obama be of any real use?

But we might just as easily draw the opposite conclusion. The ubiquity of a particular phenomenon does not make analysis of it useless and, if anything, such omnipresence makes identifying it a more urgent and critical task. A phenomenon so diffuse it can be found throughout politics, economics, and culture is hardly an illusion, and the apparent reticence of many commentators to recognize or even acknowledge its valence as a term can only be viewed as a symptom of neoliberalism's continued stranglehold on our political, cultural, and intellectual life.

The longer something is part of your reality, the more it tends to fade from your field of focus and blur into the rest of the background. After its initially disruptive incursion in the 1980s, neoliberalism fast became a feature of our collective existence, so indelible many now seem unable to recall a time before it existed, let alone conceive a future that moves beyond it. An ideology secures hegemony at precisely the point it ceases to be considered one: its claims transform into axioms; its theories harden into dogma; its abstruse vernacular becomes the lingua franca; its assumptions are subsumed under "common sense."

That neoliberalism remains so poorly understood in the very political mainstream whose frontiers it now circumscribes is a testament to both the breathtaking scope of its counterrevolution, and the daunting task facing those of us who seek its overthrow. It is everywhere and therefore nowhere: at once so diaphanous it seems invisible; so internalized it feels inescapable. Then again, perhaps something altogether more hopeful might be drawn from this strange and apparently downbeat conclusion. As the late Mark Fisher once reminded us:

> The long, dark night of the end of history has to be grasped as an enormous opportunity. The very oppressive pervasiveness of capitalist realism means that even glimmers of alternative political and economic possibilities can have a disproportionately great effect. The tiniest event can tear a hole in the grey curtain of reaction which has marked the horizons of possibility under capitalist realism. From a situation in which nothing can happen, suddenly anything is possible again.[271]

—*A version of this essay first appeared in* Jacobin, *November 2019.*

Acknowledgements

This being my first book, I'm deeply grateful to anyone and everyone who has helped me along my somewhat unexpected path as a writer. I owe tremendous thanks to the entire staff at *Jacobin* and the magazine's enterprising founder Bhaskar Sunkara for supporting me in my work. I'm grateful to Michael and Us co-host (and friend since our student newspaper days) Will Sloan who, in our weekly podcasting sessions has inadvertently become a regular sounding board for many of my half-formed writing ideas amid various riffs about Steven Seagal, Charlie Chaplin, and Ingmar Bergman—and also to our show's many listeners far and wide. Many thanks as well to Teddy Ostrow, Colin Robinson, and the entire team at OR Books for agreeing to publish an essay collection from a first-time author, and to Meagan Day, Micah Uetrict, Ben Burgis, Daniel Bessner, Branko Marcetic, and Miles Kampf-Lassin for their advice throughout the assembly of this book. Thanks as well to *Jacobin's* Executive Editor Seth Ackerman, with whom I worked on many of these essays.

Love and gratitude to my parents and family, and to Madeleine—who helped and encouraged me throughout the writing process.

The Dead Center is dedicated to the late Michael Brooks, an irreplaceable talent whose voice, values, and humor represented the very best of the socialist left.

Endnotes

1   Irving Howe, "This Age of Conformity," *Dissent Magazine*, November 8, 2014, https://www.dissentmagazine.org/online_articles/irving-howe-voice-still-heard-this-age-of-conformity.

2   Terry Eagleton, *Ideology: An Introduction* (London: Verso Books, 1991).

3   Michael Joseph Oakeshott, "Political Education," *Rationalism in Politics and Other Essays* (Indianapolis: Liberty Fund, 1991).

4   Steve LeBlanc, "Joe Kennedy Says Democrats Should Embrace 'Moral Capitalism,'" *Boston Globe*, November 28, 2018, https://www.bostonglobe.com/metro/2018/11/28/joe-kennedy-says-democrats-should-embrace-moral-capitalism/KLx9TptSdoMpallXxfYjON/story.html.

5   Chris Sommerfeldt, "'You Are Not in North Korea': Pelosi Blasts Trump over Refusal to Promise Peaceful Transfer of Power," Yahoo! News/*New York Daily News*, September 24, 2020, https://news.yahoo.com/not-north-korea-pelosi-blasts-174700507.html?guccounter=1&guce_referrer=aHROcHM6Ly93d3cuZ-29vZ2xlLmNvbS8&guce_referrer_sig=AQAAAMMhMSUpsLaTwwmg-pQ2HuurYewJspbNFXzxQ172u3u2tbakdxqJVzI4SN2cr_iYWyo4_dl3e7X-fAzMjOB7PBmzxriernRUEVDgUWQfieEkmrQmHhfo5WtW-LZRotuM-kyrjX3jiqcn5KClXP-sEXg9-TnELbB69OM4mbt4D2mTHc.

6   Natalie Andrews (@nataliewsj), "Pelosi dismisses calls from some on the left that she should shut down the government to try to stall a Supreme Court confirmation, says public employees need jobs now more than ever. 'We're going to shut them down? I don't think so.'" Twitter, September 24, 2020, https://twitter.com/nataliewsj/status/1309149540038127622.

7   John Haltiwanger, "House Democrats Gave Trump 'Everything He Wanted' on A $738 Billion Defense Bill While on the Brink of Impeaching Him," Business Insider, December 12, 2019, https://www.businessinsider.com/democrats-gave-trump-everything-he-wants-738-billion-defense-bill-2019-12.

8   Glenn Greenwald, "The Same Democrats Who Denounce Donald Trump as a Lawless, Treasonous Authoritarian Just Voted to Give Him VAST Warrantless Spying Powers," *Intercept*, January 12, 2018, https://theintercept.com/2018/01/12/the-same-democrats-who-denounce-trump-as-a-lawless-treasonous-authoritarian-just-voted-to-give-him-vast-warrantless-spying-powers/.

9   Li Zhou, "Schumer's Deal to Fast-Track Trump Judges Makes Progressive Activists Furious," *Vox*, August 30, 2018, https://www.vox. com/2018/8/30/17797770/chuck-schumer-trump-judicial-nominees.

10 Jacob Pramuk, "House Approves Usmca Trade Deal after More than a Year of Talks, Sending It to Senate," CNBC, December 19, 2019, https://www.cnbc.com/2019/12/19/house-passes-trumps-usmca-trade-agreement.html.

11 LeBlanc, "Joe Kennedy Says Democrats Should Embrace 'Moral Capitalism.'"

12 Thomas Frank, "The Blue State Model," *Le Monde diplomatique*, March 29, 2016, https://mondediplo.com/openpage/the-blue-state-model.

13 Andrew Cuomo, "The sky is orange over California. Half a million acres are burning. This is what climate change looks like. The proof is right in front of us. This is a national emergency – it's now or never." Twitter, September 10, 2020, https://twitter.com/NYGovCuomo/status/1304043986257096709.

14 Gavin Newsom, "These pictures cry out for change. CA has invested more in wildfire prevention than any time in our history. Enacted bold climate policies. But it's not enough. We must do more. We need action at EVERY level. CA cannot do this alone. Climate change is REAL. So please – VOTE." Twitter, September 10, 2020, https://twitter.com/GavinNewsom/status/1303884781659144192.

15 Daisy Nguyen, "Approvals for New Oil and Gas Wells up in California," Associated Press, September 3, 2020. https://apnews.com/d04910d29539d39e24eaa725bcf4545f.

16 Kate Kelly, Shane Goldmacher, and Thomas Kaplan, "The Wallets of Wall Street Are with Joe Biden, If Not the Hearts," *New York Times*. August 9, 2020. https://www.nytimes.com/2020/08/09/ business/joe-biden-wall-street.html.

17 Sarah Cammarata, "Biden Promises Wealthy Donors He Would Not 'Demonize' the Rich," *Politico*, June 19, 2019, https://www.politico.com/story/2019/06/19/biden-wealthy-donors-1369957.

18 Lily Geismer, "Atari Democrats," *Jacobin*, August 2, 2016, https://www.jacobinmag.com/2016/02/geismer-democratic-party-atari-tech-silicon-valley-mondale/.

19 "Franklin Roosevelt's Address Announcing the Second New Deal, October 1936," Franklin D. Roosevelt Presidential Library and Museum, http://docs.fdrlibrary.marist.edu/od2ndst.html (accessed August 30, 2021).

20 "'The Era of Big Government Is Over:' Clinton's 1996 State of the Union," PBS, October 30, 2017, https://www.pbs.org/weta/washingtonweek/web-video/era-big-government-over-clintons-1996-state-union.

ENDNOTES

21 Richard Fording Sanford Schram and Sanford Schram, "The Welfare Reform Disaster," *Jacobin*, https://www.jacobinmag.com/2016/08/welfare-reform-clinton-twentieth-anniversary-poverty/ (accessed August 30, 2021).

22 Branko Marcetic, "Joe Biden and the Disastrous History of Bipartisanship," *In These Times*. https://inthesetimes.com/features/joe-biden-bipartisanship-nostalgia-centrism-2020.html (accessed August 30, 2021).

23 Corey Robin, "The Obamanauts," *Dissent Magazine*, March 25, 2020, https://www.dissentmagazine.org/article/the-obamanauts.

24 David Brooks, "I Was Once a Socialist. Then I Saw How It Worked," *New York Times*, December 6, 2019, https://www. nytimes.com/2019/12/05/opinion/socialism-capitalism.html.

25 "Quotes Falsely Attributed to Winston Churchill," International Churchill Society, November 24, 2017, https://winstonchurchill.org/resources/quotes/quotes-falsely-attributed/.

26 FreeToChooseNetwork, "Debate between Milton Friedman, James Galbraith, and David Brooks," YouTube, August 1, 2013, https://www.youtube.com/watch?v=idPvNSzjlfo.

27 Brooks, "I Was Once a Socialist. Then I Saw How It Worked."

28 Tony Judt, "What Is Living and What Is Dead in Social Democracy?: By Tony Judt," *New York Review of Books*, December 17, 2009, https:// www.nybooks.com/articles/2009/12/17/what-is-living-and-what-is-dead-in-social-democrac/.

29 Jim Stanford, "Opinion: Auckland Transit Blues," *Globe and Mail*, June 16, 2010, https://www.theglobeandmail.com/opinion/auckland-transit-blues/article1373160/.

30 Brooks, "I Was Once a Socialist. Then I Saw How It Worked."

31 Thomas, "The Blue State Model."

32 Ethan Cox, "Poll: Over Two-Thirds of Canadians Back a Wealth Tax," *Ricochet*, July 19, 2021, https://ricochet.media/en/2599/poll-over-two-thirds-of-canadians-back-a-wealth-tax.

33 "Canadians Overwhelmingly Support Universal Pharmacare: New Poll," *Canada's Nurses*, May 2, 2019, https://nursesunions.ca/canadians-overwhelmingly-support-universal-pharmacare-new-poll/.

34 "Here's Why Anti-Poverty Groups Agree Canada's New Anti-Poverty Strategy Does Not Reduce Poverty," PressProgress, September 13, 2018, https://pressprogress.ca/heres-why-anti-poverty-groups-agree-canadas-new-anti-poverty-strategy-does-not-reduce-poverty/.

35 Andrew Jackson, "So-Called 'Middle Class' Tax Cut Leaves out Most Canadians," Broadbent Institute, November 14, 2015, https://www.

broadbentinstitute.ca/andrew_ajackson/so_called_middle_class_tax_cut_leaves_out_most_canadians.

36   "Justin Trudeau Now Suddenly Thinks Electoral Reform Is Bad for Democracy," PressProgress, February 5, 2018, https:// pressprogress.ca/justin-trudeau-now-suddenly-thinks-electoral-reform-is-bad-for-democracy/.

37   Christopher Lasch, *The Revolt of the Elites: And the Betrayal of Democracy* (New York: W.W. Norton, 1996).

38   Amy Klobuchar, "Time to bring back bipartisan talks on healthcare. Only way to get a bill that helps all Americans is by working together. https://T.co/y2dqytjd5k." Twitter, September 25, 2017, https:// twitter.com/amyklobuchar/status/912443498258997248.

39   Amy Goldstein and Juliet Eilperin, "A GOP Senate Leader Calls for Bipartisan Compromise on ACA Marketplaces," *Washington Post*, September 6, 2017, https://www.washingtonpost.com/national/health-science/gop-senate-leader-calls-for-bipartisan-compromise-on-aca-marketplaces/2017/09/06/2e85710a-9309-11e7-aace-04b862b2b3f3_story.html?utm_term=.7aaedcf8b08c.

40   Alexander Mallin, "Trump Says He Called Schumer, Touts Prospect of 'Great' Bipartisan Health Care Bill," ABC News, https://abcnews.go.com/Politics/trump-called-schumer-touts-prospect-great-bipartisan-health/story?id=50342117 (accessed August 30, 2021).

41   Abigail Abrams, "Congressional Baseball Game: Ryan and Pelosi Speak Unity," *Time*, June 16, 2017, https://time.com/4821010/paul-ryan-nancy-pelosi-steve-scalise-shooting-bipartisan/.

42   Ken Tucker, "Jon Stewart on 'The Rachel Maddow Show': 'We Have a Special Place in Our Hearts for FOX,'" EW.com, https://ew.com/article/2010/11/11/jon-stewart-on-the-rachel-maddow-show-we-have-a-special-place-in-our-hearts-for-fox/ (accessed August 30, 2021).

43   "A Grass-Roots Answer to Gridlock," *Washington Post*, December 3, 2010, https://www.washingtonpost.com/wp-dyn/content/article/2010/12/02/AR2010120205703.html.

44   Molly Ball, "On Safari in Trump's America," *Atlantic*, November 16, 2017, https://www.theatlantic.com/politics/archive/2017/10/on-safari-in-trumps-america/543288/.

45   Rebecca Elliott, "Trump to Host Fundraiser for Booker," *Politico*, July 16, 2013, https://www.politico.com/story/2013/07/ivanka-trump-fundraiser-cory-booker-094288.

46   Zaid Jilani, "Samantha Power to Receive Prize from Henry Kissinger, Whom She Once Harshly Criticized," *Intercept*, May 29, 2016, https:// theintercept.com/2016/05/29/

samantha-power-to-receive-prize-from-henry-kissinger-whom-she-once-harshly-criticized/.

47   Debbie Encalada, "Trevor Noah Sends Tomi Lahren Cupcakes after Grilling Her and People Are Pissed," *Complex*, April 20, 2020, http://www.complex.com/pop-culture/2016/12/trevor-noah-sends-tomi-lahren-cupcakes.

48   Nathan Robinson, "People You Disagree With," *Current Affairs*, https://www.currentaffairs.org/2017/12/people-you-disagree-with (accessed August 30, 2021).

49   Van Jones, "When I Say #NeverTrump, I Don't Mean THIS Trump. #nerdprom #WHCD #CNN @cnn @EricTrump," Twitter, May 1, 2016, https://twitter.com/vanjones68/status/726600801272094720?lang=en.

50   Tierney McAfee, "Tiffany Trump and Hillary and Bill Clinton Attend the Same Star-Studded Wedding in New York City," People.com, https://people.com/politics/tiffany-trump-hillary-bill-clinton-wedding/ (accessed August 30, 2021).

51   Dana Feldman, "Hillary Clinton Inks Book Deal With Simon & Schuster," *Forbes Magazine*, February 1, 2017, https://www.forbes.com/sites/danafeldman/2017/02/01/new-hillary-clinton-book-will-include-thoughts-on-election-loss-to-donald-trump/?sh=263b4d15322d.

52   Chuck Schumer, "Tonight, I feel mostly regret at what could have been. Tax reform is an issue that is ripe for bipartisan compromise. There is a sincere desire on this side of the aisle to work with the GOP, particularly on tax reform, but we have been rebuffed, time & time again," Twitter, December 2, 2017, https://twitter.com/senschumer/status/936786346785439744?lang=en.

53   Senate Democrats, "Real bipartisan tax reform isn't handwritten behind closed doors. #Goptaxscam," Twitter, December 2, 2017, https://twitter.com/SenateDems/status/937567157936046010.

54   Gregory S. Schneider, "A Democratic Winner in Virginia Says It's Time For Bipartisanship," *Washington Post*, December 16, 2017, https://www.washingtonpost.com/local/virginia-politics/ gov-elect-northam-rode-a-democratic-wave-but-now-hes-preaching-bipartisanship/2017/12/16/689e1074-e1b3-11e7-8679-a9728984779c_story.html?tid=sm_tw&utm_term=.2f75ca01f018.

55   Bill Clinton, "Americans Must Decide Who We Really Are," *New York Times*, December 4, 2017, https://mobile.nytimes.com/2017/12/04/ opinion/bill-clinton-travelban.html?rref=collection%2Fsectioncollection%2Fopinion&action=click&contentCollection=opinion®ion=stream&module=stream_unit&version=latest&contentPlacement=3&pgtype=sectionfront&referer=http%3A%2F%2Fm.facebook.com%2F.

56 Byron Tau, "When the Kochs Gave to Dems . . ." *Politico*, March 19, 2014, https://www.politico.com/story/2014/03/koch-brothers-democrats-104787.

57 Hibah Yousuf, "Wall Street Overwhelmingly Backs Romney," CNNMoney, November 6, 2012, https://money.cnn.com/2012/11/06/investing/stocks-election-obama-romney/index.html.

58 Having performed poorly in a 2012 debate, Barack Obama reportedly said: "Everyone's out there working their hearts out, and now I've made it harder for them. I'm sure I've disappointed them as well. I care more about not doing that again even more than winning." With due respect to the former president's gift for oratory, this doesn't read as particularly Periclean to me. But, according to Plouffe, it sounded "like an implausible line, written by Aaron Sorkin for President Bartlet in *The West Wing*," which, given its source, is probably meant to be taken as even higher praise.

59 David Plouffe, "Introduction," *A Citizen's Guide to Beating Donald Trump* (New York: Penguin Publishing Group, 2020).

60 Ibid., 65.

61 Ibid., 66-67.

62 Ibid., xviii.

63 Juli Weiner, "How Aaron Sorkin's *West Wing* Inspired a Legion of Lyman Wannabes," *Vanity Fair*, March 6, 2012, https://www.vanityfair.com/news/2012/04/aaron-sorkin-west-wing.

64 Ibid.

65 Joyce Millman, "'Don't Blame Me, I Voted for Martin Sheen!" Salon.com, September 25, 2011, http://www.salon.com/2000/09/11/ emmys_2000/.

66 Michael Ollove, "'West Wing's' Bartlet Is the President Voters Wish For," *Los Angeles Times*, November 7, 2000, https://www.latimes.com/archives/la-xpm-2000-nov-07-ca-48120-story.html.

67 Maureen Dowd, "Aaron Sorkin Conjures a Meeting of Obama and Bartlet," *New York Times*, September 20, 2008, https://www.nytimes.com/2008/09/21/opinion/21dowd-sorkin.html.

68 Emily Heil, "President Bartlet for Hillary: Actor Bradley Whitford Says Fictional Prez Would Be for Clinton," *Washington Post*, April 19, 2019. https://www.washingtonpost.com/news/reliable-source/wp/2016/04/05/president-bartlet-for-hillary-actor-bradley-whitford-says-fictional-prez-would-be-for-clinton/?utm_term=.d9edf67cbfc4.

69 Rob Lowe, "Watching Bernie Sanders. He's hectoring and yelling at me while he's saying he's going to raise our taxes. Interesting way to communicate," Twitter, January 26, 2016, https://twitter.com/roblowe/status/6918 07380703703046?lang=fi.

ENDNOTES

70 "Make this election about smart, and not. Make it about engaged, and not. Qualified, and not. Make it about a heavyweight. You're a heavyweight. And you've been holding me up for too many rounds." —Toby Ziegler, *Hartsfield's Landing* (season 3, episode 14).

71 Jeremy W. Peters, "The 'Never Trump' Coalition That Decided Eh, Never Mind, He's Fine," *New York Times*, October 5, 2019, https://www.nytimes.com/2019/10/05/us/politics/never-trumper-republicans.html.

72 Ibid.

73 L. Brent Bozell III, "Conservatives Should Ask, 'Does Trump Walk With Us?'" *National Review*, May 25, 2021, https://www.nationalreview.com/2016/01/donald-trump-brent-bozell-conservative-fake/.

74 Liam Stack, "Glenn Beck Says Opposing Trump Is 'Moral, Ethical' Even If It Means Clinton Wins," *New York Times*, October 11, 2016, https://www.nytimes.com/2016/10/12/us/politics/glenn-beck-says-opposing-trump-is-moral-ethical-even-if-it-means-clinton-wins.html.

75 Lee Moran, "Glenn Beck Suggests Trump Is One of the Last Male Role Models and It Doesn't Go Well," *HuffPost Canada*, March 7, 2019, https://www.huffingtonpost.ca/entry/glenn-beck-donald-trump-male-role-models_n_5c8104a8e4b0e62f69ea2aa0?ri18n=true.

76 George T. Conway, Steve Schmidt, John Weaver, and Rick Wilson. "We Are Republicans, and We Want Trump Defeated," *New York Times*, December 17, 2019, https://www.nytimes.com/2019/12/17/opinion/lincoln-project.html.

77 The Editors, "Against Trump," *National Review*, May 25, 2021, https://www.nationalreview.com/2016/01/donald-trump-conservative-movement-menace/.

78 Luke Savage, "Frumocracy," *Jacobin*, https://jacobinmag.com/2018/03/trumpocracy-david-frum-review-trump-republicans (accessed August 30, 2021).

79 Martin Longman, "'Never Trump' Conservatives Won't Save Us." *Washington Monthly*, April 18, 2018, https://washingtonmonthly.com/magazine/april-may-june-2018/never-trump-conservatives-wont-save-us/.

80 Barack Obama, "Music has always played an important role in my life—and that was especially true during my presidency. In honor of my book hitting shelves tomorrow, I put together this playlist featuring some memorable songs from my administration. Hope you enjoy it. Pic. twitter.com/xWiNQiZzNO," Twitter, November 16, 2020, https://twitter.com/BarackObama/status/1328458351869644806.

81 Matt Taibbi, "Obama Is the Best BS Artist Since Bill Clinton," Alternet.org, February 14, 2007, https://www.alternet.org/2007/02/obama_is_the_best_bs_artist_since_bill_clinton/.

82 Barack Obama, *A Promised Land* (New York: Penguin Books Ltd, 2020).

83 Ibid., 4.

84 Ibid., 5.

85 Ibid., 210.

86 Ibid., 9.

87 Ibid., 48.

88 Ibid., 196.

89 Ibid., 136.

90 Ibid., 107.

91 Ibid., 310-312.

92 Ibid., 305.

93 "Barack Obama's Remarks to the Democratic National Convention," *New York Times*, July 27, 2004, https://www.nytimes.com/2004/07/27/politics/campaign/barack-obamas-remarks-to-the-democratic-national.html.

94 "Barack Obama's Remarks in St. Paul," *New York Times*, June 3, 2008. https://www.nytimes.com/2008/06/03/us/politics/03text-obama.html.

95 "Former Caltech Provost Steven Koonin Nominated for Under Secretary for Science," California Institute of Technology, March 25, 2009, https://www.caltech.edu/about/news/former-caltech-provost-steven-koonin-nominated-under-secretary-science-1521.

96 Steven E. Koonin, "Climate Science Is Not Settled," *Wall Street Journal*, September 19, 2014, https://www.wsj.com/articles/climate-science-is-not-settled-1411143565.

97 Ezra Klein, "Obama's Gift," *American Prospect*, January 4, 2008, https://prospect.org/article/obama-s-gift./.

98 Obama, 136.

99 Matthew Creamer, "Obama Wins! . . . Ad Age's Marketer of the Year," *Ad Age*, October 17, 2008, https://adage.com/article/moy-2008/obama-wins-ad-age-s-marketer-year/131810.

100 Taibbi, "Obama Is the Best BS Artist Since Bill Clinton."

101 Obama, 67.

102 Ibid., 77.

103 Ibid., 210.

104 Ibid., 57.

105 "Is Obama All Style and Little Substance?" NBCNews.com, March 27, 2007, https://www.nbcnews.com/id/wbna17811278.

106 Ezra Klein, "A Lack of Audacity," *American Prospect*, May 30, 2007, https://prospect.org/article/lack-audacity/.

107 Andrew Cline, "How Obama Broke His Promise on Individual Mandates," *Atlantic*, June 29, 2012, https://www.theatlantic.com/politics/archive/2012/06/how-obama-broke-his-promise-on-individual-mandates/259183/.

108 Taibbi, "Obama Is the Best BS Artist Since Bill Clinton."

109 "Transcript: Obama's Speech against The Iraq War," NPR, January 20, 2009, https://www.npr.org/templates/story/story.php? storyId=99591469.

110 "Remarks by the President at the Acceptance of the Nobel Peace Prize," National Archives and Records Administration, December 10, 2009, https://obamawhitehouse.archives.gov/the-press-office/remarks-president-acceptance-nobel-peace-prize.

111 Nathan J. Robinson, "Obama's Words." Current Affairs, October 9, 2020, https://www.currentaffairs.org/2020/10/obamas-words.

112 Taibbi, "Obama Is the Best BS Artist Since Bill Clinton."

113 Adolph L. Reed Jr., "Obama No," Progressive.org, April 28, 2008, https://progressive.org/magazine/obama/.

114 Micah L. Sifry, "Inside the Fall of Obama's Grassroots Army," New Republic, August 31, 2021, https://newrepublic.com/article/140245/obamas-lost-army-inside-fall-grassroots-machine.

115 Obama, 78.

116 Ibid., 118.

117 Ibid., 13-14.

118 Ibid., 226.

119 Ibid., xv-xvi.

120 Ibid., 71.

121 Ibid., 366.

122 Ibid., 305.

123 Louis Jacobson, "PolitiFact - Obama Says Heritage Foundation Is Source of Health Exchange Idea," @politifact, April 1, 2010, https://www.politifact.com/factchecks/2010/apr/01/barack-obama/obama-says-heritage-foundation-source-health-excha/.

124 Nathan J. Robinson, "The Kind of Policy We Must Never Make Again," Current Affairs, February 6, 2019, https://www.currentaffairs.org/2019/02/the-kind-of-policy-we-must-never-make-again.

125 Obama, 354.

126 Ian Millhiser, "How to Kill the Filibuster with Only 51 Votes," American Prospect, January 29, 2010, https://prospect.org/article/kill-filibuster-51-votes/.

127 Michael A. Cohen, "End the GOP's Filibuster Folly," Politico, November 17, 2009, https://www.politico.com/story/2009/11/end-the-gops-filibuster-folly-029581.

128 Obama, 316.

129 Garance Franke-Ruta, "Obama's Deficit Speech (Transcript)," Atlantic, April 13, 2011, https://www.theatlantic.com/politics/archive/2011/04/obamas-deficit-speech-transcript/237274/.

130 Ezra Klein, "11 Shocking, True Facts about Simpson-Bowles," *Washington Post*, December 4, 2012, https://www.washingtonpost.com/news/wonk/wp/2012/12/04/11-shocking-true-facts-about-simpson-bowles/.

131 Obama, 210.

132 Bernard E. Harcourt, "Cover-Up in Chicago," *New York Times*, November 30, 2015, https://www.nytimes.com/2015/11/30/opinion/cover-up-in-chicago.html.

133 Obama, 218.

134 Mi Lee, "Book: Geithner Ignored Obama Order," *Politico*, September 17, 2011, https://www.politico.com/story/2011/09/book-geithner-ignored-obama-order-063673.

135 Ryan Cooper, "Obama the Pretender," *The Week*, November 24, 2020, https://theweek.com/articles/950908/obama-pretender.

136 Obama, 270-271.

137 Ibid., 304-205.

138 Jesse Eisinger, "The Chickenshit Club," Simon & Schuster Canada, 2018, https://www.simonandschuster.ca/books/The- Chickenshit-Club/Jesse-Eisinger/9781501121388.

139 Jed S. Rakoff, "Why the Innocent Plead Guilty and the Guilty Go Free," Macmillan, 2021, https://us.macmillan.com/books/9780374289997.

140 Obama, 305.

141 Ricky Kreitner, "Wall Street Responsible for One-Third of Obama's Campaign Funds," Business Insider, July 22, 2011, https://www.businessinsider.com/wall-street-responsible-for-one-third-of-obamas-campaign-funds-2011-7.

142 Mark Gongloff, "Holder: Banks Too Big to Prosecute," HuffPost, March 7, 2013, https://www.huffpost.com/entry/eric-holder-banks-too-big_n_2821741.

143 Aruna Viswanatha and Brett Wolf, "HSBC to PAY $1.9 Billion U.S. fine in money-laundering case," Reuters, December 11, 2012, https://www.reuters.com/article/us-hsbc-probe-idUSBRE8BA05M 20121211.

144 Zaid Jilani, "Obama Wanted to Cut Social Security, Then Bernie Sanders Happened," *Intercept*, June 2, 2016, https://theintercept.com/2016/06/02/obama-wanted-to-cut-social-security-then-bernie-sanders-happened/.

145 Emily Stephenson, "Obama Renews Call to End Saturday Mail Delivery," Reuters, February 13, 2012, https://www.reuters.com/article/us-usa-budget-postal/obama-renews-call-to-end-saturday-mail-delivery-idUKTRE81C20N20120213.

146 "Reverend Wright Transcript," ABC News, April 27, 2008, https://abcnews.go.com/Blotter/story?id=4719157&page=1.

147 Obama, 120.

148 Thomas, "Fox Anchor Calls Obama Fist Pound a 'Terrorist Fist Jab.'"

149   Byron Tau, "Obama: 'If I Had a Son, He'd Look like Trayvon.'" *Politico*, March 23, 2012, https://www.politico.com/blogs/politico44/2012/03/obama-if-i-had-a-son-hed-look-like-trayvon-118439.

150   Obama, 395.

151   Luke Savage and Nathan J. Robinson, "The Real Obama," *Current Affairs*, June 1, 2017, https://www.currentaffairs.org/2017/05/the-real-obama.

152   Matt Bruenig and Ryan Cooper, "How Obama Destroyed Black Wealth," *Jacobin*, July 12, 2017, https://jacobinmag.com/2017/12/obama-foreclosure-crisis-wealth-inequality.

153   Jonathan Chait, "In Conversation with Barack Obama," *Intelligencer*, December 9, 2020, https://nymag.com/intelligencer/2020/12/in-conversation-with-barack-obama.html.

154   Ibid.

155   John Ivison, "Why Justin Trudeau's New Guiding Light Could Have a Dramatic Impact on Canadian Public Policy," *National Post*, February 21, 2014, http://nationalpost.com/g00/opinion/john-ivison-why-justin-trudeaus-new-guiding-light-could-have-a-dramatic-impact-on-canadian-public-policy/wcm/2138f0e7-f2be-4c18-9440-aab75ab5b079? i1Oc.referrer=https%3A%2F%2Fwww.google.ca%2F.

156   Aida Chavez, "Rolling Stone Magazine asks: Why can't Trudeau be our president?" The Hill, July 26, 2017, http://thehill.com/blogs/blog-briefing-room/news/343849-rolling-stone-magazine-asks-why-cant-trudeau-be-our-president.

157   "Justin Trudeau Says Canadians Want Justin Trudeau, Not Electoral Reform," PressProgress, September 27, 2017. https://pressprogress.ca/justin_trudeau_says_canadians_want_justin_trudeau_not_electoral_ reform/.

158   "Justin Trudeau Was Questioned on Indigenous Rights in the Middle of a Selfie. This Was His Reaction," PressProgress, January 18, 2017. https://pressprogress.ca/justin_trudeau_was_questioned_on_indigenous_rights_in_the_middle_of_a_selfie_this_was_his_reaction/.

159   Peter Kuitenbrouwer, "Federal Liberals Look to Ramp up Weapons Sales in Middle East," *National Post*, March 18, 2016, https:// nationalpost.com/news/politics/federal-liberals-look-to-ramp-up-weapons-sales-in-middle-east/wcm/7b0ee8fd-7ff1-4bf2-810d-af84d172604f.

160   Andrew Jackson, "Private Infrastructure Bank Not in the Public Interest," Broadbent Institute, October 29, 2016, https://www.broadbentinstitute.ca/andrew_ajackson/private_infrastructure_bank_not_in_the_public_interest.

161   Jackson, "So-Called 'Middle Class' Tax Cut Leaves out Most Canadians."

162   "Canada's Trudeau Calls for Wider Social Benefit from Economy," Reuters, February 17, 2017, https://www.reuters.com/article/us-canada-eu-trudeau-idUSKBN15W2DF.

163 Justin Trudeau, "History shows that this country works best when we all work together to solve the problems that matter most to Canadians. #CdnPoli #LPC." Twitter, February 6, 2015, https://twitter.com/justin-trudeau/status/563810349548179456.

164 "Trudeau Swings for the Fences, but Reviews Are Mixed," HuffPost Canada, August 7, 2015, http://www.huffingtonpost.ca/2015/08/07/trudeau-speech-macleans-debate_n_7955070.html.

165 "Justin Trudeau Promises to Grow the Economy 'from the Heart Outwards' - Whatever That Means," *National Post*, August 12, 2015, http://nationalpost.com/news/politics/justin-trudeau-grow-the-economy-from-the-heart-outwards.

166 "Speech by Liberal Party of Canada Leader, Justin Trudeau, at the 2014 Biennial Convention in Montreal," Liberal Party of Canada, February 22, 2014, https://www.liberal.ca/speech-liberal-party-canada-leader-justin-trudeau-montral-qc-2/.

167 Justin Trudeau, "Justin Trudeau: Why It's Vital We Support the Middle Class," *Globe and Mail*, April 15, 2013, https://www.theglobeandmail.com/news/politics/justin-trudeau-why-its-vital-we-support-the-middle-class/article11209063/.

168 Ashifa Kassam and Laurence Mathieu-Léger, "Justin Trudeau: 'Globalisation Isn't Working for Ordinary People'," *Guardian*, December 15, 2016, https://www.theguardian.com/world/2016/dec/15/justin-trudeau-interview-globalisation-climate-change-trump.

169 C. Taylor, *Reconciling the Solitudes: Essays on Canadian Federalism and Nationalism* (Montréal: McGill-Queen's University Press, 1993).

170 Althia Raj, "Here's Why the Liberals Are Really Supporting Bill C-51," HuffPost Canada, March 10, 2015, http://www.huffingtonpost.ca/2015/03/09/liberals-are-supporting-b_n_6835700.html.

171 Joe Hagan, "Riding around with Beto O'Rourke as He Comes to Grips with a Presidential Run," *Vanity Fair*, March 13, 2019, https://www.vanityfair.com/news/2019/03/beto-orourke-cover-story.

172 Nathan J. Robinson, "All About Pete," *Current Affairs*, March 29, 2019, https://www.currentaffairs.org/2019/03/all-about-pete.

173 Nathan J. Robinson, "Pete Buttigieg Is the Democrats' Flavour of the Month. Just Don't Ask What He Stands For," *Guardian*, April 16, 2019, https://www.theguardian.com/commentisfree/2019/apr/16/pete-buttigieg-democrats-flavour-month.

174 Alexander Burns, "Pete Buttigieg's Focus: Storytelling First. Policy Details Later," *New York Times*, April 14, 2019, https://www.nytimes.com/2019/04/14/us/politics/pete-buttigieg-2020-writing-message.html.

ENDNOTES

175   Sydney Ember, "Bernie Sanders: Lion of the Left, but Not the Only One Roaring," *New York Times*, November 23, 2018, https://www.nytimes.com/2018/11/23/us/politics/bernie-sanders-president-2020.html.

176   Jennifer 'pro-voting' Rubin, "Beto Fundraising Number Suggests Bernie Now Officially Yesterday's News, Faces Stiff Competition for Youth Vote," Twitter, March 18, 2019, https://twitter.com/JRubinBlogger/status/1107625123253755904.

177   Jonathan Chait, "Why the Bernie Movement Must Crush Beto O'Rourke," *Intelligencer*, December 28, 2018, https://nymag.com/intelligencer/2018/12/bernie-sanders-beto-orourke-feud-2020-campaign-democratic.html.

178   Hagan, "Riding around with Beto O'Rourke as He Comes to Grips with a Presidential Run."

179   Beto O'Rourke, Medium Post, November 16, 2018, https://medium.com/@BetoORourke/i-woke-up-after-a-good-nights-sleep-9999308c103e.

180   John F. Harris, "Can the F-Bomb Save Beto?" *Politico Magazine*, September 6, 2019, https://www.politico.com/magazine/story/2019/09/06/beto-orourke-f-bomb-228038/.

181   Nate Silver, "How Amy Klobuchar Could Win the 2020 Democratic Nomination." FiveThirtyEight, February 10, 2019, https://fivethirtyeight.com/features/amy-klobuchar-2020-democratic-nomination-kickoff/.

182   Nate Silver, "Klobuchar probably has one of the best electability arguments in the field, so the fact that she's tied for last here is a sign that voters don't really think about electability in the same way that political analysts do." Twitter, September 12, 2019, https://twitter.com/natesilver538/status/1172183389631328261?lang=en.

183   Musadiq Bidar, "@Amyklobuchar says candidates promising free college or eliminating all student debt 'know that they most likely won't go through because they don't make any sense.' She adds that people 'like to hear that they're going to get everything free.'" Twitter, October 4, 2019, https://twitter.com/Bidar411/status/1179944598556336128.

184   Molly Hensley-Clancy, "Staffers, Documents Show Amy Klobuchar's Wrath toward Her Aides," BuzzFeed News, December 19, 2020, https://www.buzzfeednews.com/article/mollyhensleyclancy/amy-klobuchar-staff-2020-election.

185   Molly Redden, "When Staff Sought Better Jobs, Amy Klobuchar Tried to Undermine Them," HuffPost Canada, February 26, 2019, https://www.huffingtonpost.ca/entry/amy-klobuchar-sabotages-job-opportunities-for-staff_n_5c706f8fe4b03cfdaa553cdd?ril8n=true.

186   Jonathan Chait, "This line makes me want to vote for Klobuchar: 'I would trade three of you for a bottle of water,'" Twitter, February 22, 2019, https://twitter.com/jonathanchait/status/1099030782604201986.

187 Jennifer Rubin, "Exactly," Twitter, February 22, 2019, https://twitter.com/JRubinBlogger/status/1099033788926038017.

188 "Pete Buttigieg Claims Victory amid Delayed Iowa Results," YouTube, February 3, 2020, https://youtu.be/cTnM87OCCu8?t=54.

189 Robinson, "All About Pete."

190 Tony Blair, "New Politics for the New Century," *Independent*, https://www.independent.co.uk/arts-entertainment/new-politics-new-century-1199625.html.

191 "Biden's Speech to Congress: Full Transcript," *New York Times*, April 29, 2021, https://www.nytimes.com/2021/04/29/us/politics/joe-biden-speech-transcript.html.

192 Seth Ackerman, "Biden's COVID Relief Bill Is the Biggest Anti-Poverty Program In . . . months." *Jacobin*, https://www. jacobinmag.com/2021/03/joe-biden-relief-bill-child-benefit-anti-poverty (accessed August 31, 2021).

193 Matt Karp, "No, Joe Biden Won't Give Us Social Democracy," *Jacobin*, https://www.jacobinmag.com/2021/03/american-rescue-plan-covid-relief-joe-biden-democrats (accessed August 31, 2021).

194 Noam Chomsky and Edward Herman, *Manufacturing Consent* (London: Random House, 2008).

195 Rick Perlstein, "Pundits Who Predict the Future Are Always Wrong," *The Nation*, April 5, 2001, https://www.thenation.com/article/archive/pundits-who-predict-future-are-always-wrong/.

196 "Tucker Carlson Confronts Newsweek Bias," YouTube, December 15, 2016, https://www.youtube.com/watch?v=7OphbxIiaF8&t=1s.

197 Clayton Purdom, "Newsweek's Kurt Eichenwald Was Just Looking at Tentacle Porn for His Family," *The A.V. Club*, August 23, 2017, https://news.avclub.com/newsweek-s-kurt-eichenwald-was-just-looking-at-tentacle-1798263101.

198 Krystal Ball, "Krystal Ball Breaks down MSNBC Stages of Bernie Grief," YouTube, February 24, 2020, https://www.youtube.com/watch?v=6ZAFIq-JQDdI.

199 Marina Pitofsky, "Carville Says That Nevada Caucuses Are 'Going Very Well' for Putin," The Hill, February 22, 2020, https://thehill.com/blogs/blog-briefing-room/news/484217-carville-says-that-nevada-caucuses-are-going-very-well-for.

200 "Chris Matthews Warns of 'Executions in Central Park' If Socialism Wins," YouTube, February 8, 2020, https://www.youtube.com/watch?v=g5MRDEXRk4k.

201 Mark Leibovich, "The Aria of Chris Matthews," *New York Times*, April 13, 2008, https://www.nytimes.com/2008/04/13/magazine/13matthews-t.html?pagewanted=1.

202 Ibid.

ENDNOTES

Ibid.

204 "Jon Stewart Gives Chris Matthews a Book Interview from Hell," VideoSift, https://web.archive.org/web/20161021173132/ https:/videosift.com/video/Jon-Stewart-gives-Chris-Matthews-a-book-interview-from-Hell (accessed August 31, 2021).

205 Samuel C. Spitale, "Post-Truth Nation," HuffPost, December 14, 2016, https://www.huffpost.com/entry/to-family-friends-and-peers-who-voted-for-trump_b_582e6b1fe4b08c963e343d23.

206 Rune Møller Stahl and Bue Rübner Hansen, "Donald's Myths." *Jacobin*, https://jacobinmag.com/2017/05/donald-trump-post-truth-fake-news-fact-checking (accessed August 31, 2021).

207 Cuomo Prime Time. "Democrats Are Allowing a 'Noisy Wing of Our Party Define the Rest of Us," Says James Carville. 'These People Are Kind of Nice People..they're Naive and All into Language and Identity, and That's All Right. They're Not Storming the Capitol, but They're Not Winning Elections." ." Twitter. Twitter, July 14, 2021. https://twitter.com/CuomoPrimeTime/status/1415125207430356998.

208 Nwanevu, Osita. "I Think This Is Supposed to Make the IDENTITY Left Seem Small, but For COMPARISON, African-Americans and Hispanics Comprise about 19 and 13 Percent of the Democratic PARTY Electorate Respectively. Very BIG-IF-TRUE Bit of Speculation Here! HTTPS://T.CO/COTMS9RM6F HTTPS://T.CO/ZFTEZJYHNP." Twitter. Twitter, July 14, 2021. https://twitter.com/OsitaNwanevu/status/1415338338953973760.

209 Wildeman, Mary K. "Clyburn Has Taken More than $1 Million in Pharma Money in a Decade, Far Surpassing Peers." *The Post and Courier*, September 14, 2020. https://www.postandcourier.com/health/clyburn-has-taken-more-than-1-million-in-pharma-money-in-a-decade-far-sur-passing/article_62b10180-d956-11e8-9122-4f50316f66fa.html.

210 Caygle, Heather, and Sarah Ferris. "Dem Leaders Warn Liberal Rhetoric Could Blow Georgia Races." *Politico*, November 5, 2020. https://www.polit-ico.com/news/2020/11/05/house-democrats-warn-caucus-left-434428.

211 Concha, Joe. "Carville Fires Back at Sanders For 'Hack' Slam: 'at Least I'm Not A Communist'." *The Hill*, February 14, 2020. https://thehill.com/homenews/media/483054-carville-fires-back-at-sanders-for-hack-slam-at-least-im-not-a-communist.

212 Wayne, Leslie. "From Campaign Trail to Celebrity Circuit." *The New York Times*, April 18, 2004. https://www.nytimes.com/2004/04/18/us/from-campaign-trail-to-celebrity-circuit.html.

213 Turkewitz, Julie, and Maggie Astor. "Michael Bennet Drops out of the 2020 Presidential Race." *The New York Times*, February 12, 2020. https://www.nytimes.com/2020/02/11/us/politics/michael-bennet-drops-out.html.

214 "Democratic Write-Ins." NH.gov. New Hampshire Secretary of State. Accessed August 30, 2021. https://sos.nh.gov/elections/elections/election-results/2020/2020-presidential-primary/democratic/democratic-write-ins/.

215 Stanton, Zack. "The Worst Predictions of 2020." *Politico*, December 29, 2020. https://www.politico.com/news/magazine/2020/12/29/worst-predictions-about-2020-451444.

216 Paul Heideman, "Joe Biden Is Not Ready to Confront Corporate America," *Jacobin*, https://jacobinmag.com/2021/01/joe-biden-corporate-america?fbclid=IwAR17sRl7IQon1K4FGf5OoXXKGRN_QqXqHvMeNTl2qR8t_OUDOCfxTFOqPwg (accessed August 31, 2021).

217 Zachary D. Carter, "Biden's $1.9 Trillion Package Is a Good Start. But It's Only a Start." HuffPost Canada, January 15, 2021, https://www.huffingtonpost.ca/entry/joe-biden-19-trillion-dollar-package_ n_6001e6e8c5b6e-fae62f87991?ril8n=true.

218 Peggy Noonan, "Obama and the Runaway Train." *Wall Street Journal*, November 1, 2008, https://www.wsj.com/articles/SB122539802263585317.

219 The Editors, "A Liberal Supermajority," *Wall Street Journal*, https://www.wsj.com/articles/SB122420205889842989.

220 David Brooks, "A Moderate Manifesto," *New York Times*, March 3, 2009, https://www.nytimes.com/2009/03/03/opinion/03brooks.html.

221 Clive Crook, "The Budget Reveals the Liberal Obama," *Financial Times*, March 1, 2009, https://www.ft.com/content/e9049900-069211de-ab0f-000077b07658.

222 Paul Krugman, "The Obama Agenda," *New York Times*, November 7, 2008, https://www.nytimes.com/2008/11/07/opinion/07krugman.html.

223 Paul Krugman, "Franklin Delano Obama?" *New York Times*, November 10, 2008, https://www.nytimes.com/2008/11/10/opinion/10krugman.html.

224 Edward Rothstein, "In Desperate Times, the Rise to Take the Reins and Take on Fear Itself," *New York Times*, December 20, 2008, https://www.nytimes.com/2008/12/20/arts/design/20fdr.html.

225 Steve Friess on 06/01/20 at 5:00 AM EDT, "Joe Biden, the Moderate, Plans the Most Radical Overhaul of the U.S. Economy since FDR." *Newsweek*, June 8, 2020, https://www.newsweek.com/2020/06/12/joe-biden-moderate-plans-most-radical-economic-overhaul-since-fdr-1507674.html.

226 George Packer, "The New Liberalism," *New Yorker*, November 8, 2008, https://www.newyorker.com/magazine/2008/11/17/the-new-liberalism.

227 David Brooks, "When Obamatons Respond," *New York Times*, March 5, 2009, https://www.nytimes.com/2009/03/06/opinion/06brooks.html.

228 Michel Foucault, *The Birth of Biopolitics: Lectures at the College De France, 1978-1979* (New York: Palgrave Macmillan, 2011).

229 Naomi Klein, *The Shock Doctrine: The Rise of Disaster Capitalism* (London: Penguin, 2014).

230 Margaret Thatcher, "Interview for *Sunday Times*," 3 May 1981, https://www.margaretthatcher.org/document/104475.

231 Mark Fisher, *Ghosts of My Life: Writings on Depression, Hauntology, and Lost Futures* (London: Zero Books, 2014), p. 8–9.

232 "Full Pepsi Commercial Starring Kendal Jenner." YouTube, April 6, 2017, https://www.youtube.com/watch?v=uwvAgDCOdU4.

233 Shannon Liao, "Amazon Warehouse Workers Skip Bathroom Breaks to Keep Their Jobs, Says Report." *The Verge*, April 16, 2018, https://www.theverge.com/2018/4/16/17243026/amazon-warehouse-jobs-worker-conditions-bathroom-breaks.

234 Ian MacDougall, "How McKinsey Helped the Trump Administration Carry Out Its Immigration Policies," *New York Times*, December 3, 2019, https://www.nytimes.com/2019/12/03/us/mckinsey-ICE-immigration.html.

235 Mark Fisher, *Capitalist Realism: Is There No Alternative?* (Winchester, UK: Zero Books, 2010).

236 Louise Dransfield, "Battersea Power Station Is Sold for £1.6bn," Building.co.uk, January 18, 2018, https://www.building.co.uk/news/battersea-power-station-is-sold-for-16bn/5091622.article#:~:text=Malaysian%2520sovereign%2520wealth%2520fund%2520Permodalan,Station%2520for%2520%25C2%25A31.6bn.

237 "'Chimney Lift' and Large Events Space Planned for Battersea Power Station." CLAD, https://www.cladglobal.com/CLADnews/architecture_design/news/339486?source=search (accessed August 31, 2021).

238 T.J. Stiles, *The First Tycoon: The Epic Life of Cornelius Vanderbilt* (New York: Alfred A. Knopf, 2011).

239 Steve Fraser, "The Misunderstood Robber Baron: on Cornelius Vanderbilt," *The Nation*, June 29, 2015, https://www.thenation.com/article/archive/misunderstood-robber-baron-cornelius-vanderbilt/.

240 Ibid.

241 Ibid.

242 "A Great Monopoly," *Atlantic*, November 10, 1999, https://www.theatlantic.com/magazine/archive/1999/11/a-great-monopoly/306018/.

243 Sarah Jorgensen and Joe Sterling, "West Virginia Teacher Strike Set to Continue Tuesday." CNN, February 27, 2018, https://www.cnn.com/2018/02/26/us/west-virginia-teachers-strike/index.html.

244 All these numbers are from page 9 of this doc. Quotes in the subsequent paragraph are also from the doc. https://peia.wv.gov/benefit_coordinators/Documents/Open%20Enrollment%20Plan%20Year%202019%20web%20v.pdf.

245 "PEIA Open Enrolment Meeting," 2019, https://peia.wv.gov/benefit_coordinators/Documents/Open%20Enrollment%20Plan%20Year%20 2019%20web%20v.pdf.

246 Manuel Klausner, "Inside Ronald Reagan," *Reason*, December 20, 2019, https://reason.com/1975/07/01/inside-ronald-reagan/.

247 "Ronald Reagan's First Inaugural Address," Wikisource, https://en.wikisource.org/wiki/Ronald_ Reagan%27s_First_Inaugural_Address (accessed August 31, 2021).

248 "Radio Address to the Nation on Welfare Reform," The Ronald Reagan Presidential Foundation & Institute, https://www.reaganfoundation.org/ronald-reagan/reagan-quotes-speeches/radio-address-to-the-nation-on-welfare-reform/ (accessed August 31, 2021).

249 Raphael Samuel, "Mrs. Thatcher's Return to Victorian Values," The British Academy, 1992. http://publications. thebritishacademy.ac.uk/pubs/proc/files/78p009.pdf.

250 Ibid.

251 Tim Barker, "The People's Flag Is Palest Pink," *Dissent Magazine*, January 9, 2019, https://www.dissentmagazine.org/article/the-peoples-flag-is-palest-pink.

252 Samuel.

253 Franklin Foer and Noam Scheiber, "Nudge-Ocracy." *New Republic*, August 31, 2021, https://newrepublic.com/article/61724/nudge-ocracy.

254 Bill Clinton, "Address before a Joint Session of the Congress on the State of the Union," The American Presidency Project, January 23, 1996, https://www.presidency.ucsb.edu/documents/address-before-joint-session-the-congress-the-state-the-union-10.

255 Premilla Nadasen, "How a Democrat Killed Welfare," *Jacobin*, September 2, 2016, https://www.jacobinmag.com/2016/02/welfare-reform-bill-hillary-clinton-tanf-poverty-dlc/.

256 Foer and Scheiber, "Nudge-Ocracy."

257 David V. Johnson, "Twilight of the Nudges," *New Republic*, August 31, 2021, https://newrepublic.com/article/138175/twilight-nudges.

258 Foer and Scheiber, "Nudge-Ocracy."

259 Johnson, "Twilight of the Nudges."

260 Jane Mulderrig, "The Language of 'Nudge' in Health Policy: Pre-Empting Working Class Obesity through 'Biopedagogy'." Critical Policy Studies, https://www.academia.edu/34974263/The_language_of_nudge_in_health_policy_pre-empting_working_class_obesity_through_biopedagogy (accessed August 31, 2021).

261 Jonathan Chait, "Reminder: Liberalism Is Working, and Marxism Has Always Failed," *Intelligencer*, March 23, 2016, https://nymag.com/

ENDNOTES

intelligencer/2016/03/reminder-liberalism-is-working-marxism-failed. html.

262 James Traub, "It's Time for the Elites to Rise up against the Ignorant Masses," *Foreign Policy*, July 23, 2019, https://foreignpolicy. com/2016/06/28/its-time-for-the-elites-to-rise-up-against-ignorant-masses-trump-2016-brexit/.

263 Blair, "New Politics for the New Century."

264 Bill Scher, "Is This the Stupidest Book Ever Written about Socialism?" *Politico Magazine*, August 28, 2018, https://www.politico.com/magazine/ story/2018/08/28/chapo-trap-house-book-review-219596.

265 Tom Watson, "There are no neoliberals in the U.S. Congress - not one. Not one in any statehouse in the nation, either. City councils? Zero. Yet it's constantly bandied about by white academic left as a functioning and present ideology," Twitter, March 2, 2018, https://twitter.com/tomwatson/ status/9697218539 36840704?lang=en.

266 Jonathan Chait, "How 'Neoliberalism' Became the Left's Favorite Insult of Liberals," *Intelligencer*, July 17, 2017, https://nymag.com/intelli-gencer/2017/07/how-neoliberalism-became-the-lefts-favorite-insult.html.

267 Ben Chu, "Opinion: The European Union Is Not a 'Neoliberal Conspiracy' – and It's Disturbing That Some in the Labour Party Apparently Believe This Nonsense." *Independent*, , May 14, 2018, https://www.independent. co.uk/voices/european-union-neoliberal-conspiracy-labour-party-brexit-jeremy-corbyn-a8349316.html.

268 Ed Conway, "Sky Views: What Is Neoliberalism and Why Is It an Insult?" Sky News, May 15, 2018, https://news.sky.com/story/sky-views-what-is-neoliberalism-and-why-is-it-an-insult-11373031.

269 Ezra Klein, "Leftists, Liberals, and Neoliberals Share a Problem: Congress," Vox, September 20, 2019, https://www.vox.com/ policy-and-politics/2019/9/20/20874204/obama-farhad-man-joo-neoliberalism-financial-crisissanders-warren?fbclid=IwAR2xnGQ_ CbyF8m_EbClBc3fv-j9stOQ-oUc5SXxv5ETTCmnIlIOK87Ewpzs.

270 Corey Robin, "More than an Epithet," *Jacobin*, March 5, 2016, https://www. jacobinmag.com/2016/05/jonathan-chait-charles-peters-mont-pelerin.

271 Mark Fisher, *Capitalist Realism: Is There No Alternative?* (Winchester, UK: Zero Books, 2010).

About the Author

Luke Savage is a staff writer at *Jacobin Magazine* and a leading voice on the millennial left. His work has also appeared in *The Atlantic*, *The Guardian*, *Current Affairs*, *The New Statesman*, *The Literary Review of Canada*, and elsewhere. A graduate of the University of Toronto, he holds a BA in political science and history, and an MA in political theory.